MW01100715

PEACE PROCESSES
AND PEACE ACCORDS

SOUTH ASIAN PEACE STUDIES

Series Editor: Ranabir Samaddar

OTHER TITLES IN THE SERIES

Volume 1: Peace Studies: An Introduction to the Concept, Scope, and Themes (edited by Ranabir Samaddar)
Volume 3: Women in Peace Politics (edited by Paula Banerjee)
Volume 4: Human Rights, Human Rights Institutions and Humanitarian Crisis (edited by Ujjwal Kumar Singh)

EDITORIAL ADVISORY BOARD

Daya Varma, Professor, McGill University, Montreal, President CERAS, Montreal, Canada

Ghislaine Glasson Deschaumes, Founder and Director of the international journal of critical thought *Transeuropéennes*, Paris, France

Itty Abraham, Social Science Research Council, George Washington University, Washington DC, USA

Jyrki Kakonen, Jean Monnet Professor, Department of Political Science and International Relations, University of Tampere, Finland

Oren Yiftachel, Professor, Department of Geography, Ben Gurion University, Beer Sheva, Israel

Paul Joseph, Professor of Sociology, and Peace and Justice Studies, Tufts University, MA, USA

Rada Ivekovic, Professor, Department of Sociology, Jean Monnet University, Saint Etienne, France

Stefano Bianchini, Director, Europe and the Balkans International Network, University of Bologna-Forli Campus, Forli, Italy

EDITORIAL BOARD FOR THIS VOLUME

Paula Banerjee
Shibashis Chatterjee
Samir Kumar Das
Parimal Ghosh

PEACE PROCESSES AND PEACE ACCORDS

Edited by Samir Kumar Das

SAGE Publications
New Delhi • Thousand Oaks • London

Copyright © Mahanirban Calcutta Research Group (MCRG), 2005

All rights reserved. No part of this book may be reproduced or utilized in any form or by any means, electronic or mechanical, including photocopying, recording or by any information storage or retrieval system without permission in writing from the publisher.

First published in 2005 by

Sage Publications India Pvt Ltd
B-42, Panchsheel Enclave
New Delhi 110 017
www.indiasage.com

Sage Publications Inc  **Sage Publications Ltd**
2455 Teller Road 1 Oliver's Yard, 55 City Road
Thousand Oaks, California 91320 London ECIY ISP

Published by Tejeshwar Singh for Sage Publications India Pvt Ltd, phototypeset in 10/12 Century Schoolbook by Star Compugraphics Private Limited, Delhi and printed at Chaman Enterprises, New Delhi.

Library of Congress Cataloging-in-Publication Data

Peace processes and peace accords/edited by Samir Kumar Das.
    p. cm. — (South Asian peace studies; v. 2)
    Includes bibliographical references and index.
    1. Social conflict—South Asia. 2. Conflict management—South Asia. 3. Peace-building—South Asia. 4. Pacific settlement of international disputes. 5. Peace treaties. 6. Reconciliation. I. Das, Samir Kumar, 1961– . II. Series.

HN670.3.Z9S62   303.6'9'0954—dc22   2005   2005019371

ISBN: 0–7619–3390–5 (Hb)   81–7829–532–6 (India–Hb)
         0–7619–3391–3 (Pb)   81–7829–533–4 (India–Pb)

Sage Production Team: Madhuparna Banerjee, Shweta Vachani, Radha Dev Raj and Santosh Rawat

IN HONOR OF RAJNI KOTHARI

Contents

Section III: Peace Accords

Series Note

Peace has become a maximal concept, refusing to accept a minimalist version that stops with the master-idea of security. This was never so apparent than the present time, when draconian laws, outright aggression, plunder, global control of monopolies, resource wars, immigration control, and new racism—all are being justified in the West, particularly in the United States, in the name of security against terrorism and a new global order. At the same time, the world is being told that this is the pathway to peace. This series is intended to address the critical time as this. It brings together writings, which refuse to accept the dominant ideas on peace given to us by national and international security establishments.

The first volume of the South Asian Peace Studies introduces the concept, scope, and themes of peace studies. The second volume deals with peace accords in this region. The third volume narrates experiences of women in conflict and peace. The fourth volume deals with human rights institutions in this region.

This series of volumes is different from the usual conflict and conflict resolution studies that revolve around interest-based approaches and game theories. While it remains uncertain as to how much these studies have contributed to an enriched understanding of conflicts and the dynamics of their resolution, now it is reasonably clear that these while focusing on conflicts neglected ideas and visions of peace, justice and reconciliation, and were often used as post-facto justification of the way in which a particular conflict was handled, the most well-known example in this region being the Indo-Pakistan wars over Kashmir. Conflict studies by and large divorced the idea of conflict resolution and peace from practices of democracy and justice. More important, in this kind of studies, there was little recognition of the social and political realities of the colonial and post-colonial world. Peace with justice seems to be an impossible agenda to the conflict and conflict resolution theorists and practitioners. The South Asian Peace Studies series has been planned as an exercise against that politics of excluding justice and democracy from conflict resolution and peace—by bringing into light practices of human rights, justice, dignity, reconciliation, and democracy, and lodging them at the heart of peace studies. In a world characterized by structures of dominance and inequality and the received histories of freedom, the volumes will show that peace studies will have to be of a critical nature.

Ranabir Samaddar
Calcutta Research Group, Kolkata

PREFACE

The first volume of the series on South Asian Peace Studies (SAPS) was intended to set forth the general framework of all its subsequent volumes. While promising to familiarize us with the scholarship developed on the subject particularly during the last 10 years, it also laid down in our minds, at least three broad themes, running through the readings, that are contained or expected to be contained in them. First, the question of peace will have to be understood independently of the binary of conflict and war. In more positive terms, these studies propose to understand it as an integral part of the agenda of rights, justice, and democracy.

Second, and as a corollary to the first, peace is premised on the problematic of conflict and war insofar as it emanates from the desire of securing democracy against the "undemocratic" forces, and anything that is perceived as a threat will have to be kept at bay through constant conflict and war. It is strange that the great proponents of democracy, starting from the ancient Greeks down to the philosophers of our times, seem to have no answer to the question of how such threats can be tackled by way of observing the same democratic norms and principles. As a result it is yet to develop any theory of its *outside*. The so-called undemocratic forces are called upon either to democratize themselves by observing some "basic" rules laid down by the contemporary theoreticians of democracy (Habermas' "pragmatic universals" and Rawls' "rule of the peoples" being two eloquent illustrations) or to face the consequences of "just war" waged by the democratic powers against them. Democracy as one hears particularly after 9/11 is after all for those who respect it. As democracy creates its vast outside, the desire of securing it ironically escapes the democratic logic. Thus, security invariably becomes incommensurate with democracy. The point is best exemplified by "the democratic capacity to wage colonial wars and commit genocide". Democracy thereby turns into a monologue—a conversation with its own self. SAPS, in short, underlines the importance of recognizing the specificity of this experience and making good the "democratic deficit" as a means of establishing peace whether in South Asia or else-where. The main purpose of SAPS is to gather these insights from the emerging peace historiography of the region, and ac-cordingly plead for bringing dialogue back into democratic theory.

Third, SAPS also warns us against the commonplace tendency of leaving peace to the "immanent goodness" of human beings. The assumption that human beings in their pristine state are inherently good and peaceful, and war and conflicts are only a temporary aberration in our long, tortuous yet inevitable jour-ney towards peace does not seem to recognize the importance of dialogue and moral reasoning in that journey. The series seeks to understand how various modes of moral reasoning and reconciliation prevailing in South Asian cultures were irre-deemably appropriated by and subsumed under the dominant democratic monologue since their encounter with colonialism, and how democracy can be made to observe its own norms and principles while dealing with these historically honoured modes and practices. The imperative of reconciliation and moral rea-soning imposes on us the abiding obligation of taking *critical* lessons from them. If democracy were to survive in culturally varied contexts, it must be ready to renegotiate the terms of its relationships with such multiplicity of modes and practices. SAPS is only a preliminary attempt at reminding us of the possi-bility of alternative pathways to peace that histories of the region offer us.

While elaborating on the themes mentioned above, the present volume proposes to dwell more specifically on peace processes and peace accords in its second and third sections respectively. The opening section seeks to introduce the sub-sequent sections by way of sensitizing us to the emerging theor-izations on the subject. The volume being part of the series also follows the same style and format set forth by the first.

It is indeed difficult, if not impossible, to push the distinction between peace processes and peace accords beyond a certain point. There is, of course, the temptation of viewing accords as

the culmination of peace processes triggered off by fairly pro-
longed spells of conflict and war. Thus conflict, peace process
and accord are supposed to follow an evolutionary schema in
which one follows the other in a neat and precisely defined se-
quence. Signing of an accord, according to this framework, is
celebrated as the end of conflict, as much as the failure in signing
it is regarded as a continuation of its opposite. The studies included here almost unequivocally point out how the very act of
signing an accord could mark either the continuation of the
same conflict or simply its metamorphosis. Accords, in short,
are implicated in the same framework of conflict that neces-
sitates them. While it would be instructive to define peace as
process, accord is only a moment in the process, which is by no
means inexorable or irreversible.

The essays included here provide a useful morphology of violence and conflicts. Contrary to what grand narratives (like
"clash of civilizations") would have us believe, the faultlines of
conflict are never clearly drawn with the effect that each instance of conflict reflects a "cacophony of competing tunes". With
the hardening of positions of the parties engaged in conflicts,
"the competing tunes" are pushed into oblivion. The surfacing
of a conflict implies submergence of a wide variety of them
underneath it. As a sequel to it, war and violence always push
people to the margins. Caught in the crossfire between two
highly hardened positions, the hapless and unarmed people in
every instance are called upon to bear the brunt of war and
conflict. The objectification of people through war and conflict
is a permanent stumbling block to peace.

Establishing peace on the triadic foundations of rights, justice
and democracy is a normative exercise in restoring people's subjectivities to the peace agenda of our times. One of the major
thrusts of SAPS has been to implicitly redefine human nature
in accordance with this objective. The essays included in this
volume look upon human beings essentially as moral beings
without of course any predefined and unchanging essence. For,
the presence of such essence is likely to contribute to the hardening of positions and eruption of war and conflict in human
societies. Accordingly, negotiation is redefined as "joint problem-
solving" on a long-term and sustainable basis rather than "one-
off hard bargaining" and communication between the warring

parties implies not just communication of their differences but of "communicable differences". Reason is not self-interest; it consists in our ability to understand and appreciate our differences. Our case for dialogue is bound to disrupt any essentialist understanding of human nature.

The editors thank the contributors and the publishers for having agreed to permit their writings to be included in this volume. They also thank Ranabir Samaddar for his precious and thoughtful advice and Shekhar Shil for readily preparing a part of the bibliography for the volume. They express gratitude for the assistance of the staff of the Calcutta Research Group in preparing the manuscript. Finally, we owe a special word of thanks to Sage Publications for literally translating our grand idea into a reality.

SECTION I

THEORIZING PEACE

INTRODUCTION

Shibashis Chatterjee

In spite of mankind's apparently natural preference for peace, the history of peace is shamefully tenuous to say the least. Correspondingly, the academic interest in peace studies has been rather negligible compared to an overwhelming interest in war and conflict, in their myriad dimensions and complexities. As a result, conventional approaches to peace studies developed more as a reflex of conflict resolution exercises, ranging from highly positivistic, quantitative studies establishing the complex correlation of a plethora of factors to peace to albeit qualitative understanding on the subject. In all such approaches, peace was seen as incidental to war, either as a normative goal the realization of which compelled an understanding of the dynamics of war-making, or as a quiescent phase before the unavoidable cycle of violence. The recognition of the pervasiveness and ubiquity of conflict relegated peace into the footnotes of International Relations that, because of its very epistemic identity, denies autonomy to peace. The predominance of political realism within the discipline did not quite encourage a critical sociological inquiry into peace. It is not surprising therefore that scholars who sought to rehabilitate peace studies in International Relations came from outside the discipline. The articles that go into the making of this section open up a small yet significant window of opportunity to appreciate the articulation of critical peace studies discourses in recent years, discourses that attempt very consciously and vigorously to sever their connection with political realism and its corollaries.

The articles are essentially experiments in a new sociology of peace. They are more epistemological than ontological, concerned more with understanding of peace than peace itself, remarkably free floating in terms of actors, referents and levels of pegging, and provide an uncharacteristically new form of radicalism that self-consciously abhors the temptation of living up to the realist grand narratives of peace through conflict resolution. There is little thematic common ground linking the pieces, although the authors seem to converge on their method (anti-positivistic and broadly humanistic), definition (peace as social state that can and has to be understood independently of the binary of war or conflict), and process (preferring agency to structure).

Broadly speaking, the three essays enter the conceptual domain of peace through three not altogether different pathways—territoriality, identity, and reconciliation. Samaddar's essay dwells on broad issues of identity, and develops an argument that releases peace from the burden of territoriality. Yiftachel's work, in contrast, points out the continuing grip of territorial imagination in the minds of two conflicting peoples, who are unable to transcend their hostility by invoking a new deterritorialized political imagination powerful enough to shake their obsession with homelands. Bose's essay on the other hand, seeks to trace the bases of peace by understanding anthropologically the processes of reconciliation in tribal societies. While Bose's essay is an exercise in drawing lessons from microstudies conducted in para-state societies, Yiftachel's treatment pivots around state's role. If peace is predicated on political imagination, Samaddar seeks to decouple it from the stranglehold of territoriality.

The title of Samaddar's essay is a good clue to its contents. In his attempt at discarding peace-as-security argument, he feels the need for understanding peace without its "other" (war). In this context the author discusses the themes of friendship, trust, dialogue, inequality, etc., to define a politics of understanding and an ethic of accommodation built on desire, concern and care as a substitute for the conflict-centric understanding of peace. Samaddar's brilliant exposition of the role of a maximalist notion of friendship being responsible for an equally maximalist idea of conflict, mistrust, and enmity, finds parallel(s) in Yiftachel's concern for the Israeli/Arab failure in understanding the predicaments and compulsions of the other, and Bose's findings on the problems of and opportunities for reconciliation of differences amongst groups.

The alternative to a maximalist model of friendship is best illustrated by intimacy. Intimacy threatens absorption and thereby pre-empts dialogues. Pessimism and despair are bound to set in once the desire for intimacy meets with resentments.

Bose surveys conflict resolution mechanism at various levels of social grouping and shows that reconciliation processes that are in operation are governed by the respective social and cultural matrices. Viewed thus, there is no universally applicable democratic structure of conflict resolution. Such structures will have to be culturally localized and sufficiently embedded in the particular communitarian settings to prevent unilateral, hence forced, imposition of democratic norms by the dominant cultural groups.

Yet, the problems of conflict often lie "in" the very communitarian settings including the nations where the spirit of trust, dialogue, and democracy never cuts across their narrow boundaries, and generates the narcissism of the worst kind. Both Samaddar and Bose are in search of strategies that may be rediscovered from within the existing cultural symbols and resources and constructed by way of re-signifying them and adapting them to the requirements of peace.

Oren, however, prefers to reverse the argument. His essay implies a categorical rejection of the highly territorialized notions of nationalism informing the tale of two estranged people—the Arabs and the Israelis. Where territoriality has been the most significant determinant of adversarial psychology and memory, any political project of peace and reconciliation is unlikely to make any headway. It is the idea of the homeland that, according to him, creates its genealogy, and not the other way round as most analysts (including Samaddar) would have us believe. Peace therefore has to encounter a common space where adversaries get involved in a protracted conflict over claims of ownership.

The struggle for peace is much more difficult than the challenge of war. More than resolving conflicts, peace is ultimately a question of establishing justice. The interesting part of this section is that it prepares us for taking peace as peace, for approaching it from the window of civil society, culture, identities, and differences. The three essays, despite all their divergences and diversity of locales, share this common commitment.

1

THE POLITICS OF UNDERSTANDING*

Ranabir Samaddar

NOTHING SPECIAL, A MATTER OF PRUDENCE

"On the road to science, social science has lost what politics formerly was capable of providing as prudence," thus commented Jurgen Habermas in *Theory and Practice*.[1] Following that advice, let us for once leave the high road of international politics and nest in what Habermas calls "prudence." Probably more than theory, prudence or common sense will enable us to write of friendship, trust, and understanding, of the politics of understanding, and in the process something about the understanding of the politics of democracy. It revolves round the fundamental issue: How do we understand each other? How do we appeal? How do we dialogue among ourselves? In other words, what is the politics of appeal, the politics of familiarity, the phenomenological form of familial proximity? Do the nations and the peoples of this region feel the need to love each other, that is to say, do they feel that it is advisable to love to be loved, to understand in order to love, in short, to love so that they can understand? These questions refer to a politics of understanding, also a model of that understanding.

MAXIMALIST NOTION OF ACCOMMODATION

It is obvious that the nations of this region will fail miserably if we take a maximalist model of accommodation. Such a model

* Originally published in *Economic and Political Weekly* with the title "Friends, Foes, Understanding"; vol. 36, no. 10, March 2001.

will tell that it has to be a maximum of friendship, the friendship has to cover all issues of existence, and that such friendship cannot permit the loved and the beloved to be incommensurable in any way. Such a model of mutual understanding disallows asymmetry, because the risks of asymmetry complicate the egalitarian schema of friendship; disallows any difference between the effective and the virtual, between a fragile friendship and death. A maximal model does not admit of the possibility that sympathetic understanding may erupt from a loss of union, mourning may give rise to renewed partnership, and anguish may inspire understanding and tolerance. In such judgement, no instability in friendship is allowed. Stability is crucial. Brotherhood, and from brotherhood complete identity of life is primary, primal.

It is apparent that the nations of South Asia, particularly the three nations of the erstwhile united land, do not follow the maximal model, and by that judgement cannot be friends. Yet, do they have no understanding of each other? If the maximal model is not practised here, must that mean that there are no discernible laws of understanding in this region? Before we answer that question, we must probe into the reasons of the impossibility of a maximum alliance, understanding and friendship.

Imperatives to a Maximalist Alliance

Behind friendship lies the architecture of a desire—the desire to live, to achieve liveability, to prefer, and to love; in short, there is morphology of accommodation. The impossibility of absolute friendship shows the impossibility of the laws of equality, and indicates the attempts to make the impossible possible, a possibility of periodic upheavals, and of recurring testimonies. Alliance is a weight, an overwhelming weight. It is the weight of the attempt to ally, to reconcile, to make others conform, and to constitute the incompatible values in compatibility. This also suggests a truth. It raises the issue: what truth is there in the proximity that lies at the heart of a friendship, the differences that this proximity produces, proximity's pangs, without presence, therefore without resemblance, without attraction, therefore without dissociation, and without the possibility of significant or reasonable preferences? There are all kinds of partisans and partners: born partners, jealous partners, partners of solitude, and partners of differential understanding. Often the partners invite each other to be members of a singular community, an anchored community—another name of secret society. They are like owls in the full light of day. Such partisanship is in the long run the premonitory sign of a breakdown. In maximizing the essence of partnership and the mutual obligation to answer, such partisanship takes the notion of common good to the point of ridicule. We shall then say, what can be common has ever but little value; common good is a contradiction, and at the end of the day, it can be found by only conjuring up secrecy. Belonging to the kingdom of a spiritual and therefore a hyper-political community, it assures only currency, presence—a contemporaneous life. Belonging to contemporaneous life, it experiences harrowing tremors of existence.

A maximal friendship (like Cold War friendship) depends on maximum enmity, not only that, maximum hostility. In its imperatives, we find reconstituted enmities, reconstitutive enmities (like post-Cold War enmities). The logic of total friendship is ineluctable. It kills understanding. Its testament becomes an epitaph on accommodation, an elliptical justification of hostility. It begins with democracy, but soon turns against it, stabs it with the dagger of absoluteness, totality.

Understanding Difference

There is another model of understanding whose key is difference. Accommodating difference, reconciling to the permanence of difference bespeak a strategy whose stakes are limitless when placed in the history of the relations in the region. In short, we speak of democracy—a different *politics of understanding*.[2] In arguing for a politics of understanding as the core of democratic politics today, it is obvious that I have begun with Derrida's argument about politics of friendship, but I want to carry it further in the context of a possible politics of democracy for reconciliation and justice.

Reflexivity and an Alternative Argument

In opposition to the maximal idea presented above, I wish to present here briefly an alternative argument of partnership and friendship relating to the history of post-colonial South Asia. It not only contradicts the model discussed earlier, but denies and defies the very wisdom of that history of claiming total union that led nations of this region to desire total friendship, demanding total surrender of the self to the other, or vice versa. I may confess that this alternative argument may seem a kind of mythography.

I shall give the example of the politics of understanding Bangladesh. The 53 years of "our" (India's) independence and 30 years of "their" independence are historical facts. These are two different countries, sovereign neighbors. India is a Hindu majority country. Bangladesh has a Muslim majority. India is more industrialized. Bangladesh is less. India never had a military rule; Bangladesh, for 15 years, was ruled by the army. In our attempt to understand Bangladesh, we are to give due respect to these facts. In other words, we accept "South Asia" as the *given* region, composed of *given* nation-states, and we accord respect to the state system *given* to us. We are to hold our contrahistory in rein so that the desire to belong to our past does not oppose history. But alas, in understanding a neighbor this is often not possible. The relations of past continue to structure the present and this I term as the problem of reflexivity. I hope to make clear in the process what I indicate as contra-history.

What is reflexivity? The *Oxford English Dictionary* meaning of the word suggests that, "the action of the verb is performed on its subject." In other words, we may say, it implies the dynamics of mutuality in space(s), word(s), time(s), and text(s), with knowledge and existence, both caught in that dynamics. It is a principle that tells how the object and the subject are perennially reversed in their relation. It speaks of how the self is thus constituted. If one definition of nationalism is that it is a system of cultural signification, this signification thrives on reflexivity—in other words, a nation does not by itself only determines its signs. The signs are determined by an element of "other" that helps in constituting the signs. Nations thus rarely avoid the problem of reflexivity. Even if we stop short of generalization, we can see at the least, how the nation in India constitutes itself by reflecting on its neighbors and how the existence of a neighbor, an intimate knowledge of it, becomes crucial for determining India, in other words Indianess. Reflexivity features in the strategy of finding similarities and differences.

Linguistic nationalism has been problematized by religion in this subcontinent. Anti-colonial nationalism was similarly problematized by religion. A nationalist strategy that seeks identity in common factors (like language, geography, anti-colonial resistance), at the same time probing into differences (like their language/our language, their religion/our religion) thus becomes inevitable. The dynamics of understanding thrives on the chiaroscuro of identity and difference, they always raise the possibilities of contra-history, that is to say, the history of the desire to go against history, only to deny it immediately after. Given this context, in understanding Bangladesh, the Indian has to appreciate this psychology of the margin. Many crucial cultural, social and psychological artefacts, such as autobiographies, thrive on the margins—margins of fact and memory, history and literature, identity and difference, nation and the person, conflict and accommodation, and desire and resolution. It is impossible therefore to deny these artefacts, such as autobiographical writings and the memorial accounts, a place of utmost importance in appreciating the dynamics of understanding in South Asia.

Intimacy—A Corollary of Reflexivity

One can argue in the vein of Ashis Nandy, that it is the intimacy that creates multiplicity as well as the rigid one-dimensionality that then submerges multiplicity.[3] There is some merit in this observation. Ashis Nandy of course speaks of intimacy in a different context, where colonialism so much mixes with or engulfs the native self that the latter is lost and has to be first recovered before it is free from imperialism. Speaking in our context, we may see that intimacy brings in its wake a certain kind of reflexivity which does not sink our "multiple self" into oblivion, but makes it sensitive and reciprocal, responsive to the stirrings of mind, matter and heart. Polar ends such as the

South Asian universal versus the parochial, the nation-state centric material versus the spiritual, the achieving or the competitive versus the non-achieving, and the rational versus the emotional do indeed meet inasmuch as they are created because of our intimacy with our neighbors. It is this intimacy that always raises the possibility of contra-history, contra-facticity—an alternative mythography.

This point needs a little elaboration. Reflecting on the political understanding of Bangladesh, we can say that we of this Bengal know them so much. They too know us. We know our mutual betrayals, hopes, and despair. Thousands of people cross border and ferry news from here to there and there to here. Our rivers, ecological-agricultural regions, transportation networks, clan ties, affinitive links, folk regions, remain spread across the entire land. Above all, we know what they write, how they think; they too know of us. To deceive ourselves of the pangs of proximity, we have changed categories into opposites: migration is infiltration, border trade is smuggling, empathy is interference, area study is policy prescription, and neighborhood is near abroad. But while this metamorphosis shows a rigidity of mind born of intimacy, our memory, literature and our thousand and one responses speak of the multiplicity of selves too. It is not enough to say that this is a remainder of Partition. Of course, social sciences, journalism, state policies, and other elements of the language of power seek to impose our standards on Bangladesh, completely misreading her self (selves). This should no doubt be resisted. But, more fundamentally, it is a question of alternative history, seeking other possibilities, seizing the signs of multiplicity born out of intimacy, dialogue, and hence reflexivity. After all, each history leaves in its trail a remainder, each historical act other possibilities. Reflexivity thrives on that. The question of open choices producing reflexivity, therefore, turns past as present, then to a fractured present, to a remade past, onto a new past—a lingering hope, almost a despairing hope of a different future.

We are, it seems then, hopelessly caught in a bind. For, to define ourselves, we have to now define our neighbors. Our liberal present has to produce a not so liberal neighbor, our secularism has to find a fundamentalism there, our modernity faces someone's traditionalism, and our economic progress is counter-posed to her poverty. And this we do, not only to define our tri-umphant self, we do it to resolve the quarrel and tensions in our many voices. In order to Westernize our present, we must non-Westernize others, just as in order to challenge the given present, we must reopen a settled past. The first produces history out of half-truth, the second counterpoises possibility to history in order to drag history into the region of mytho-graphy. Our attempt to understand our neighbor cannot settle for either. More than the scholarly articles of international re-lations, the literary accounts ... reflect that fluidity. ...

Reflexivity therefore calls for a politics of new language of understanding a neighbor. The received language of inter-national politics is illegitimate in this task. It is very difficult to shake off the image of the "Bangladeshi Mussalman" from Bengali upper class or the Assamese upper caste Hindu minds, which think of the former as a primal force, representing un-tempered and unmediated primitive impulses. This image will cease to be legitimate only when we stop offering primacy to the military metaphors of fear and security in our understanding of Bangladesh, which pass off as politics. This politics is after all only current history. In other words, desire and contra-facticity have no place in it. It implies that the language of understanding our neighbor cannot be primarily of fear and anxiety. In fact, that language of living in empathy exists by ceasing to accord primacy to the metaphors of a politics of security. It relives a failed past, an act often termed as cultural, to re-deploy the fluidity. ...

... (Now) I begin with an attempt to examine the elements that lie beneath the political dynamics of dialogue constituting friendship, accommodation, and understanding. And from that I want to make an attempt to understand the rules of formation of the language of dialogue.

TRUST, DIALOGUE, UNDERSTANDING

There are two ways in which my argument of pitching friendship and understanding (indeed as will be soon clear, I am here arguing for a democratic inquiry) on the theme of dialogue may be construed. These two ways are ironically contradictory. First, it may look like an ethical or a pious tract. Second, it may seem a leaf straight out of a book of enlightened self-interest. Let me place my response to these two assumptions at the outset, for these clarifications will put the submissions that follow in this (essay) in a clearer light. First of all, I am neither contesting here the ethical underpinning of what is argued here, nor am I denying the factor of interest. But in pointing out the ethical dimension of understanding and the process of accommodation of interests, I am only suggesting a historical course. It is a course through which desire for friendship refuses to be satisfied with historical verdicts and furrows long tunnels imperceptibly within this history to be able to face it with what I have called mythography. I am also suggesting that the accommodation of varying interests, reconciliation, partnership, and partisanship are best understood as historically achieved relations.

In trust, dialogue, and understanding, we have, therefore, the working of history that contains within it the desire to step beyond the historically set limits of accommodation. These are the "truth games" that make relations unstable, but in an assuring manner they encourage a politics of trust, and trust in building up an ethics of friendship. To clarify this point of historicity of relations, on which trust and understanding build up, I want to make a move here by way of picking out certain contemporary themes in inter-state and inter-nation relations in this region. I wish to hold them up in the mirror of the politics of accommodation to show how a historically predicated argument of relations that admits the nuances of contra-history is a better tool for understanding the dynamics of dialogue.

Trust

I want to begin with the crucial theme of *trust*. Trust (or, the idea that the logic of trust is operational only within networks of "traditional," that is already formed, relations constituting a network, and therefore by logic is not operational where this tradition is not evinced to naked eyes[4]) occupies a critical place in the military metaphors also. Often we hear from men of strategic circles that X country is not to be trusted, is untrustworthy, and hence can be trusted at one's own peril. This argument is then extended inward from inter-state and inter-nation relations in this region to classify certain groups of people in the country as trustworthy and untrustworthy. We can hear any day that Pakistan committed "treachery," that LTTE went back on cease-fire and broke trust, or that X country cannot be trusted in view of her behavior. Likewise, we are told that Chinese assurances can never be taken at face value in view of their persistence in their own design, or, X community is essentially untrustworthy for their allegiance to Z country, or, Y people at the frontier do not have faith in the nation. In *The Marginal Nation* (1999), in my discussions on trans-border migration in South Asia, I showed how the issue of trust, that expressed itself in a philosophy of not trusting, acts as a pillar in the security architecture of India.

But this raises the question, why do people trust? There are three answers. One, A can trust B because A by trusting B gains. Two, A trusts B because B trusts A and therefore A's gains can be calculated in terms of the accumulated gains of A and B whose mutual trust increases the stock of dividend of trust. Three, A has no other option than trusting B, for B in relation to A invokes trust so much that A has to engage with B in this game of trust to find out the trajectory of relation and relational gain. True as all these explanations are, it is clear that these three explanations are built on an exchange-scenario.[5]

Even when the explanation is that people trust each other *within* an entity (network or collective such as family, locality, community) because that is how they live, or because only that is how they can live, in the process increasing the total volume of social capital, such explanation cannot avoid the fundamental argument of mutual exchange.[6] In a desperate attempt to escape the hold of a neo-classical bind, it has been argued that, "Trust is a key by-product of the cooperative social norms that constitute social capital" or "Trust, it should be recalled, is not in itself a moral virtue, but rather the by-product of virtue; it arises when people share norms of honesty and reciprocity and hence are able to cooperate with one another."[7] This neo-Weberian scenario does not explain three things.

First, it has to depend on a circularity of arguments. For it may be asked, if trust is a by-product of virtue, what begets virtue? If the answer is, trust in norms that constitute social capital begets virtue, then the question would be, if trust is born from social capital, what begets social capital? If the answer is cooperative social norms, that is to say trust, what begets trust? It seems that unlike physical capital (land, machine, money, stock) social capital does not have to reproduce itself on an expanded scale, so that we can continue depending on the holy trinity of virtue–trust–social capital for continuity of "social goods." Second, it does not explain why trust breaks down, except resorting to long term structural explanations of the kind Fukuyama undertakes in *The Great Disruption*, and yet cannot deny that moments of increase and collapse of trust are historically noticeable political periods. Third, what is the purpose in which trust is put to use? Is it to run day-to-day life, or to increase prosperity, or to tide over adversity?

In other words, in trying to avoid the compulsive scenario of exchange, the discourse on trust enters into a bind. This is because it avoids a simple historical–political truth that trust augments in *actions, moments of historical actions*, that reveal to the people their capacity to trust, need to trust, the willingness to trust in times of contention, more appropriately living in the time of contentious history. The only other way is to admit that trust results from a realization of the profitability of exchange. That is to say, that the game is played out in the mirror house of market. While, as I admit, trust may be induced by the notion of gain, the point to note is that such a mirror-arrangement that makes perceptions of the dividends of trust possible is faulty on two counts. First, it cannot take into account the huge stock of trust available in society, because not all stocks can be represented in the mirror of exchange. Second it has no way of explaining why, if trust benefits from exchange, the total stock of trust does not always increase as in many cases. In other words, the game of gains scenario even when accepting a dynamic format cannot explain why people trust each other, why people should trust each other. My plea is therefore for a historically conditioned search for the roots of trust, for a search engine that can negotiate the galaxy inhabited by networks, ties, relations of affinity, histories of mutually conditioned entities, histories of political actions, and of course, a universe of morals that marks this galaxy.

This is a more fruitful way. We shall then open our eyes to acts of altruism that may occur in pursuit of morals, or in an appreciation that such altruist act can bring in a net increase of the fortunes of a group/community/nation, or simply because such acts entail "satisfaction." But in all these increases we shall see the net stock of trust also increasing. History presents before us ample evidences of all these three reasons. Charity, compassion, altruism, trust—all these are based on historically evolved ways of understanding, accommodating, and reconciling.[8] Since values are collectively produced, these become the collective goods of society where goodness and volunteerism become social actions beyond the comprehension of the rational action theorists. Indeed it can be shown in a detailed analysis how co-operation and contention have not been mutually exclusive in popular history. In what Charles Tilly calls "contentious politics," we find trust playing critical role in building up solidarity of various kinds.[9]

Mutiny, war, revolution, strike have produced great moments of trust; similarly, exodus and disasters have also produced trust which have then resolved into great social residue in various forms and ties, ultimately increasing the net social stock of trust. Historians of Naga politics have wondered, why the Naga rebels refused to take advantage of the crisis in 1971 in cornering India and securing gains.[10] Similarly, every student of India–Pakistan relations knows that Pakistan declined to take advantage of the situation in 1962 against India. China did not push for any advantage in 1999 when the border war between India and Pakistan was being waged, even after the bitterness between the two countries following the Pokhran II nuclear test by India. India does not take advantage of the Tibetan issue in a big way in spite of mutual irritants between the two countries over Tibet, that always seem to cloud the fundamental norm of co-existence. Or, let us think of the following questions posed by some chapters of contentious history of India.

What leads the host population to offer shelter to the immigrants who may be aliens? All accounts, nationalist and cosmopolitan, agree that without the massive quartering of the aliens by the host population the aliens cannot survive so much so that nationalists and patriots say that the country's borders are shrinking inwards.[11] Again, how does one explain from the standpoint of the rational theory of trust the genesis of the Khilafat alliance in 1919–21 in the nationalist times in India, before that to the Lucknow Pact of 1916 between Gandhi and Jinnah, and after that to the C.R. Das–Fazlul Haq pact, better known as the Bengal Pact?[12] Or, how does one take note of the complete political character of the steps undertaken by the West Bengal government into initiating the recently concluded pact on Farakka (1998) between India and Bangladesh?[13] Conversely, we have to also take note of the extreme disillusionment among Muslim nationalist minds, when Congress rejected the Bengal Pact, or refused to leave any ground for the Muslim League in the ministries in 1936–37, or when it rejected the Cabinet Mission plan.[14] Again, a historical study of the post-colonial Naga political history will tell us the extreme disillusionment of the Nagas when the government of India broke the Akbar Hydari Accord with them, or of the Kashmiris, when the government went back on promises built on Article 370 with respect to Jammu and Kashmir.[15] Or, when the prime minister of Nepal, B.P. Koirala and Chairman Mao Ze Dong met in Henchow in March 1960 during Koirala's visit to China, what led them into resolving in their conversation not to aggravate the India–China tension over borders that were already building up?[16] Trust, and/or then a sudden cataclysmic loss of trust, were the answer in all these cases.

Evidently, what are considered as fairness, justice, commitment are important. They insulate trust networks. Conversely, a lack of these jeopardizes the trust-stock. The fortunes of democracy depend on how insulated these networks are and how the total stock is able to increase on the basis of familiarity that trust induces. This holds true not only within a country, but in a democratic framework of relations among peoples, nations, and states also. In both we can observe the growth of trust-stock through the growth of trust networks. As Tilly shows, the growth can be gleaned in the observable shift from individual to the network, separate beliefs to shared stories of fortune and woe, from distinct and separate cognition to conversation, unilateral action to interaction, and deliberation to everyday talk. The transformed locus and basis of trust point out that the strategic height in the politics of accommodation is not the individual participant (I include the state also in the list of individual actors), but the collective process that generates trust. The challenge is to understand the process—the mechanisms, sequences, outcomes, reproductions, and then fathom and fashion an appropriate politics of peace.[17] In Palestinian peace politics this is called "amanah," which means trust reposed in someone who has to keep it, a responsibility, and a treasure. In fact, in Hanan Ashrawi's autobiographical chronicle of public politics of peace, *This Side of Peace*, the concept of trust comes back again and again as leitmotif.[18]

Discussion of trust leads us to the theme of *inequality*. Though the issue of inequality itself is of significance in discussions of social relations, my concern here specifically relates to the issue of how inequality affects trust, thereby political accommodation. Apart from the basic fact that inequalities are produced from the ways all kinds of social goods and capital are produced and traded, and reinforce the power structure or create new power structure, inequality is a product of various classificatory modes. These are the classificatory modes in which we observe, gaze, exchange, relate, correspond, converse—in short, we make our appearance. Again I am speaking here of individuals and groups as well as individual states and groups of states engaged in relational acts.

It should not be difficult to see how our ways of taxonomy induce inequalities. The arrival of modern economy in this region has ensured that individuals have to pass "scanners" to land up in various slots with determined attributes and formats, in the process joining people having similar characteristics. In an ironic way therefore taxonomy skews social mobility. Efforts, inheritance, connections, learning, do not make much difference in this space, which is in reality a segmented market, based on classifications of various kinds. Classification produces hierarchy and from that, inequality. Markets, serving as scanners, sort out individuals according to the marginal increases in productivity caused by incremental inputs of the resources they embody or control. These scanning monitors can classify individuals and groups according to indices of attributes, which in modern economy are financial capital, machines, land, and now with increasing importance, information and knowledge. But if that is how the social sensors work, why do societies not break up in unworkable boxes deaf to each other?

The point is that as against these sensors classifying and slotting individuals and groups, we have also individuals and groups conversing with each other. Assuming that inequality will remain in some amount, and has always remained, we need to study the dynamics that temper the inequalities produced and exacerbated by markets. I refer to the mechanics of *dialogue*.

Dialogue

Dialogists, as interlocutors, build on previous experience, improvize, and bring new ideas, values, and goods through intercourse. The collective production of ideas and identities does not necessarily produce symmetry in relations, but the mechanics compel continuous engagement and prevent a party from running away with all the goods. The "social colloquy" that Tilly speaks of is a dynamic for engaging with inequalities. Thus while inequalities may result from economic domination, patterns of interlocking that produce unequal networks, asymmetrical control over resources, unequally paired categories, opportunity-hoarding, and categorical distinctions, and we cannot claim that dialogues undo any of these, yet dialogue increases the strength to negotiate inequalities.

The practice of dialogue is significant for three reasons:

1. Certain specific modes of dialogue reactivate the residue of morals, which are then transformed into moral capital in fighting inequalities.
2. Dialogue by locating the fault-lines in structures of coercion weakens organized centres of coercion, which have always thrived on inequalities.
3. Certain forms of dialogue augment trust and trust builds up solidarity against inequalities.

Indeed, it will be worthwhile to see how the relations between the three elements I am referring to here—inequality, dialogue, and trust—work in a dynamic format. Grossly we can say that, increase of inequality weakens trust. Increase of dialogue strengthens trust and weakens inequality. Decrease of dialogue shows increase of inequalities and a decrease of trust. This scenario holds greater relevance in the current global context, also in our own regional context. For in this context, the three factors—finance capital (more potential as it becomes more volatile), control and management of information, and control of science and technology—reinforce inequalities and have the capacity to twist the mechanics of dialogue to make the latter compatible with the former. Ironically, civil wars, genocide, proliferation of arms, and mercenary activities in state and non-state forms have created a situation that invokes the need for dialogue with increasing frequency. But this is precisely the situation that can invoke dialogue without necessarily reducing inequalities. Here we have the most intriguing element in the dynamic scenario that I have just sketched above. An increase of dialogue may not necessarily decrease inequality or correspond to decreasing inequality, while increasing inequalities will certainly affect the total stock of trust.[19]

Yet there is more to the issue of the relation between dialogue and inequality that brings us to one more aspect of this relation besides the three mentioned above. What we have not said explicitly so far is the issue of inequality of power, the asymmetries of position. The question hence arises, if trust breaks down completely and the asymmetries of power assert themselves so much that conversation collapses, how will dialogue be restored without which democracy cannot proceed? One answer is that democracy comes by the powerful (authoritarian) route; "we must break the egg" to bring in place the right sort of institutions, set the governmental order, and discipline anarchic social forces. That was the logic of Samuel Huntington, when he appreciated the political legitimacy of modern rule in Turkey in his thesis on "political order in changing societies."

That is again the logic of the way Russia has been democratized; this process of democratization of Russia after 1991 is again a process of "breaking the egg," when hundreds of thousands of Russians had to perish, sink under poverty, and had to endure the emergence of the mafia at all levels. The parliamentarians had to be gunned down, the parliament house had to be bombarded, and the political society had to accept the humiliation of forced participation in repeatedly rigged electoral order—all this so that Russians could become subjects of democracy. Apart from the moral ground, the problem with the metaphor, as Alexander Motyl, one of the most astute observers of Soviet and East European politics pointed out, is that we do not know how many eggs have to be broken before the omelette can be served.[20] In any case the social cost of ruining trust and dialogue is bleeding for democracy. The result is in fact what Antonio Gramsci had termed "passive revolution," whereby the state emerges victorious over democracy, and authoritarianism permanently inscribes a democratic order. We are, then, left with the other route—the route of dialogue, familiarity, and rebuilding trust. But how can that route be operational in a situation of complete breakdown of trust, and then dialogue? And faced with several such situations in many of the post-colonial regions in the world today, are not situations worsened by our inherent liberal idea about our own capacity to understand others? To say the least, such idea and capacity both suffer from a paradox, akin to almost the liar's paradox. For example, John Rawls at the end of his celebrated essay, "The Law of Peoples" (1993), asks and answers:

> If it should be asked whether liberal societies are, morally speaking, better than hierarchical societies, and therefore whether the world would be better place if all societies were liberal, those holding a comprehensive liberal view could think it would be. But that opinion would not support a claim to rid the world of non-liberal regimes... Political liberalism holds that comprehensive doctrines have but a restricted place in liberal democratic politics in this sense.[21]

In other words, liberalism cannot become comprehensively liberal without negating its essence. Surprisingly, Rawls has not seen the logical fallacy of this position that arises when a doctrine of democracy is not built on a theory of dialogue. What is termed as barbarity and total loss of civility, is often the total breakdown of trust between communities, and hence of dialogue. As much as this is true between communities, it is also true of the relation between countries, and peoples. How can trust be restored?[22] How and why will the weak, the victims of asymmetries of power, agree to dialogue? How and why will communities agree to restore their relation to some form of co-existence or familiarity? How will dialogue become the key to restoration of trust and thus reconciliation? In other words, how the reconciling practice, that is, restoration of trust and dialogue, can inhere justice, can conceptualize minimal justice as the path to peace and democracy?[23] How can the victims, say of genocide, regain their dignity in situations where regimes, both at the national and international levels, have failed to address the question adequately due to their own divisions, interest groups and "high politics?" Or, how can dignity be restored where memories and trauma imprison their lives and history, because justice has not been given the opportunity to address the crime of genocide, and perpetrators of murders have been politically rehabilitated in positions that have the capacity of influencing the course and conduct of national and international politics? Or, haunted by memory and the desire to escape and occasionally take revenge, the victims turn into permanent escapees? This is a major question, which calls for separate discussion. But one can say at least a few things here on the contribution of truth telling to dialogue, justice, and reconciliation, before we proceed further.

If truth about injustices is about ending judicial immunity/ impunity of the perpetrators of crimes, and helping a society to put the past behind it, it requires nothing short of full knowledge about atrocities committed (on both sides). We still do not know how exactly the truth telling heals or succeeds in bringing about reconciliation. But the right and the ability to tell the truth restore pride and dignity in the abused. Since truth telling can also become banal, as it is fast becoming a staple in the diet of transitional peacekeeping, truth itself is becoming a victim of the daily truths of maneuver and manufacture of silence under new conditions. Truth telling is often de-linked from the process of justice. Lawmakers and judges ignore the vast amount of truth about injustices and abuses revealed by truth commissions. As a result reconciliation becomes another unequal act. It also shows the almost bottomless difficulties in reconciling truth with office, state, and justice. Truth commissions are only commissions. In South Asia, citizens' and state-recognized human rights commissions sometime engage in dialogues with the victims; they also, organize, occasionally dialogues of the victims and bring out the truth about injustices. But rarely commissions have enforcing powers of the courts, though they practice broader mandate in dialogues with the abused. Truth commissions are different from international tribunals also, such as, the International Criminal Tribunal for the former Yugoslavia, and the International Criminal Tribunal for Rwanda. These are established in response to massive state violence and may function with powers and purpose of a court, but they are singularly incapable of restoring trust and dignity, for beneath the international hype there is very little scope for the truth to come up and make the victim stand up in confidence to negotiate the transition to a less violent and constitutional politics. And, as far as country-specific cases are concerned, in country after country, commission reports are prohibited from having judicial effect, as in Guatemala. On the other hand, as in South Africa, where the commission has the power to pardon if the perpetrator of abuse comes out with truth, and nothing short of full truth with specified time, truth may have some effect on the process of justice.

Here is the role of dialogue. As victims press hard and testimonies mount, truth, if not resulting in direct justice in courts, contributes to making justice possible in the long run by incorporating the truth about injustice into public politics, and making it part of democratic politics. This is what happened after the report of the Shah Commission, which inquired into the excesses committed in India when the national emergency was declared in 1975, came out. Revelation of truth leads to few trials, but it establishes a broad pattern of events of crimes, impunity, and injustices. Thus it is important to inquire, how is the dialogue for truth organized? How is past dealt in public sphere? What are the relationships between the adversaries when truth is spoken? How many (versions of) truths are coming out? Does truth telling encourage the process of justice? Does it get acknowledgment from broad sections of society? What is the process through which society encourages truth? Is truth telling in front of a commission instituted through national legislation, number of drafts, dialogues between parties and other political forces? In other words, we are once again pushing for a relational account—truth, yes; but relating to what, related to what, relates to what? We are again emphasizing the need to study the institutional practices of dialogue, dialoguing for truth that combines demands, desires, and responses.[24] At least this much is clear: first, the mechanics of dialogue for minimal justice would have to be such that dialogue is not subsumed under the asymmetries of power; second, the middle space (often called the humanitarian space) will be able to organize the mode/modes of dialogue so that truth about (how populations became) victims, inequalities, and injustice comes out to reinforce the point that reconciliation and justice are inseparable; third, truth and reconciliation become the reason of dialogue; fourth, the truth about the destruction of trust, about barbarity, cannot be single. Dialogue becomes what I term in discussing the politics of reconciliation—"multilogue," or "plural dialogues."[25]

In having many themes and many audiences the dialogists widen the question of justice. Hanan Ashrawi writes:

Once I was asked how many audiences I had in mind when I gave public briefings or responded to official questions. I began counting. The strata of listeners became a host of internal ghosts fighting for my soul and speech. Was I expected to keep them separate, to identify each one and address in its own parlance? Would I speak to our own constituency, a people under occupation, the same I would address Israeli public opinion? Did I exercise self-censorship when targeting the ears of the leadership in Tunis? Which Arab constituency or government did I envisage when speaking the language of our torn world? As a woman was my discourse gender-based? Was I slipping into Western garb and an occidental mindset when I faced the foreign media? ... Suddenly I faced captive of the Word, which I had revered and severed for so long. The *logos*, formidable as an enemy and overwhelming as a friend, had become both master and slave. I began to resent the original question, how many audiences I had in mind, which had opened up such a Pandora's box of linguistic and existential self-consciousness.[26]

This is the point where the iron grip of state over the link between dialogue and political order becomes weak. Society repeatedly dying for reconciliation brings into life plural dialogues that not only reflect the plural process of truth and reconciliation, but they become a factor constantly predicating the existent inequalities. In other words, democracy becomes a condition of reducing inequality.

Situations often arise where instead of an outright victory of one party in the battle for justice (Bolshevik victory in Russian civil war, Allied victory in the Second World War, or the communist victory in China in 1949), there is a stalemate. A negotiated settlement ensues, and the shift from illegitimate authoritarianism to democracy is gradual, democracy is fragile, and popular unity is precarious. The capacity of the outgoing regime is still enormous. But equally strong is the memory of all injustices, asymmetries, and the determination to prevent recurrence of such massive human rights violations and oppression. And finally, the spirit of the constitution, that is to say, the mood of framing new rules and abiding by them, marks the beginning of the new order. In short, in such a situation, dialogue is not ensuing from the constitution. Rather the constitution bases itself on the spirit of truth about injustices, the desire to heal the wounds, and the overwhelming urge to combine the desire to punish the guilty with the desire to restore justice through dialogue, procedure, and an agonizing inquiry. It is a long way, from Nuremberg Trial to the present Geneva trials, for crimes against humanity. It shows the inadequacy (I admit the necessity) of these modes and the urgency of the politics of restoration of agency/autonomy to the victim. Dialogue to find out truth, to speak out the truth, to inflict shame on the perpetrators and accomplices of injustice, to voice the imperatives of accountability and to demand procedures to punish the guilty, cannot erase asymmetries of power. But it becomes a necessary mechanic in facilitating the transition from injustice and occasional retributive justice to restorative justice (restoration of dignity and the combination of justice with reconciliation), and recognition of past injustices.[27] Here is what one correspondent wrote of dialoguing for restoration of dignity by stressing on justice:

The diminutive witness struggled unsteadily to gain her feet and
then launched into a story that had been seared into her memory
over the six decades since the events: Wan Aihua was eleven when
Japanese soldiers stormed her North China village, killing her parents, raping her, and beginning her enslavement as a "comfort
woman" to Japanese forces. Under the repeated prodding of the tough
young Chinese prosecutor, her story cres-cendoed to an emotional
peak and she collapsed on the stage, requiring emergency hospitaliz-
ation. Her testimony was among many presented by 75 former
comfort women to the Women's International War Crimes Tribunal
on Japan's Military Sexual Slavery... The tribunal offered a unique
perspective for posing issues pertaining not only to Japanese war
crimes, but also to those committed by other nations.[28]

Dialogue that speaks of reconciliation on the basis of truth,
justice and restitution, thus restores the moral content of trust,
brings out the fallacies of a "rainbow nation," and thereby
strengthens the political ethic of democracy. In other words,
we are engaged with the perennial theme of democratization of
relations, because as in the case of trust and inequality predicating
the mechanics of understanding, the factor of democratization
of relations also reflects on understanding and accommodation.
Admitting the complexities in the three-way figure of inequality,
dialogue, and trust, it becomes necessary to see, first, how democracy becomes a casualty if understanding evaporates, and second, how democracy aids understanding and vice versa. It is
clear that I am again taking here a relational stand. We do not
have to go into the controversies in democratic theory now, though
what I am going to argue may indicate the way the issue of
democracy can be looked at in our context.

The significant issue to note in the context of studies of democracy is that, democracy today arouses two kinds of discussions.
One is the theme of transition, second is the theme of institutions. The moment policymakers, analysts, and scholars in this
region sit together to mull over democratic issues, the issues
invariably are: Is the state of affairs democratic enough? How
can these be made democratic, or more democratic? What are
the causal mechanisms for a democratic transition? What are
the requisites? These questions belong to the theme of transition. Similarly they discuss: Why are certain institutions not

democratic? How to insulate democracy? What are the procedures and institutional practices of democracy? These questions belong to the theme of institutions. It is not difficult to see why democracy is perched today on these two themes—transition and institutions—clearly, it is the post-restoration period beginning with 1989, the *annus mirabilis*. But this is significant, for with these themes being internalized in democratic theory, the latter creates democratic hierarchy, a ranking of more, less, and never democratic, and relegates to the back the issue of justice, equality, and understanding. Inside the country, we have the stereotypical case of Bihar unendingly lampooned in the elite-controlled national media as lacking inherent democratic strength. Outside, Pakistan is placed absolutely low in a similar ranking order, for it cannot have democracy because democratic institutions are not sustainable there. We also have some kind of paradigmatic truth in the political culture of the rulers here, that Islam is unsuitable for democracy. In these examples and explanations, either the requisite mechanism for transition is held to be absent, or the institutions for democratic functioning are considered weak. In this reappearance of the structural-comparative school, we can locate the justification for democratic hierarchy, more accurately democracy producing its deficit.[29] The reason why democratic theory produces this is because the route is non-relational, static. As against this I am advocating a relational route that places dialogic relation at the heart of democracy. Only in this way can we re-inscribe in democratic theory, the themes of public rights and public claims to justice, trust in the procedure and consequences of mutual approval of the norms of justice, and an expansion of political society. That is the only way in which orphans of time can become heirs of their own history of peace making and reconciliation.[30]

But how can we do that? Let us remember what has been argued above on inequality and trust. The regime of relations existing in the region may promote inequality by making the weakening of trust networks its explicit goal. Such weakening may result in confrontation, colonization, civil war, and sometimes, outright annexation. We have ready instances of all these. Deficits if suddenly become too big, or shocks to democracy too strong, relations can become more asymmetrical, more disengaging, more dissociating. Trust-stock will plummet affecting democracy in a serious way. It is important therefore to critically analyze phases of sudden appearance of deficits and shocks (1946–48, 1974–77, 1991–93 in India, 1970–72, 1974–76 in Bangladesh, 1995–2000 in Sri Lanka, 1998–2000 in Nepal) to understand why inadequate democratization makes accommodation and understanding difficult. ...

... while democratic theory acknowledges the element of dialogue, it has yet to answer to the fact that contentious dialogue marks the perennial inadequacy of democracy. Dialogue, in other words, is not always the great harmonizer that liberal theory would have us believe, its operation is often contentious, and there is a dialectic in its relation with democracy. Contentious dialogue is the mark of democratic deficit, but dialogue also builds trust and acts as a supplement. One can say in that sense, it strengthens popular democracy. ...

I urge for this relational understanding, because it is not abstract notions such as "civil society" that is going to take the politics of democracy further. The relational route makes possible for democracy to have multiple ways of achieving its goal arriving constituted by a variety of collective political actors, organizations, institutions, exchanges, and forms of participation. These paths may range from protected polity, expanded political society, widened citizenship, heightened collective identity or republicanism, contentious conversation to tolerance, widening of networks, and innovation of new mechanisms of dialogue.

The truth is that the amazing variety of ways in which democratization occurs depends on combinations and concatenations of three basic elements—expansion of trust-stock, negotiation with inequalities, and spurt in dialogues. This also explains why mobilization–repression–bargaining scenario (the nationalist period in India) or techniques of co-optation, containment, dissolution of coalitions, imposition, and categorization (the post-colonial period in Sri Lanka), cannot block the elemental democratic thrust. Indeed, in the relational scenario that I am sketching, democracy as a political order may have all these in order to keep itself steady. It may use the former strategy in order to control the forces of challenge. In the second scenario, its conduct may be marked by a strategy to co-opt these challengers to democracy. It may confine the contending forces, may dissolve old coalitions, may impose new rules, and may try to block the sudden surges of dialogue threatening democratic order by categorizing participants in various orders. Indian democracy adopted the last mode when confronting the challenge from the Left. It simply categorized them into civilized Left, and the non-civilized and unconstitutional Left. But, thereby creating deficit in the stock of trust, reducing familiarity, and increasing inequalities, democracy creates its own supplement—a dangerous supplement in form of further desire for democracy that may push the day-to-day existence of democracy to the point of possible nullity.

In short, the problem of accommodation and understanding that I have been discussing is absolutely a political problem. And that is why, a theory of multiculturalism as a way to negotiate plurality is inadequate for critical engagements with the issue of democracy. The stakes are high here. The three themes, once we view them in the glass of a politics of accommodation, suggest serious intellectual inquiries into issues of friendship and enmity, war and peace in this region. The task of understanding is irreducibly political. I do not deny that a pursuit of understanding entails issues of culture; some wistfully say that we need a "civic culture" of accommodation that can strengthen trust and civilize public politics. But the practice of trust, dialogue, of contending with inequalities, of pointing out the incessant production of democratic deficit, is a political task. And there I part company with those in search of the elusive civil society, also those in search of retrieving collective memory of democracy for rectification of democracy and restoration of friendship.

Rules of a Dialogic Act

By now I hope to have made my arguments clear as to where my fundamental critique of the military metaphors around friendship and enmity lie. All military metaphors are moved by the "fear of the masses." Fear of the masses in this age of delirium has not only evoked direct military metaphors leading to the emergence of notions of "peacekeeping army," "waging peace", and "peace-building," but has also led to a virtual zeroing in on madness, distrust, quarrel, and restoring sanity. The same fear has led to finding out the rules of "decomposition and recomposition of the multitude," in short, rules of making democracy a fully functioning regime, which means making democracy work as its own mask. Thus we have strange bedfellows in post-colonial democracies, that are so, because they are paired as binaries—distrust/trust, insanity/sanity, anarchy/democracy, and collapse/reconciliation. These binaries make possible for democracy, stricken with fear of the masses, to co-exist with the various military metaphors.[31]

In showing the complex relations between democracy and understanding, the intention was double. First, I wanted to examine at least the possibility of a different logic of accommodation that is not grounded in the binary of security or morals. That path is a tried one and critical theorists of democracy should look for possibilities of understanding elsewhere— fundamentally, in the inadequacies and adequacies of democratic politics, in the capacity of democratic politics at a given moment to encourage trust and understanding.[32] Auden had written in his poem, *New Year Letter*, "...true democracy begins with free confessions of our sins." By such logic the military metaphors also can be shown to be a part of the scenario of "breaking trust, breaking ties and breaking homes." Second, I wanted to locate the roots of the inadequacy of the language of accommodation that is available with us now. It is not enough to say that the rational actor approach cannot develop the language of accommodation. For, if behind accommodation lies understanding, we have to formulate its own politics, which may sometimes look like a self-interest theory or an ethical theory of friendship and of brotherhood/sisterhood. But make no mistake, such a politics will have its own language. The initial similarities, if there are, are but tokens of the newness of the new formulations. But can we locate some of the basics of the new language of the politics of understanding on the basis of observing the rules of accommodation?

Understanding the Politics of Understanding

Here are some very tentative answers for colleagues in democracy research. At least, the direction of my own work will be along these lines. Let us recall that in the beginning we had defined understanding as understanding difference. If things were identical, there remains nothing to understand. But if trust, dialogue, the reflexive dynamics, and the ever-continuing process of democratization are based on understanding, what helps understanding? What are its rules? Of course we can say that understanding is based on trust, dialogue, and the ever-recurring process of democratization. And these facilitate the former. There is nothing to disagree on this, except that causal theories always lead to chicken and egg explanations. Beyond an immediate point they do not help us to come to terms with a problematic. We must look into the rules of its formation, and not origin–accounts.

Understand difference? This immediately leads us to ask how do we perceive things are different? We obviously look for signs, representations, and symbols. But our wisdom is compromised there, for in that act of locating difference we may be only looking at ourselves, a voyage of vindication of what we stand for in this world. Since symbols of difference are often cultural, we shall always lapse into what Edward Said had called in a different context "orientalism." The problem is therefore, how do we eschew the inevitable narcissistic acts in understanding difference? Two broad rules may be suggested, may be rules of thumb. (Therefore allow many exceptions, revisions, and modifications.) First, never look for symbols, but take what strikes your gaze as elements of a different order, and if at all you have to accept them as signs, take them as empty signs. In other words, do not rush into judging your neighbor who appears to you not as neighbor, but because of your act of perceiving differences, as the "faraway land." This means in a fundamental sense, take them as elements of an order, and not as signs of "something," that something over the spiritual destiny, of which you can preside. Second, when something has caught your gaze, look into it with your history of obscurity, not manifested in your "density of narcissism." In other words, the "different" is someone with whom we relate, because this "difference" belies our truth, our god, our existence. What appears as different is so, because we have related, and difference is nothing but the mediation between my presence, and my functions and acts. Unless we understand these two, we shall be at a loss to comprehend the limits of a liberal language of understanding. Tolerating difference will be nothing but just a high act of piety. Clearly we are pushing here for a thoroughly relational account of dialogue, accommodation, and understanding.

The awareness of a different language of dialogue that takes into account the differences, the longing, belonging, and the relations lying in various repositories, requires a non-referential conception of language to be applied to the study of dialogues that incessantly take place in society, and among nations. Concretely, it means exploring the systemic relationship between terms and propositions within the language rather than viewing these terms and propositions as only having some putative experiential reality, of which, they are assumed to be the expressions. In order to rewrite the political history of dialogues that will be able to indicate the dynamics of understanding, that is to say understanding of differences among the nations and peoples of this region, we have to start therefore from the other side of the chain. An attention to the language of dialogue will imply discarding a simple notion of dialogue as some reflection of the degree of consciousness of dialogue among social beings and political entities. In other words, the political language of dialogue cannot be decoded beyond a point to reach a thesis about the conflict of primal and material interests; indeed it is the structure of the political language of dialogue that conceives and defines interests.

In political theory, dialogue has held a mysterious place. Political theory has not been as yet able to solve in its 2,400 years of history whether dialogue signifies a pedagogical enterprise, or a mode of production of knowledge, or a neutralizing discourse, a trope, or a matter of resolving identity through a critically existential encounter. In the *Great Dialogues of Plato*, for example, while it is clear that the dialogues serve as discursive ploy, it also appears as a way of life as Dion Chrysostom describes of the Hellenic city of AD 70. Long after Plato, Mao Ze Dong had said that dialogue was crucial for the correct handling of contradictions among the people, implicitly conveying the argument at the same time that only a certain political consciousness and a certain political leadership could ensure the culture of dialogue. Else, in a world of asym-metries of power, it becomes a dialogue of the deaf.[33] In the ideas of Antonio Gramsci, the place of dialogue remains complicated and is connected to his discussions on state and civil society. Gramsci had argued that it always happened that individuals belonged to more than one private association, and often to associations that were objectively in contradiction to one another. A totalitarian desire aimed at ensuring that members of a particular party would find in that party all the satisfactions that they had formerly found in a multiplicity of organizations, that is to say, such party aimed at breaking all the threads that bound these members to extraneous cultural organisms. It also aimed at destroying all other organizations or incorporating them into a system of which the party was the sole regulator. Gramsci saw in this desire a paradox—the parallel existence of progressive and regressive aspects. Such desire occurred when the given party was the bearer of a new culture, also when the given party wished to prevent another force, the bearer of a new culture, from materializing.[34] What Gramsci wrote of parties is no less true of nations.

Dialogue is communication. With the growth of institutions of communications we have now what Jurgen Habermas has defined as the "public sphere." The emergence of a public sphere belongs neither to the state nor to the individual citizen. It becomes a mediating sphere that mediates between society and state, in which the public organizes as the bearer of public opinion. Yet we must remember that this public sphere is often a degraded public life, where the public faces its various particularisms, and long-term political disempowerment in the backdrop of short-term empowerment in the arena of the public. Thus the public sphere in the nation induces communication and dialogue only to retard it later. Dialogues are thus something to be managed. The institutions of dialogue such as Assembly debates, diplomatic notes, exchanges and meets, state–community accords, the various social and political contracts, or say, trade union negotiations, become crucial to the science of government. The more power takes on what Foucault called "capillary form," the greater is the importance of dialogues. Dialogue becomes a tool of governance, it becomes crucial in constituting the field that he terms as governmentality. It becomes the form of a transactional mode on which modern state and state relations base themselves. Faced with such a reality, dialogue even though emanating from a more fundamental phenomenon of reflexivity remains tantalizingly perched on the ethic of the nation.

One fruitful way of understanding the tension around the concept of dialogue is to stress its character of mediation. In fact, the question of resolving or reaching identity through critically existential encounters, that is, through dialogues, belongs to the domain of mediation. Since there is an inerasable asymmetry in social identities, we shall be forever searching for a "subject supposed to liberate" identities from asymmetries to enable them to engage in an equal and fair dialogue, and then finding in place of such a subject, the existence of a constitutive lack. In simple words, this means a hegemonic power negotiating the asymmetries is often only a short-term reality, while dialogues, that is, the mediating encounters, are the long-term phenomena of society. It is the lack that constitutes the reason of dialogue.

Two important corollaries follow from this. First, since the lack (of hegemonic power) constitutes itself as the subject, that is, such a lack promotes the mediating nature of dialogue, it implies a series of signifiers of lack, "of the absentfullness," which are constantly produced in politics. These also signify the presence of a communicative order, something akin to what Habermas describes as "communicative rationality." Second, since the lack itself is the subject, making dialogue the reason of a communitarian and communicational existence, identities are therefore always transient and precarious in a politically managed society. Identification always fails to achieve a full-fledged identity. Dialogue becomes thus the condition of the management of an incomplete society forever trying to be civilly and politically complete. We have to remember that dialogues today, for all the reasons recounted above, constitute a new politics of knowledge and politics of cultures. In this new politics of knowledge the dominant mode still remains hierarchical, for the dialogic structure carries the elements of inequalities residing in society, and therefore represses constantly *the other* within. And hence whenever dialogue occasions friendship and increases trust, the dialogic situation is marked by an implicit recognition of equal right to interpretation, a rejection of the comparativist legacy, a willingness to open oneself up for remark and involvement.[35]

In the theatre of dialogues, others are thus being constantly reproduced—"they cannot be taken in, they cannot be expelled." They give "yes" to reconciliation and then they give it the slip. Dialogues are thus never finished. They do not produce harmony. They ensure the conditions of unstable stability. They ensure the existence of others, that is to say, the remaining of the past, the existence of the beyond, in the selves. They see to it that the "assured horizon of a hermeneutic question" remains impossibile.[36]

Difference, accommodation, dialogue, trust, partnership, friendship, partisanship, reconciliation—these are the themes to be recounted again and again in order to understand the language of democracy. This is what I term as *understanding*. Understanding eschews absolute friendship. Understanding is the understanding of differences, understanding through dialogue. In short, understanding is the culture of democracy. Yet it would not be enough to say so. Two points need immediate attention on the basis of which we can develop our ideas little more. First, if neither identity nor difference is absolute, it means understanding is a function and product of what I have termed as "plural dialogue" in the context of Pakistan–India conversation.[37] Second, understanding would mean further, as I indicated (elsewhere), the development of a middle ground, not in the meaning of compromise but in the sense of a "politics of communication" as well as "a communication of politics," and the "politics of democratization against the politics of democracy." It is this aporia that will face us eternally. Therefore we are not speaking of a rational field of communication where actors understand each other to create an understanding of which Habermas tells us, but we are speaking of the problematic of a production of consensus that lies at the heart of the issue of dialogue. Etienne Balibar writing of the politics of Spinoza posed the problem in this way: "How can one produce a *consensus*, not just in the sense of the communication of pre-existing opinions, but above all as the condition of the creation of *communicable opinions* (that is, opinions which are not mutually exclusive)? And how can this consensus be produced since, as we have seen, the 'matter' of politics is constituted not of isolated individuals but of a *mass*, whose most frequent passion is fear, and to which everyone belongs, rulers and ruled alike? For a mass, in this sense, is a fearful thing, not only to those who govern, but even to itself."[38]

From these few broad rules, we can now probably try to proceed a little more. If understanding were to be an act that could go without relating, it would have been only a matter of speculation. And, indeed, that is what we see in the everyday state affairs in this region. Fortunately, or unfortunately, that luxury of understanding without relating is not allowed in a world of varying systems which are bent upon stamping the flat space of representations with their orders. Understanding being a relational practice, our engagements are marked by an unusual and therefore remarkable parsimony of self-gaze. Imagination with its voluptuous treasure of curious relations and appreciation elbows out narcissistic projects. For once then, we have to accept, that in acts of understanding we have dispensed with, rather willingly, the profundity of meanings in what we observe, profundity of our gaze. What remains then in those that we take as symbols of different meanings? Not deeper meanings, but as Bertolt Brecht had said once, interweaving of references, assertions, codes, distancing modes, autobiographical gestures— a space not of some metaphysical appeal, but simply another theatre, quite simply another soul. In the practice of understanding we have therefore the transmutation—understanding difference to be understood as difference as understanding, or better still difference replaced by understanding. The breach of meaning, the sovereign act of the powerful, is final.[39]

What will be the result of this inversion and the like? Dialogue will become plural, in other words "multilogue." And, what will be the loss? The sacrifice will be the centred space—the space of a Delhi-centred India and India-centred South Asia. Uncentred (de-centred), the political space of accommodation becomes irreversible. Turn, as Roland Barthes had once said, the gallery upside down, nothing would change except some inconsequential inversion of top, down or right, left.[40] For, we would have irretrievably dismissed hierarchy. We shall be able to live without the agonies of being chained to, and therefore, carrying the anxiety of protecting the centred space of which we are a part, for we have related as parts to a centre.

NOTES AND REFERENCES

1. Jurgen Habermas, *Theory and Practice*, John Viertel (trans.). Cambridge, 1996, p. 44.
2. See for a critique of the modern politics of friendship, Jacques Derrida, *The Politics of Friendship*. London, 1992.
3. Ashis Nandy, *The Intimate Enemy: Loss and Recovery of Self Under Colonialism*. Delhi, 1983. On reflexive nationalism, see the introduction to Ranabir Samaddar (ed.), *Reflections on Partition in the East*. Delhi, 1997. On the notion of reflexivity, see Pradip K. Bose, "Text of Language, Language of Text—The Post-modern Dilemma," *Margins*, February 2000 (earlier published in Bengali in *Anushtup*, vol. 27, no. 1, 1992).
4. For such a view of trust in most succinct form, see chapters 2 (particularly pp. 47–60) and 12 (pp. 194–211) in Francis Fukuyama, *The Great Disruption—Human Nature and the Reconstitution of Social Order*. New York, 1999, Trust indeed in this logic is seen as social virtue residing in "traditional goods" with historical impulses little to do with the building or maintaining these "goods" or creating social "bads." The difference of my argument that rests on relations and historical events with this argument will be clear from the way I approach the issue. For the network-centric discussion, see also Francis Fukuyama, *Trust—The Social Virtues and the Creation of Prosperity*. New York, 1995.
5. On this, Susan Cross and Robert Rosenthal, "Three Models of Conflict Resolution—Effects on Inter-group Expectations and Attitudes." *Journal of Social Issues*, vol. 55, no. 3, 1999, pp. 561–80. Cross and Rosenthal speak of distributive bargaining (hard, competition-based, agreement oriented approach with lose/zero-sum gain disputes), integrative bargaining (concession-making and search for mutually profitable alternatives), and interactive problem-solving (parties recognize the issue to be a problem for them that calls for interaction).
6. Again I am summarizing Fukuyama's argument here. See also, Herbert Kelman, "The Interdependence of Israeli and Palestinian National Identities—The Role of the Other in Existential Conflicts," *Journal of Social Issues*, vol. 55, no. 3, 1999, pp. 581–600, where Kelman reminds us of what he terms as "negative interdependence" in the zero-sum view of national identity and the "existence in reality of positive interdependence between Israelis and Palestinians." Readers can see how my argument here proceeds along a different direction on the question of dependence and its acknowledgment.
7. Fukuyama, *The Great Disruption*, pp. 49–51. See also Diego Gambetta, *Trust—Making and Breaking Cooperative Relations*. Oxford, 1988.

8. Related to this, see Victoria Kahn, "The Duty to Love—Passion and Objectivity in Early Modern Political Theory," *Representations*, vol. 68, 1999, pp. 84–107.

9. On contentious history and politics Charles Tilly has written enormously. The reader can at least have an idea of Tilly's history and politics from his *The Contentious French—Four Centuries of Popular Struggle*. Cambridge, Mass, 1986.

10. On this see Subir Bhaumik, *India's Northeast—Insurgency Crossfire*. Delhi, 1996.

11. I write on that in detail in *The Marginal Nation—Trans-border Migration from Bangladesh to West Bengal*. Delhi, 1999.

12. I have analyzed the consequences of the disillusion among the Bengali Muslim leaders following the collapse of the Bengal Pact in terms of the evolution of a Muslim public in Bengal; see Ranabir Samaddar, "Leaders and Legacies—Stories in the Time of Transition," *Indian Economic and Social History Review*, vol. 37, no. 4, 2000.

13. How lack of trust played a crucial role in the deadlock over negotiations on Farakka waters becomes clear in the narrative of negotiations in Ben Crow (with Alan Lindquist and David Wilson), *Sharing the Ganges—The Politics and Technology of River Development*. Delhi, 1995; Harry W. Blair, "Democracy, Equity and Common Property Resource Management in the Indian Subcontinent," *Development and Change*, vol. 27, 1996, pp. 475–99; also Ranabir Samaddar, "Flowing Waters and the Nationalist Metaphors," *Studies in Conflict and Terrorism*, vol. 20, no. 2, 1997.

14. On the reaction of Jinnah and his disappointment over the behavior of Congress in 1930s–40s, particularly during the Cabinet Mission period, see the collection of essays in Mushirul Hasan (ed.), *India's Partition—Process, Strategy, and Mobilization*. Delhi, 1993.

15. The story of broken promises is described in details in chapter 7; see also chapter 9.

16. The complete transcript of the discussion between Mao Ze Dong and B.P. Koirala (1960) is now available in *Mao Zedong on Diplomacy*. Beijing, 1998, and reproduced in "BP and Mao," *Nepal Times*, May 25–31, 2001, pp. 1 and 7. In the verbatim record, Mao is recorded as refusing to blame only India for the tension around India–China border, thanks Nepal for refusing to take any side in a dispute between India and China, speaks of resolution of issues between Nepal and China, and speaks repeatedly of the need for trust between developing nations. Similarly, B.P. Koirala speaks honestly of differences between Nepal and China, of his desire to remain neutral in disputes between India and China, and shares his views on ways to develop friendly relation between the two countries.

17. The recent writings of Charles Tilly on trust and inequality and relation to democracy have seemed to me significant. See for example, Charles Tilly, *Durable Inequality*. Berkeley, 1998; "Contentious Conversation," *Social Research*, vol. 65, 1998, pp. 491–510; "Power—Top Down and Bottom Up," *Journal of Political Philosophy*, vol. 7, 1999, pp. 330–52; "Where Do Rights Come From?" in Theda Skocpol (ed.), *Democracy, Revolution, and*

History. Ithaca, 1998, pp. 55–72. I am very much grateful to Charles Tilly for suggesting me these essays and allowing me access to his recent writings. On the role of everyday talk, I am indebted to the writings of Jane Mansbridge; for example, "Everyday Talk in a Delib-erative System" in Stephen Macedo (ed.), *Deliberative Politics—Essays on Democracy and Disagreement*. New York, 1999, pp. 210–39; "Feminism and Democracy," *American Prospect*, vol. 1, pp. 127–36; and, "Using Power/Fighting Power—The Polity" in Seyla Benhabib (ed.), *Democracy and Difference*. Princeton, 1995.

18. Hanan Ashrawi, *This Side of Peace*. New York, 1995, pp. 31, 142, 154–55, 229, 262. Hanan describes at one place how the women of Hamas come in a delegation to her house to dissuade her from joining peace talks in Madrid when so many husbands and brothers of Palestinian women have been illegally jailed and deported by the Israeli authorities and they remind her of her responsibility. At other places in the internal quarrels in the Palestinian peace camp each one is reminded of trust that the people of the occupied territories has placed in them, and she writes that on one occasion how the entire citizens' delegation wanted to resign because of the irresponsible behavior of the PLO and the Palestinian Council reminding the latter of the responsibility that was on their shoulders as they themselves were from the occupied territories.

19. To be clear I am indeed pushing here for a thoroughly relational account as opposed to a static account of a relational category. Donna Luff speaks of "moments" of dialogue in her essay, "Dialogues Across the Divides—Moments of Rapport," *Sociology*, vol. 33, no. 4, 1999, pp. 687–703.

20. Alexander Motyl in an unpublished comment in a seminar on "Democracy and the Margins" organized by the University of the Negev, Beer Sheva, May 19–22, 2000.

21. John Rawls, "The Law of Peoples" (1993) in Samuel Freeman (ed.), *Collected Papers of John Rawls*. Cambridge, Mass, 1999, p. 563.

22. For an instructive discussion that links reconciliation with justice, see, Rajeev Bhargava, "The Moral Justification of Truth Commissions" in Charles Villa-Vicencio and Wilhelm Verwoerd, *Looking Back Reaching Forward—Reflections on the Truth and Reconciliation Commission of South Africa*. London and Cape Town, 2000, pp. 60–67; hereafter *Looking Back Looking Forward*. A longer exposition of his arguments was delivered in his lecture, "Between Revenge and Reconciliation—The Significance of Truth Commissions," in the first peace studies orientation course of the South Asia Forum for Human Rights, Kathmandu, February 7, 2000, mimeo.

23. N.J. Kitz (ed.), *Transitional Justice—How Emerging Democracies Reckon with Former Regimes*. Vol. 2, Washington D.C., 1995; K. Asmal and others, *Reconciliation through Truth—A Reckoning of Apartheid's Criminal Governance*. Cape Town, 1996; Donna Pankhurst, "Issues of Justice and Reconciliation in Complex Political Emergencies—Conceptualizing Reconciliation, Justice and Peace," *Third World Quarterly*, vol. 20, no. 1, 1999, pp. 239–56.

24. On the need to take a concrete look into the practices of truth telling, see Priscilla B. Hayner, "Fifteen Truth Commissions, 1974–1994—A Comparative Study," *Human Rights Quarterly*, vol. 16, 1994, pp. 597–655; also her, "Commissioning the Truth—Further Research Questions," *Third World Quarterly*, vol. 17, no. 1, 1996, pp. 19–29.

25. Ranabir Samaddar, "Plural Dialogues" in Ranabir Samaddar (ed.), *Space, Territory and the State*. New Delhi, 2002.

26. Hanan Ashrawi, *This Side of Peace*, no. 18, pp. 154–55.

27. For this, see three other essays in Charles Villa–Vicencio and Wilhelm Verwoerd, *Looking Back Looking Forward*—Johnny De Lange, "The Historical Context, Legal Origins and Philosophical Foundation of the South African Truth and Reconciliation Commission," pp. 14–31; Wilhelm Verwoerd, "Towards the Recognition of Past Injustices," pp. 158–65; and Mxolisi Mgxashe, "Reconciliation, A Call to Action," pp. 210–18.

28. Mark Selden, "On Asian Wars, Reparations, Reconciliation," *Economic and Political Weekly*, vol. 36, no. 1, 2001, p. 25; see also, chapter 12, "The Redress of Past Grievances—The Nanking Massacre," in Richard Falk, *Human Rights Horizons—The Pursuit of Justice*. London, 2000, pp. 199–216. Yet, it will be wise to note, how these are termed as "past," not "present"— grievances that continue. In chapter 7, I show in the analysis on accords, how past grievances are matters of the present. The question is, how past does it have to be in order to be past?

29. See in this context, Umbarto Eco, "Tolerance and the Intolerable," *Index on Censorship*, vol. 1, no. 2, 1994, pp. 47–55.

30 In discussing the relation mentioned here, the writings of Robert Putnam are well known. See Robert D. Putnam, *Making Democracy Work—Civic Traditions in Modern Italy,* NJ: Princeton, 1993; "The Strange Disappearance of Civic America," *American Prospect*, vol. 24, 1996, pp. 34–48; and "Bowling Alone—America's Declining Capital," *Journal of Democracy*, vol. 6, 1995, pp. 65–78. However, it will be clear to the readers that the path I am taking here will differ significantly from Putnam's.

31. Etienne Balibar, "Spinoza, The Anti-Orwell—The Fear of the Masses" in Etienne Balibar, *Classes, Masses, Ideas—Studies on Politics and Philosophy Before and After Marx*. London, 1993, pp. 3–37; also Warren Montag, "The Pressure of the Street—Habermas' Fear of the Masses" in Mike Hill and Warren Montag (eds), *Masses, Classes, and the Public Sphere*. London, 2000, pp. 132–45. Michael Mann's discussions on what he says "the dark side of democracy" are relevant in this context; they show how democracy has always been a companion of ethnic cleansing. In his forthcoming book, *Murderous Ethnic Cleansing*, he devotes considerable attention on "the colonial dark side of democracy" with reference to the experiences of Mexico, Australia, United States, and particularly the genocide of Hereros, 1904–05. <http://www.theglobalsite.ac.uk>

32. Chantal Mouffe brings this out in *The Democratic Paradox*. London, 2000. She writes, "... the 'constitutive outside' [is] not a content which would be asserted/negated by another content which would just be its dialectical opposite—which would be the case if we were simply saying that there is no 'us' without a 'them'—but a content which, by showing the radical

undecidability of the tension of its constitution, makes its very positivity a function of the symbol of something exceeding it: the possibility/impossibility of positivity as such," p.12; and "... the condition of the possibility of a pluralist democracy is at the same time the condition of impossibility of its perfect implementation. Hence the importance of acknowledging its paradoxical nature," p. 16; See also her essay in this context, "Deliberative Democracy or Agonistic Pluralism?," *Social Research*, vol. 66, no. 1, 1999, pp. 745–58. She writes, "Awareness of the fact that difference allows us to constitute unity and totality while simultaneously providing essential limits is an agonistic approach that contributes in the subversion of the everpresent temptation that exists in democratic societies to naturalize their frontiers and essentialize their identities," p. 758.

33. Mao Ze Dong, "On Correct Handling of Contradictions Among the People" and "On Ten Major Relationships" in *Selected Works of Mao Ze Dong*, vol. 4, Beijing, 1989.

34. Antonio Gramsci, *Prison Notebooks*. Indian edition, Hyderabad, 1996.

35. I am in agreement here with Ashis Nandy's thumb rules for an egalitarian dialogue, except that these almost look like constructing an ideal situation, "east set up against west." The point is, if all are equal in dignity, power, and an appreciative readiness, what is there to dialogue? See Ashis Nandy, "Defining a New Cosmopolitanism—Towards a Dialogue of Asian Cultures," *Identity Culture and Politics—An Afro-Asian Dialogue*, vol. 2, no. 1, 2001, pp. 46–57.

36. Terence Ball, "Deadly Hermeneutics; Or, Sinn and the Social Scientist" in Terence Ball (ed.), *Idioms of Inquiry—Critique and Renewal in Political Science*. N.Y.: Albany, 1987, pp. 95–110.

37. Ranabir Samaddar, "Plural Dialogue" in Ranabir Samaddar (ed.), *Space, Territory and the State—New Readings in International Politics*. Hyderabad, forthcoming, pp. 151–68.

38. Etienne Balibar, *Spinoza and Politics*. Peter Snowdown (trans.). London, 1998, p. 119.

39. This crucial question is brought out in a collection of essays, Anuradha Dingwaney and Carol Maier (eds), *Between Languages and Cultures: Translation and Cross-cultural Texts*. Delhi, 1996.

40. Roland Barthes, *Empire of Signs*. Richard Howards (trans.). New York, 1982, p. 109.

2

TERRITORY AS THE KERNEL OF THE NATION: SPACE, TIME, AND NATIONALISM IN ISRAEL/PALESTINE*

Oren Yiftachel

The article deals with the relations between time and space in
the making of modern nations, focusing on conditions of territorial conflicts in general, and on expansionist "ethnocratic"
societies in particular. Under such conditions, it is argued, territory (the "where" of the nation) becomes a most vital "kernel"
of national mobilization, while the history of national origins (the
"when") tends to become mythical and homogenous, used chiefly
to boost the territorial struggle. A geographical critique of dominant theories of nationalism is presented, focusing on their
"spatial blindness", and analytical fusion of nation and state.
These deficiencies are conspicuous in ethnocratic societies, where
the "national project" does not aspire to merge nation and state,
but, on the contrary, to essentialize and segregate group identities. While the "when" and the "where" of the nation are still
intimately intertwined, it is the latter that provides the core of
nation-building. The claim is substantiated through a detailed
account of Zionist and Palestinian nationalisms. In recent decades, the struggle over land has shaped the two national cultures
as intensely territorial, with a wide range of symbols, values, and

* Despite numerous attempts to secure permission, the Editor of this volume
and the author of this article did not get a response from the publisher, Frank
Cass. We herewith acknowledge that this article was previously published in
Geopolitics, vol. 7, no. 2, 2002 with the title "Territory as the Kernel of Nation
in Israel/Palestine."

practices intimately attached to settlement and land control, pitting Jewish *hitnahalut* (settlement) versus Palestinian *sumud* (steadfastness). Territorial issues, however, remain the "kernel" of Zionist and Palestinian national mobilization[1].

> The Land of Israel was the birthplace of the Jewish people. Here its spiritual, religious and political identity was shaped. Here it first attained statehood, created cultural values of national and universal significance ... After being forcibly exiled from their land, the people kept faith with it throughout their Diaspora and never ceased to pray and hope for their return ... By virtue of our natural and historic right ... we hereby declare the establishment of a Jewish state in the Land of Israel (*Israel's Declaration of Independence, May 15, 1948*).[2]

> Palestine ... is where the Palestinian Arab people was born, on which it grew, developed and excelled ... [Their] willed dispossession and expulsion ... was achieved by organized terror. In Palestine and in exile, the Palestinian Arab people never faltered and never abandoned its conviction in its rights of Return and independence ... and the right of sovereignty over territory and homeland ... The Palestinian National Council ... hereby declares the establishment of the State of Palestine on our Palestinian territory ... (*Palestinian Declaration of Independence, November 15, 1988*).[3]

INTRODUCTION

The territory known as "the Land of Israel" or "Palestine" (or *Eretz Yisrael* and *Filastin* in Hebrew and Arabic, respectively) stretches over an area demarcated by the British as "Palestine" in 1921. Over the years, it has been subject to multiple national and religious claims, drawing on rivalling interpretations of historical origins (the "when") and place (the "where") of collective identities. During the last 100 years, the land has become associated with a bitter struggle between Zionist–Jews and Palestinian–Arabs, both claiming the territory to be their own national homeland.

Given this context, the chapter seeks to show that due to the inconclusive struggle over the land, the type of nationalism developed by both Zionists and Palestinians is highly ethno-territorial. Hence, territory is the main—though by no means sole—shaper of the nation. This is incongruent with the thrust of leading theories on nationalism, which generally privilege national time, culture, or economy over the dynamics and intricacies of collective space. The territorial emphasis is well illustrated by the Israeli and Palestinian Declarations of Independence quoted above. Both documents place great importance on grounding their national identity and claim in a specific *location*, which embodies their histories, memories, cultures, religions, and desired futures.

The article begins with a theoretical account and critique of leading nationalism theories, and continues with a detailed analysis of the historical and geographical making of the Zionist and Palestinian national movements. These form the basis for suggesting a more refined understanding of nationalism in "ethnocratic" settings, marked by geographic, political, and economic *expansion* of a dominant ethnos. In such settings, the "national project" does not aspire to merge nation and state, but on the contrary, attempts to essentialize and segregate group identities.

While the "when" and the "where" are still intimately intertwined in ethnocratic settings, it is contended that the sharper the territorial struggle, the greater the emphasis on the "where," and the greater its influence on the making of national identities. This is so even when processes of globalization and privatization erode the mobilizing power of nationalism in other regions, and seriously threaten the ability of territorial control to protect collective safety and prosperity, in what Zygmunt Bauman has recently termed "the end of the era of space."[4]

To be sure, conceptions of national origins and history remain highly important, but over the course of the conflict have become mythical and homogenous. The "when" of the Zionist and Palestinian narratives provides both sides with rigid historical accounts, geared to justify their claim to temporal *priority* (and hence legitimacy) in their current territorial aspirations.[5] Consequently, many of the political, cultural, and practical emphases of Zionist and Palestinian nation-building have been shaped by an acre-by-acre struggle for land control.

The territorial thrust has spawned another transformation: during the last three decades, the heart of the conflict has shifted from a previous pre-occupation with history and sufferings of

Jewish *galut* (exile, diaspora) and Palestinian *manfah* or *ghourba* (dispersion, estrangement), to a focus on *contemporary* political spaces shaped by the people living in Israel/Palestine itself. Consequently, the main feature of the conflict during the last three decades has pitted expansive Jewish settlement (*hityashvut, hitnahalut*) versus Palestinian resistance and steadfastness (*sumud*).

Given the overlapping definition of Palestinian and Zionist homelands, and the geography of Israeli rule since 1967, the article treats Israel/Palestine (that is, Israel and the occupied Palestinian territories) as a single political unit. Hence, the existing Israeli–Jewish regime cannot be regarded as democratic, but "ethnocratic," ruling in the name of a dominant ethnos over a bi-national and multi-ethnic territory.[6] The population of Israel/Palestine at the end of 2001 was 9.6 million, of whom 53 percent were ethnic Jews, 44 percent Palestinian-Arabs, and 3 percent other groups. Population projections show that Palestinian-Arabs will constitute a majority in Israel/Palestine by the year 2020, without counting possible return of Palestinian refugees.[7]

CONCEPTUALIZING NATIONALISM

In a review of the developments of nationalism studies, Anderson notes:

> There is no disagreement that nationalism has been "around" ... at the very least for two centuries. Long enough, one might think, for it to be readily understood. But it is hard to think of any political phenomenon which remains so puzzling and about which there is less analytic consensus.[8]

This observation underscores both problems and challenges facing researchers into the immensely powerful force of nationalism. The problems relate to the treatment of nationalism by "global" theorists such as Anderson, Smith, Hobsbawm, Gellner, and scores of other leading scholars as all-embracing (albeit flexible) global phenomenon, which needs to be "readily understood."[9] This, despite the enormous variety in the goals, characteristics, and consequences of movements described as "national."

The challenge—to be partially addressed in this article—is to "breathe life" and *geographical dynamism* into our accounts of the very different types of self-determination movements currently lumped under the title "nationalism."

"Global" theories of nationalism are breathtaking in their sweeping scope and ambition. It attempts to explain the entire transformation of the world's political, social, cultural, and economic order during the last two centuries, and connect disparate events in time and space, such as the emergence of self-government in South America, the breakdown of European empires and colonial rule, the expansion of multi-ethnic states such as Indonesia or Turkey, the rise of western European "uniting nationalism," the later emergence of "divisive nationalism" in eastern Europe, or the rise of anti-colonial nationalism in Asia and Africa. A cursory glance reveals that this is a tall order indeed!

An intense, and highly illuminating scholarly debate developed, dominated by three leading interpretations: instrumental, historical–ethnic and social constructivist. The *instrumental approach*, as typified by the works of Earnest Gellner,[10] but also shared by a number of Marxist and materialist analysts,[11] perceives the reorganization of human societies into nation-states as a most efficient mechanism to govern the transition of pre-modern societies towards a new industrial capitalist order. Being a grand modernist project of socio-cultural engineering, nation-building entailed "invention of traditions," and elite manipulation of mass consciousness and political mobilization.[12] The (temporal and cultural) emphasis on modernist reconstruction led Gellner to observe: "It is modernity which produces nationalism ... and ... it is nationalism which engenders the nation, and not the other way around."[13]

An alternative *historical–ethnic interpretation*, spearheaded by the works of Anthony Smith, focuses on the historic "layers" of cultural meanings and collective memories as the foundation of contemporary national identities. Thus, it argues that nationalism cannot be a mere elite-driven project to reconfigure the power bases of the privileged, as implied by most Marxist scholars. It is rather a transformation into the politics of modernity, which remains predicated on deep-rooted attachments to a collective past. This sentiment is manifested in the concept of the "ethnic"—a more primordial locus of cultural, religious and political heritage, born out of a mythical belief in common origins, shared texts, and specific territories.[14]

A third, *constructivist approach* breaks the deadlocked debate on the "invented" versus "real" nature of the nation, by focusing instead on the dynamic modes of *identity construction*. Led by Benedict Anderson's groundbreaking work[15] and the notion of "imagining," this approach portrays nationalism as a constant process of building collective imaginations about the commonality of the nation. The process is intimately tied to modernity, secularism, and capitalism, which trigger the diffusion of the written word ("print capitalism"), and hence the development of collective political mobilization. The emphasis thus shifts to the ceaseless *process* of identity-building and social construction, which replaces a previous scholarly pre-occupation with primordiality and modernity. The centre of attention moves to the prevailing similarities in the dynamics of national "imaginings," in a globalizing order characterized by the existence of "modular" and exportable "components" of national consciousness.[16]

Notwithstanding conflicting interpretations, the three schools of thought appear to concur on several key assumptions, including the existence of nationalism as one global phenomenon, its powerful dominance over the world's political order, and the ultimate aim of nationalism to *merge nation and state*. As explained later, these assumptions are questionable when viewed from the perspective of critical political geography. The brief review presented here pertains only to global nationalism theories; many groundbreaking theoretical works on nationalism, which pertain to other scales, are not covered here (for notable examples, see, Bhabha, H. (ed.), *Nation and Narration*, London: Routledge 1992; Chatterjee, P., *The Nation and Its Fragments*. Princeton: Princeton University Press, 1993).

A GEOGRAPHICAL CRITIQUE

Despite the valuable insights offered by most nationalism theories, they display several deficiencies, which emanate from their global scope and all-encompassing explanatory ambition. Three such deficiencies are noted here: the chronic confusion between nations and states, the bypassing of relevant geographic scholarship, and subsequently, the privileging of the dynamics of time over space. The critique draws inspiration from the seminal works of Gramsci[17] and Lefebvre[18] who perceived nation-building, inter alia, as a sophisticated and highly effective way of expanding the domination of upper strata, through discourses and practices of spatial transformation, including conquest, settlement, boundary setting, and development.[19]

Many theories of nationalism too readily collapse, confuse, or ignore the critical gap between nation and state. Hence, they tend to erroneously equate the processes of *state-building* with *nation-building*. This is clear from the various definitions of nationalism offered by leading theories, which emphasize a joint political institution, common economy, and shared territory.[20] Scholars such as Smith, Anderson, Hobsbawm, and Gellner are undoubtedly aware of the frequent prominence of one group within the new political community defined as the "nation." But these scholars often interpret such a setting as a *temporary gap* between the historical nation (or "ethnic"), and the state. This gap is likely to close gradually through inclusive political mobilization and cultural homogenization. As Billig notes, the legitimacy of the "hyphen" in the term "nation-state" is now taken as "banal."[21]

Despite its prevalence, this is not a universal view, with other notable scholars pointing to a chronic, and even sharpening, disparity between nation and state.[22] Others have pointed to irredentism—a stark illustration of the gap between nation and state—as one of the core expressions of twentieth-century nationalism.[23] Notably, this tension has also been raised by Anderson who reflects critically at his own previous interpretation, and anticipates "an impending crisis of the hyphen that for two hundred years yoked state and nation."[24]

Given the dominant analytical perspective which fuses nation and state, most social science scholarship has assumed a priori the (contentious) existence of the "nation-state." The research activity of an entire generation of scholars has been based on state statistics, textbooks, maps and state-based images of "society."[25] As such, it has legitimized the nation-state construct, in an approach termed by John Agnew "methodological nation-alism."[26] But clearly, the "nation-state" rarely exists as such. The lack of analytical distinction between nation and state has made most theories of nationalism overlook the abuse of the nation-state model, in cases where one ethnos appropriates the state apparatus, while legitimizing its domination in the name of the "national interest."

In highly conflicting cases, the actions of a dominant and ex-pansionist ethnic group may result in the emergence of *ethno-cratic regimes*. Such regimes exploit the international legitimacy and autonomy bestowed on the "nation-state," as the sole expres-sion of "national" self-determination, to facilitate the expanding political and material resources by the dominant ethnic group, often at the expense of minorities and peripheral groups.[27] Hence, ethnocratic regimes simultaneously draw on the legit-imacy of the nation-state order, but at the same time undermine some of its major tenets, such as equal citizenship, inclusive self-determination, protection of minorities, and the possibility for all citizens to participate in the making of the nation-state. Ethnocratic regimes, which are chronically unstable, can be found in cases such as Serbia, Northern Ireland, Estonia, Latvia, Sri Lanka, Cyprus, and Malaysia, to name but several notable examples.

The nation-state mismatch leads to a second critique, focusing on the *spatial blindness* of leading accounts of nationalism. This is expressed by both a lack of analysis on the links between space on nationalism, and a conspicuous paucity of reference to a rich tradition of geography and geographers. Commonly, theories of nationalism "flatten" the state's human space, over-looking the dynamic geographical contours of ethnicities, classes, genders, borders, and development, so critical for shaping the nature of political community.[28] These dynamic "spatialities" often run across, "below" or "above" the putative, flat and stable "national territory."[29] Therefore, analysis of national movements must hinge on the understanding of "active space" which is not merely a backdrop or a container of social change, but exerts a *vital influence* on group identities and relations. The links be-tween space, development, collective identities, and group re-lations are thus *reciprocal*.[30] That is, while political processes create spatial outcomes, these outcomes, in turn, create new political dynamics.

In particular, we must perceive space as a key factor in the generation and reproduction of collective identities. Group "spatiality" may include the degree of ethnic concentration or mix, the proximity of inter-state brethren, the degree of its peripherality, the level of its ideological territoriality, and the process of "territorial legitimization" involved in its identity construction.[31] These factors usually exert a decisive influence on group identity, shaping collective memories, cultural norms, accents, networks, accessibility to material and symbolic resources, socio-economic status, and position vis-à-vis the "others." Hence the division and struggle over space reflects, but also shapes, the social, ethnic, and national landscapes.[32] This is so at all scales, from neighborhood demarcations to the violent partition of states in the name of "peace."[33]

The article will also critique the main theories of nationalism for often privileging the dynamics of *time over space*. This is a common theme, exemplified by a pivotal debate between two prominent theoreticians of nationalism—Anthony Smith and Ernest Gellner. Their continuous debate has focused almost entirely on the question of national "invention" or continuity ("do nations have a navel?"). The essence of modern nationalism was thus perceived in terms of its temporal development. While the two scholars do refer in their work occasionally to territory and homeland, it is likened to a passive "nest" of the nation, not an active determinant of national trajectory and identity. Hence, Smith centres the nation-building project on accumulation of memories, experiences, and histories.

> The nation is a deposit of the ages, a stratified or layered structure of social, political and cultural experiences and traditions laid down by successive generations of an identifiable community ... the contemporary situation of the nation is explained as the outcome, the precipitate, of all its member's past experiences and expressions ... the ethnic past explains the national present.[34]

For Anderson, the very rise of nationalism is positioned against the decline in religiosity, which required new *collective perceptions of time*:

What was then required was a secular transformation of fatality into continuity, contingency into meaning ... [F]ew things were (are) better suited to this end than an idea of the nation. If nation-states are widely conceded to be "new" and "historical," the nations to which they give political expression always loom out of an immemorial past, and still more important, glide into a limitless future.[35]

Indeed, these and other articulations of national time, history, and memory, constitute influential pieces of scholarship.[36] Yet, national time, so prominent in these works, can never be divorced from the on-going construction of national territory. National history is "made" by a ceaseless interweaving of time and space. That is, there can be no credible account of historical development without fathoming the thick enmeshment of political structures and actors within the discursive and material aspects of places, spaces, and territories.

The mere undoing of spatial blindness is not enough. What is needed is a serious consideration of the ceaseless geographical processes which shape and reshape political relations, through the "grids of power" endlessly operating over space and place.[37] A notable example is the making of "ethnocratic" and settler societies, which can never be treated as static political communities, but rather as arenas of constant struggles over the very geography of the polity in question.[38]

In such settings, the link between geography and political power, and the essentialized nature of group identities, often fuel a drive to exclude and marginalize groups which do not "belong." Therefore, the spatial and political project of such movements is rarely driven by a will to merge nation and state, and assimilate minorities into the dominant cultural unit, as portrayed by leading theories of nationalism.[39] Quite the opposite, they attempt to keep "alive" the tension between ethnonational belonging and formal citizenship, as a form of legitimizing further ethnic expansion and segregation. In ethnocratic societies, space, then, is not only influential, but also dynamic. It constantly produces new ethnic geographies, and thus new conditions for socialization and mobilization. In such societies, it is argued, space becomes a main kernel of national identity, as shown below in the case of Israel/Palestine, to which we now turn.

THE PALESTINIAN–ZIONIST CONFLICT: FROM TIME TO SPACE

Historical Roots: Diasporas, Colonialism, and a Contested Homeland

Both Zionists and Palestinians claim *priority status*,[40] which, in their own narratives, grants them a higher moral claim for contemporary control over Israel/Palestine. The Jews draw on the divine promises contained in ancient Jewish texts, on the actual reign of Hebrew Kingdoms over the territory as described in the biblical text, on a myth of forced eviction, and on continuous spiritual connection to the land.[41] The Palestinians concentrate on their unbroken residence on, and cultivation of, the land, on their recent (partial) expulsion and dispossession, and on their current status as a stateless nation.

Jewish narratives of an ancient biblical "golden age," followed by defeat and forced dispersal, provide vivid images for constructing the historical narrative of contemporary Zionists. Yet, historical sources show that following the last defeat of their kingdoms (associated with the destruction of the Second Temple in AD 70), Jews remained on the Land of Israel in significant numbers for centuries. At the same time, other Jews emigrated and formed a chain of diaspora communities in Middle Eastern, North African, and European countries.[42]

Over the ensuing centuries Jews maintained a religious connection to the land, mainly through an inter-generational cultivation of texts and myths of the "promised land."[43] In recent years, Palestinians have also begun to construct ancient narratives of belonging to the land, focusing on their historical links with the Canaanite and Jebusite tribes believed to have resided on the land prior to the Hebrew biblical conquest.[44]

In later periods, the Land of Israel/Palestine was conquered by the Greek, Assyrian, Roman, Persian, Arab, Crusader, Byzantine and Ottoman empires. The name "Palestine" derives from the Roman title for their local province—Palestina, which in turn was based on the supposed location of the biblical Philistine people. The people known today as Palestinians are probably a mixture of groups (Hebrew tribes and other communities) who remained on the land, converted to Christianity and Islam; and later joined by migrants of Arab descent.[45]

The Ottoman empire conquered the land in 1516 and ruled for 400 years. In the middle of the nineteenth century, the population of the area reached 510,000, of whom 6 percent were Jews. It was during this period that both Jewish and Palestinian movements began to emerge. Jews were profoundly affected by the ethno-national, often anti-Semitic, nationalism appearing in central and eastern Europe (where most of them lived), as well as by the assimilating emancipation promised in the more liberal West. Both anti-Semitism and assimilation posed serious threats to Jewish collective existence, either through exclusion and physical oppression, or through the new openings into previously impregnable paths of societal integration and assimilation.

Zionism emerged in the late nineteenth-century Europe as a direct response to these threats. It encouraged Jews to emigrate to the remembered Land of Israel as a form of collective survival. The nascent Zionist movement sought to compete with other camp, such as the Bund, which called for Jewish autonomy in Europe, or with mass Jewish migration to the West. Their efforts, however, were largely unsuccessful, as the early Zionists remained a small minority among world Jewry. In 1914, for example, only 60,000 Jews were living in Israel/Palestine, comprising less than 1 percent of the world's Jewry, and about 8 percent of the local population.[46] In general, immigration of Jews to Palestine proceeded almost only when Jews faced pressing circumstances, and were denied the option of emigrating to the West. Hence it can also be conceptualized at this stage as a "colonialism of the displaced."[47]

Time – space interactions became crucial for Zionism. It was embodied in the perception that resurrecting Jewish *history* is only possible in the *Land* of Israel. But given the very pressing practical territorial, and economic agendas of early Zionists, the historical origins of Jewish nationalism quickly became mythical and homogenous, rarely subject to open debate over the dynamic and diverse national past(s). For example, the explorations of Jewish antiquities and archaeologies were, in the main, tools for validating present Jewish colonization, rather than prompting genuine interest in national histories and trajectories.[48] National time became, in effect, a-historical, providing a unified, linear, and repeatedly recited backdrop for contemporary practices of territorial expansion.[49] The aims and energies of the Zionist movement became territorial par excellence: purchase land, attract immigrants, build cities, develop agriculture, establish industries, settle colonies, and launch an international struggle for Jewish political sovereignty.[50] From an early period, then, space, place, and territory became the kernels of the Zionist project.

But as Shafir notes, Zionist space was to be "pure," attempting to maximize both Jewish control and exclusivity—territorial, economic, and social.[51] A corollary move was to represent the country (*Eretz Yisrael*, the Jewish homeland) as "terra nullus"— an empty land awaiting its Jewish redemption after centuries of "neglect." The Zionist movement thus coined the now infamous idiom: "a people without land to a land without a people." The territorial double strategy (create a new Zionist nation while denying the existence of Palestinian nationalism) remained effective until the early 1990s! It illustrated both the prevalence of *spatial control* as a major national goal, and the effective use of nation-state imagery of ethnic self-determination ("Jewish state in *Eretz Yisrael*"), to seize a contested territory and marginalize its indigenous population.

In parallel, the Palestinian national movement was also surfacing. During the twilight of Ottoman rule, they conducted life as a typical Middle-Eastern agrarian society, spread over 950 villages and a dozen urban centres, and were undergoing gradual modernization and urbanization.[52] The Arabs of Palestine started to form a collective consciousness, mainly inspired by an Arab national "awakening" resonating throughout the region, and by a common local culture shaped through centuries of settling and working on the land.[53]

In 1917, Britain conquered the land and issued the Balfour Declaration promising to facilitate a "Jewish national home" in Palestine, but remaining careful not to mention a Jewish "state," or sacrifice the rights of local populations. The land was renamed "Palestine" and its (current) borders were demarcated for the first time.[54] The newly shaped territory quickly became embedded in the collective imaginations of the two national movements. "Palestine" began to define the Palestinians (its Arab

inhabitants), but the same unit also became "Eretz Yisrael"—
no longer an abstract and vague icon present in Jewish myth
and prayer, but a concrete, bounded, territory to be claimed
and seized.[55]

Following the demarcation of Palestine in 1921, the Palestinians
began to focus their consciousness on a collective claim to the
land. This was facilitated by the 1916 Hussein–McMahon correspondence in which Britain also committed itself to assist
the establishment of an Arab state in the region.[56] It is likely
that, in the absence of Jewish immigration to the land, Palestinians
would have formed a typical anti-colonial national movement
similar to the cases of Egypt or Syria. Palestinian nationalism
was developing, then, with a strong territorial focus. However,
it was markedly different to Zionist engagement with territory:
whereas the Palestinians saw their collective territorial identity
as inclusive (that is, all people residing in Palestine were considered Palestinians, including "pre-Zionist" Jews), Zionists only
regarded Jewish newcomers as part of the nation. Palestinian
nationalism was, then, on course to develop incrementally as a
modernizing territorial political organization typical to in situ
collectivities.

During the 1920s and 1930s, the Land of Israel/Palestine was
shaped as a "geo-body"—a powerful symbolic spatial icon held
by most national movements.[57] To date, the identical map of
the Land of Israel/Palestine functions as the clearest collective code and mobilizing image, used commonly by Jews and
Palestinians in official and unofficial maps, on shirts, murals,
pamphlets, and political publications. Since the British mandate
period, then, the Zionist–Palestinian struggle became an all-
consuming race for territorial control. The spatial practices and
ideologies of each movement profoundly influenced the other,
in what Portugali termed "implicate relations."[58] The goals of
land control also became a major axis to guide the nation-building
efforts of the two communities, culturally, economically, and politically. Aspired territory became the kernel of the two national
movements.

The collective memory of centuries of Jewish persecution, the
plight of most Zionist Jews from European anti-Semitism, and
the immediate dangers emanating from Arab political and violent

opposition also shaped Zionism as a particularly *intransigent* movement. During the first half of the twentieth century it may be conceptualized as *colonialism of ethnic survival*, with a major goal to "Judaize" territory in the ancient homeland as a safe Jewish haven. Notably, Zionism represented itself as a movement of (anti-colonial) liberation, not conquest, thereby gaining internal Jewish legitimacy and international support. Hence, from the early years, Zionism developed a seemingly contradictory dual identity. On the one hand, it evolved as a colonial project, attempting to maximize the landholding and economic strength in the new colonies. On the other, it presented itself as anti-colonial, attempting to "liberate" the homeland from the British, in order to build a Jewish state.[59]

This political and territorial activity spawned increasing Arab opposition, culminating in the 1936–39 "Arab revolt," which erupted over the growing Zionist threat to the Palestinian homeland.[60] The revolt was brutally put down by the British, who exiled much of the Palestinian leadership, and imposed harsher controls over their political rights. The three-year uprising exerted a high economic, communal, and political price, disrupting Palestinian nation-building and political institutionalization.[61] This despite gaining some policy concessions, such as greater British control over Jewish immigration and land purchase. However, the main goal of the Arab revolt—halting the Zionist project—was frustrated, as the clouds of murderous anti-Semitism were closing on Europe, and Zionism was perceived as a highly moral rescue movement of a besieged, homeless, people.

From a Palestinian perspective, however, the justice of Zionism and the tragic plight of European Jews mattered little; Jews were perceived as foreigners whose presence in the land violated the natural rights of Palestinians.[62] This feeling was strengthened by the highly segregated manner in which Jewish society developed, separating itself almost totally from local Palestinians. This ethos of "collective survival-revival," with an Orientalist colonial attitude typical to Europeans in settler societies created a dual society, manifested in separate residential areas, education systems, cultural milieu, labor markets, and political organizations.[63]

For Zionists, the Holocaust illustrated the ultimate need to build a Jewish national state, and solidified the Zionist construction of the Jewish Diaspora as a timeless void, a disastrous "black hole" "outside history," leading to Jewish resurrection only in their own homeland. Consequently, in 1947 there were already 610,000 Jews in Palestine, constituting 32 percent of the country's population. Jewish land holdings were more modest, covering 8 percent of Palestine, mainly along the coastal plain and the northern valleys. That year, the United Nations proposed a partition of the land, awarding 55 percent of Palestine to the Jews, although this included the sparsely populated (and mainly Bedouin-Arab) southern desert as land for the future absorption of Jewish refugees. The UN proposal was accepted by the Zionist Movement after a fierce debate, but rejected by most Palestinian leaders and Arab states.

The subsequent 1948 war, known to Jews as the "war of independence" and to Palestinians as "the disaster" (*al-naqbah*), became a watershed in the territorial struggle over the land and the shaping of national identities. Jewish forces responded to Arab attacks by enlarging their territorial holdings, and at the end of the fighting controlled 78 percent of the Land of Mandatory Palestine. Moreover, some 700,000–750,000 Palestinian refugees fled or were driven out of the land by Jewish forces, and over 420 Palestinian villages were demolished.[64] A few thousand Jews also became refugees, finding haven in the main Jewish concentrations. The remaining parts of Palestine fell under Jordanian (the West Bank) and Egyptian (Gaza Strip) administration.

The Palestinian national disaster was indeed grave: most became refugees, dispersed throughout the Middle East and beyond, and prevented from returning to their homes once the war ended. Both the Palestinian *naqbah* and the Jewish *shoah*, became deeply etched in the collective memories of the two national movements as ultimate examples of their victimhood and righteousness.[65] The development of Zionist and Palestinian identities has since remained framed by the memories of immense collective losses, and formed a central "spine" of their national narratives.

In terms of time/space conceptualizations, we can pause here and interrogate the "ethnically pure" image of the ideal "nation-state," which spawned both the UN partition plan and the disastrous events which ensued. Ethnic control over space, and the "purification" of this space became the prime goal, buttressed by strong feelings of historical mission and justice.[66] Notably, both Zionist and Palestinian discourses at the times aspired to "enter history" by achieving their "own" state; that is, *entering history through territory*. This illustrates that modern nationalism, propelled by the myth of the "pure" nation-state, inherently harbours the possibility of ethnic cleansing in situations of mixed geography.

In this context, space becomes paramount, because it provides a concrete, achievable goal, and at the same time, distances rivalling groups from realizing their competing national-territorial agendas. Seizing and claiming sovereignty over contested space is closely tied with the *denial* of other's claims to that space, that is, the other's history, place, and political aspirations are presented as a menacing package to be thoroughly rejected. Israel's subsequent attempts to refute Palestine's territorial claims by denying the existence of a Palestinian nation, constantly referred to Palestinian geographical dispersal and lack of past political independence in Palestine.[67]

The Israeli "Ethnocracy": Judaization and Stratification, 1948–77

Following the 1948 war, Israel was established as a Jewish state. It enacted immediately the Law of Return, which enabled any Jew to immigrate to the country, thereby prolonging indefinitely the duration of the Judaization project. Following massive confiscation of Arab land, over 400 Jewish settlements were established in a decade throughout the state (see Figure 2.1).[68] This created the infrastructure for the settlement of Jewish immigrants and refugees, increasing its population fourfold within the first decade of independence (replacing the Palestinian refugees whose total number was similar to that of Jewish newcomers by 1952). It should be remembered, however, that nearly all Jews arriving in Israel during that period were either (*a*) refugees surviving the European holocaust, or (*b*) emigrants from the Muslim world, who were largely coerced by hostile Arab and Muslim regimes (augmented by Zionist activities) to leave their countries and to settle in Israel.[69]

Figure 2.1
The Progression of Jewish Settlement in Israel/Palestine

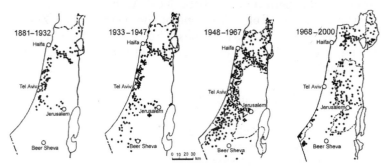

• Newly established settlement.
Source: updated from Newman (1996).

The geographical Judaization program was premised on a hegemonic myth cultivated since the rise of Zionism, and buttressed by the "nation-state" myth, that "the land" (*Ha'aretz*) belongs to the Jews, and to them only. An exclusive ethnonational culture was coded, institutionalized and militarized by the new state, in order to quickly "indigenize" immigrant Jews, and to conceal, trivialize, or marginalize the land's Palestinian past.[70]

This period illustrates one of the central points of this article, namely, the elevation of space to an all-assuming kernel of national identity constructed through territorial struggle and socialization. For Zionist culture, the "frontier" became a central icon, and its settlement was considered one of the highest achievements. The frontier *kibbutzim* (collective rural villages) provided a model, for the reviving. Hebrew language was filled with positive images drawn from religious myths of national redemption, such as *aliya lakarka* (literally "ascent to the land," i.e., settlement), *ge'ulat karka* (land redemption), *hityashvut, hitnahalut* (positive biblical terms for Jewish settlement), *kibbush hashmama* (conquest of the desert), and *hagshama* (literally "fulfilment" but denoting the settling of the frontier).[71]

The glorification of the frontier was central to the construction of a "new Jew"—an everready settler–fighter who conquers the land with his physical strength and endless poetic love.[72] As shown well by Israeli scholars, the construction of the "new" Zionist Jew was premised on building a settling and militaristic national identity in negation, and denial of two prominent "others"—diaspora Jews and the local Arabs.[73] The following song from Yoram Tehar-Lev, one of the most popular Zionist song writers, exemplifies the ethos of knowing, walking, settling, loving, and staking a claim to the land, as a way of creating the new Zionist Jew.

Arise and Walk Through the Land

> Arise and walk through the land
> With backpack and stick
> You'll surely find on the way
> To the Land of Israel again
> The paths of the good land will embrace you
> She will call you as if to a bed of love
> And the groves of olive trees
> The hidden spring
> Still guard its dream
> Our ancient dream
> And red roofs on a hill
> And children on the paths
> In that place where we walked
> With backpack and stick
>
> —Yoram Tehar-Lev, 1980

During the same period Palestinians were gradually emerging from the 1948 defeat and dispersal, and began the task of rebuilding their national movement. This project had to overcome several major difficulties, including the disenfranchised and stateless status of most Palestinians, their geographical and political dispersion, the urgent economic and social needs of the refugees, the continuing denial by Israel of their collective and individual rights, and the oppressive rule of most Arab governments.[74] During the 1960s Palestinian national activity was most prominent in Egypt, which supported the 1964 establishment of the Palestinian Liberation Organization (PLO). The PLO, which became the umbrella Palestinian organization, began during the1960s to launch an armed struggle against Israel.

The Palestinians remaining in Israel were totally separated from their brethren abroad, and were isolated in small geographical enclaves, governed by military rule. Jewish settlements surrounded their localities, while over half of their private lands were confiscated by the state. But here, too, national resistance began to emerge during the 1950s and 1960s, most prominently among the Communist Party, and the *al-Ard* (the land) movement, which effectively mobilized Arab youth, and was subsequently outlawed by Israel in 1964.[75]

Despite its "objective" weakness and geographical fragmentation, Palestinian collective identity began at this stage to form several distinct characteristics, centring around dispossession, the land, and the struggle for its protection and liberation. The total belief in superior national right over Israel/Palestine was the major driving force. This led to the emergence and glorification of key national–cultural symbols such as: *al-fida'i* (the freedom fighter), *al-balad* (the village), *al-falah* (the farmer), *al-ard* (the land), *al-zayt* (the olive tree), and *al-watten* (the homeland). The main goals were generally articulated as: *al-awda* (the return of the refugees) and *al-tahrir* (national liberation), *al-istiqlal* (national independence). These were disseminated through fledgling literature, poetry, and political discourses, which made constant use of national symbols.[76] We can hence note, again, how national identity is reshaped through territorial conflict, and how laden it is with "signs" of active space, vis-à-vis a frozen notion of national time, to be recaptured only if space is fully controlled.

The renewal of collective Palestinian consciousness was impeded by competing political agendas, most notably, Pan-Arabism, and by the hostility towards Palestinian nationalism displayed by most relevant political powers, namely, Israel, the West, and the Arab states.[77] Nevertheless, Palestinians did manage to regenerate a measure of national consciousness, albeit still weak and fragmented,[78] centring around the PLO, and around notions of homeland and liberation.[79]

A further dramatic territorial transformation of Israel/Palestine took place in 1967, following Arab threats of aggression, when Israel conquered the West Bank, Gaza, the Sinai Peninsula, and the Golan Heights. This established Jewish ethnocratic rule over the entire territory of Israel/Palestine. The 1967 war also enabled the initiation of further Jewish settlement, this time in a territory held by belligerent occupation, and hence in violation of international law. A new wave of Jewish settlement soon began to thoroughly change their ethnic geography, and with it the nature of the Zionist–Palestinian conflict.

Jewish Expansion and Palestinian Resistance, 1967–87: Settlement (*Hitnahalut*) versus Steadfastness (*Sumud*)

A decade after the conquest of the occupied territories, the Israeli ethnocracy reached its peak. Following the 1977 rise to power of the rightist Menahem Begin and his Likud party, Israeli policies began to create "irreversible facts on the ground" and prevent the possibility of the redivision of Israel/Palestine. The most conspicuous manifestation was the massive settlement program in the West Bank, and to a lesser extent, in the Gaza Strip. Motifs of Jewish survival used in the rhetoric of "Jewish survival" were used once again and manipulated to justify the new settlement project on grounds of enhancing national security. The new settlers, many of whom aligned with rightist religious groups, also argued for the necessity of biblical lands to be settled as the "bedrock of Jewish national identity."[80] Settlement was now placed in the midst of Palestinian population centres. Ancient Jewish time was thrusted again into contemporary political moves, by settling Jews at biblical sites, thereby shaping anew the nature of Zionist and Palestinian geographies and identities (see Figures 2.1 and 2.2).

The peace treaty signed with Egypt during the late 1970s ostensibly signalled territorial contraction, as contrasted to previous expansion, including withdrawal from occupied territories (the Sinai peninsula), and the dismantling of some Jewish settlements. Yet, the struggle over Israel/Palestine never genuinely included the Sinai. On the contrary, the peace with Egypt—the most powerful Arab state—actually enabled Israel to deepen its settlement and territorial control over Palestinian territories,

Figure 2.2
Ethnic Geography in Israel/Palestine 2000

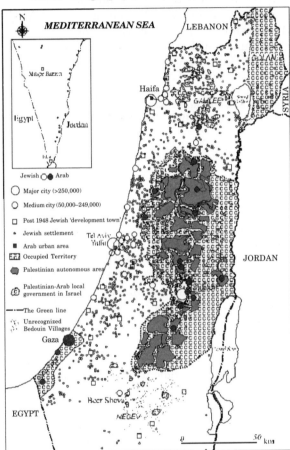

particularly in the West Bank. It also allowed Israel to launch the 1982 Lebanon War, officially in reply to Palestinian attacks on Israel's northern border, but with the clear aim to destroy the PLO, and dampen Palestinian hopes for consolidating a nation and achieving statehood in Palestine.

Not satisfied with the slow initial pace of Jewish resettlement in the West Bank, the Israeli government initiated a new strategy in the early 1980s. In an attempt to attract middle-class suburbanites, it offered subsidized housing in new well-designed

localities located on confiscated Palestinian lands. These were
situated in the occupied territories, but in near proximity to
the Tel-Aviv and Jerusalem metropolitan areas.[81] As shown in
Table 2.1, the combined push and pull factors worked to quickly
increase the number of Jewish settlers in the West Bank, which
reached 129,000 by the end of Likud's second term in 1984.

Table 2.1
Jewish Settlers and Palestinians in the West Bank
(including East Jerusalem)

Year	Jews Outside Jerusalem	Jews in East Jerusalem	Total Jews	Total Palestinians[2] (in millions)	% Jews[3]
1976	3,000	23,000	26,000	0.66	3.7
1980	11,000	39,000	50,000	0.78	6.0
1984	48,000	81,000	129,000	0.91	12.4
1988	71,000	117,000	188,000	1.02	15.8
1992	108,000	146,000	254,000	1.15	18.1
1996	148,000	173,000	310,000	1.41	21.9
2001	206,000	190,000	396,000	1.74	22.7

1. Source: Israeli Central Bureau of Statistics
2. Sources: Benvenisiti (1988); Foundation for Mid East Peace (1997);
   www.palestinemonitor.org/factssheer/settlement.html
   www.peacenow.org/programs/settlement.html.
3. Of the total West Bank population

Jewish control and settlement in the territories also caused
a major change in the representation of space: In the late 1970s
Israel erased the Green Line (the 1949 armistice lines and the
state's internationally recognized border) from official maps,
atlases, and state publications. Despite certain "remnants" of
the old border (Figure 2.2)—notably checkpoints on the roads
entering the occupied territories—the Green Line has remained
invisible in most Jewish public arenas, thereby facilitating the
de facto annexation of Jewish settlements to Israel, and spawn-
ing greater frustration and militancy among the Palestinians.
At this stage, the political objectives were clear—to cement control
over the entire "Greater Israel," that is Eretz Yisrael/Palestine.
This goal was candidly articulated by Israel's prime minister
during most of the 1980s and early 1990s—Yitzhak Shamir,
who stated in a Parliament (Knesset) speech:

This is our goal: territorial wholeness. It should not be encroached or fragmented. This is an *a priori* principle; it is beyond argument. You should not ask why. Why this land is ours requires no explanation ... Is there any other nation that argues about its homeland, its size and dimensions, about territories, territorial compromise, or anything to that effect?[82]

A major focus of the Judaization project centred around al-Quds (East Jerusalem 1) represents another telling example of manipulating Jewish history and identity for territorial gains. The Old City of Jerusalem (extending over a single square kilometre) is sacred to many Muslims, Christians and Jews; indeed, it is the ultimate "Zion." But following the 1967 war Israel incorporated some 170 sq km of surrounding lands (including some urban, rural, and vacant areas), and named the new entity "united Jerusalem." It thus invoked a most cherished Jewish symbol in order to gain Jewish land control, and marginalize the Arab residents of the city. Until very recently, the symbolic strength of Jerusalem, and the superior power of Israel in the city, enabled the issue of "united Jerusalem" to remain an "untouchable" taboo in the public discourse. That is, no leader or organized public voice was able to express support for the "redivision" of the city, without being ridiculed or gagged. Similarly, the future of al-Quds as the future Palestinian capital has remained unmoved at the heart of the Palestinian consensus.[83]

Jewish settlement in East Jerusalem proceeded rapidly, with the construction of eight large settlements/neighborhoods, totalling some 206,000 Jewish settlers at the end of 2001. But Palestinian hold on the eastern city, although weakened, has not been fundamentally undermined. The official rhetoric of the Palestinian national movement repeatedly mentioned al-Quds as the future national capital, and the existence of Islamic shrines on Temple Mount (*Har Habayit / Haram al-Sharif*) has assured continuing national and international support for a strong Palestinian presence.[84]

Jerusalem, then, has remained the geographical heart, and a microcosmos of the entire territorial conflict. Both Zionist and Palestinian cultures, which are intimately linked to the Jewish and Islamic religions, have sanctified and glorified the

city. This is highlighted by the following poetic lines, widely
known and cherished by their respective Jewish and Palestinian
peoples. The two poems reflect and recreate the glorified status
of Jerusalem, by weaving in their lyrics frequent references to
sacred texts and heroic pasts. But both poems also display the
denial and exclusion of the other—Jerusalem/al-Quds are purely
Jewish/Arab. The "other" is a present absentee, casting a shadow
over the city, but is never allowed a voice, a name, or a rightful
place in this bi-national, multi-communal city.

Jerusalem of Gold

Mountain Air, clear as wine
And the Fragrance of Pines
Stands in twilight breeze
With the sounds of bells
In the sleep of oak and stone
Captured in her dream
The City waits desolate
With a wall in her heart

Jerusalem of Gold
Of copper and light
I shall be a violin to all your poems

How the wells have dried
The market square stands empty
No one attends the Temple Mount
Inside the Old City.

And in the rocky caves
The winds are wailing
No one descends to the Dead Sea
On the Jericho road.

For your name burns the lips
Like a resinous kiss
If I forget Thee O Jerusalem
All of gold.

We've returned to the wells
The market and the square
The Shofar calls on Temple Mount
And in the rocky caves
A thousands suns are shining

We shall descend again to the Dead Sea
On the Jericho Road

Jerusalem of Gold
Of copper and light
I shall be a violin to all your poems

—Nattan/Shemer

The Flower of All Cities

For you, the city of prayers, I shall pray
For you, the city of beautiful homes,
you the flower of all cities
O al-Quds, O al-Quds, the city of prayers, I shall pray

Our eyes will follow you every day
Searching for the places of prayer
Embracing the old churches
Erasing the sorrow of mosques
O night of Israa* the path passed to the heavens
Our eyes will follow you every day and I shall pray

The faces of the child in the cave
And his mother Maria are crying
For the homeless and the abandoned...
For the defenders who died in the city gates
The martyrs of peace in the homeland of peace
And justice ceased in the gates
When the city of al-Quds fell
Love retreated and the hearts
of the world settled on war

The bitter rage has come and I am faithful
The bitter rage had come and
I shall overcome my sorrows
Through all paths, they will come
The horses of Godly fear, they will come
Like the face of the almighty God, they'will come

The gate to our city will not remain locked and I am walking to pray
I shall knock and open the gates
I shall cleanse, O Jordan River, in holy waters
And shall erase, O Jordan River
the traces of the savage foot
The bitter rage, O Jordan River, will come
with the horses of Godly fear

Will crush the face of power
The house is ours, al-Quds is ours
With our hands, we shall return al-Quds
With our hands, al-Quds, peace is coming

— Fairuz/Rahbani

* The night Muhammad soared from al-Quds (Jerusalem) to heaven, according to Islam.

Beyond the city of Jerusalem, Jewish expansion continued apace. By the mid-1980s it was estimated that 52 percent of West Bank's land was classified as Israeli "state land."[85] This was composed of (existing and planned) Jewish residential developments, other "state lands," roads, Jewish agricultural land, army installations and training grounds, and industrial estates. This expansion was backed by a tight check over the development of Palestinian villages and towns, where hundreds of houses on private lands were demolished every year on the grounds of being "illegal" or, more recently, "a threat to the security of Jewish settlers." Other forms of Palestinian commercial or public development were stifled by the restrictive policies of military government, in effect *ghettoizing* the locals to their towns and villages, and making them dependent on distant Jewish employment.[86]

Palestinian resistance during the decade in question was weakened by the geographical and political split in its leadership between those "inside" (in the occupied territories) and those "outside" (the leading institutions of the PLO and other Palestinian organizations). Resistance was further restricted by Israel's political and economic oppression, a lack of effective Palestinian organization and resources, the frequent incarceration of local leaders, and the tacit legitimacy of the occupation within Israel.[87]

If early Zionism was indeed a colonial movement of the displaced seeking survival, its later version became a case of state colonialism. The Zionist state was constantly using the "survival" and security rhetoric for goals of expansionist ethnocratic rule, and for the dispossession of local Palestinians, while at the same time, denying the relevance of the same "security" and "survival" considerations for the Palestinians.[88]

Palestinians never accepted Jewish occupation and expansion into what they perceived was nothing but remnants of their historical homeland remaining in Arab control. The protection of land remained one of the highest values among Palestinians, and its sale considered *tachween* (a traitorous act).[89] A most widespread form of resistance among Palestinians became the *sumud*—literally steadfastness in hanging on to the land, the place, the homeland. The continuation of daily practices and rituals developed by hundreds of years of agrarian living, attempts to maintain normality in difficult circumstances, came to characterize the Palestinian *sumud*. Until 1987 *sumud* was the Palestinians' main weapon, both in the occupied territories and within Israel proper.[90] Tawfiq Ziyyad's famous song, typifies this attitude:

We Are Staying Here

Here, on your chest
Here, like a fence
Here, in your throat
Like a piece of glass, like a Sabar[91]
And in your eyes
Like a storm from the fire
We are staying here

— Tawfiq Ziyyad, 1978

During the same period, an expansive Jewish settlement policy was also implemented within Israel "proper." The strategy of penetrating heavily populated Palestinian regions was carried out mainly in northern Galilee where 62 new Jewish settlements were built during the decade, and to a lesser extent along Israel's "hills axis" east and northeast of Tel Aviv, and in the southern Negev (Figure 2.1). In the north, this initiative continued the long-lasting "Judaization of Galilee" strategy. It also came as a response to growing resistance among Israel's Palestinian citizens, which culminated in 1976 mass protest known as "Land Day," during which six Palestinians were killed while protesting the confiscation of their land by the state. Land Day itself has become a prominent Palestinian annual day of commemoration, providing another key example for the intimate intertwining between the *geographical process*—the discourses, development, and struggles over land—and the construction of Palestinian *symbols and identity*.

1987–2001: Between Uprisings and Territorial Compromise

The eruption of the *Intifada* ("the awakening") in late 1987 marked the beginning of a new phase in the territorial struggle over Israel/Palestine, which firmly refocused the conflict on the land and its residents. The revolt broke out first and foremost against Israeli occupation and against the unyielding Jewish penetration into Palestinian lands, but was also a statement by local Palestinians against the ineffectiveness of the external national leadership, headed by the PLO and Yasser Arafat.[92]

The Intifada lasted six years. It began in mass demonstrations, road blocks, labor and commercial strikes, and developed into sporadic violent attacks on Jewish settlers and Israeli residents within the "Green Line." The Intifada caused a historic shift in the agenda of the Palestinian national movement, with the PLO declaring in late 1988 its acceptance of the existence of Israel. It launched a revised agenda of building a peaceful Palestinian state in the occupied territories.

Geographically, the Intifada also revived the "Green Line." A new "geography of fear" was created with most Jews ceasing to travel beyond the previous border, and Palestinians increasingly prevented from entering into "Israel Proper."[93] Another major event in the struggle between the two national movements was the arrival of some 800,000 immigrants from the former Soviet Union during the 1990s, not only strengthening Jewish economy and demography, but also imposing new costs and tensions.[94]

The Intifada imposed serious economic and political costs on Israel, becoming major factors buttressing the large Israeli peace movements, which campaigned for territorial withdrawal. This movement was never clear enough about its precise territorial and political goals, but it did influence the decline of the rightist Likud in the 1992 elections, and the rise of a less ethnocratic, more compromising, Labor administration, headed by Yitzhak Rabin.

In 1993, Israel and the Palestinians signed the Oslo accord which ended the Intifada. The accord achieved, for the first time, mutual recognition between the two national movements, and allowed the return of the PLO leadership to govern several autonomous areas to be transferred to Palestinian self-rule. The Oslo agreement sought to open the way for a gradual resolution of the conflict on the basis of a redivision of Palestine. By 1993, the Palestinians appeared to have reasserted their collective power and articulated a clear territorial agenda of liberation from Israeli occupation, and a vision of two neighboring states co-existing in peace, while Israel appeared to have gained official recognition of its most bitter rival.

Despite the high hopes, the Oslo Accords were only a five-year interim agreement, and did not specify final territorial or political ends. It reflected the skewed balance of power between Zionists and Palestinians: the latter recognized the state of Israel (and hence, abdicated their claim for 78 percent of historic Palestine), but received in return only a vague "recognition," and a concrete plan for a three-phase Israeli withdrawal from unspecified parts of the occupied territories. Central points of the territorial conflict, such as the future of Jerusalem/al-Quds, the plight of Jewish settlements, or the rehabilitation of Palestinian refugees, were shelved for later "final status" negotiations. What appeared to be leading to a historic compromise, turned sour very quickly. The vagueness of the agreement encouraged opposition groups, from both Zionist and Palestinian sides, to launch a concerted attack on the possibility of political partition.[95]

Over a stormy period, Palestinian–Zionist violence reached new heights, beginning with the 1994 mass murder of Muslim worshippers in Hebron by a Jewish settler, continuing with large-scale anti-Jewish terrorism inside Israel, and culminating with the assassination of Israel's peace-leaning Prime Minister, Yitzhak Rabin, in November 1995, by a Jew opposing Rabin's decision to transfer territories to Palestinian self-rule. In the words of the assassin: "Rabin had no right to relinquish any part of Jewish historical and God-given homeland. He is therefore a traitor who deserves death."[96]

Similarly, Mahmud Rantissi, the spokesman of the militant Islamic-Palestinian organization Hamas, declared after 25 Israelis were killed in a 1995 bus explosion set by a Hamas suicide bomber: "Palestine is the one and indivisible land of the Palestinians; the whole of Palestine, from the river to the sea is 'waqf' (Islamic asset) and can never be surrendered by Muslims."

The rhetoric of the opposition groups, coming overwhelmingly from hard-core (Jewish or Islamic) religious circles, was spatially clear: the land cannot be divided; *it belongs to us, and us only*. Nevertheless, the Oslo agreement was partially implemented. It created a highly complex and convoluted patchwork of new ethnic geography, owing to the existence of Jewish settlements (Figure 2.2). Their existence prevented the Palestinians from stretching their (limited) autonomy beyond an archipelago of disconnected enclaves.[97] Security control and management of external borders remained in Israeli hands. In 1996, Israel elected Binyamin Netanyahu—a right-wing Likud prime minister—who stalled the implementation of the Oslo agreement, while accelerating Jewish settlement activity. Following international condemnation and economic downturn, Netanyahu was replaced in 1999 by Labor's Ehud Barak, who ran on a ticket of "ending the conflict," while still allowing a rapid growth of Jewish settlement activity. This was the setting in summer 2000, when peace talks resumed between Israelis and Palestinians.

A peace summit was convened in July 2000 in Camp David, under the auspices of the US President. The summit failed to reach an agreement, although both sides made some notable breakthroughs on territorial issues. Israel offered, for the first time, to establish an "independent" Palestinian state, to withdraw from over 90 percent of the West Bank, dismantle most Jewish settlements, and establish (limited) Palestinian sovereignty in Jerusalem. The Palestinians agreed to allow the continuing existence of several large Jewish settlements, and maintain Jewish control over parts of conquered East Jerusalem.

However, peace negotiations hit a deadlock. This was due largely (although not solely) to an enduring image by Israelis that their presence on this land is "natural" and just. Transferring occupied territories to Palestinian control was represented as "Israeli generosity," and the main test for the feasibility of proposed arrangements was Israeli (not Palestinian) security.

Time–Space configurations continued to be central here too. Israeli negotiators attempted to date the beginning of the issues seeking resolution in 1967, while Palestinians sought to address their roots in 1948. Hence, Israeli leaders and media portrayed a compromise over the 1967 territories as the only obstacle to peace. But in historical terms, most Palestinians felt they had already offered their full compromise to Zionism, by recognizing Israel's right to exist securely on 78 percent of their historic homeland. The Palestinians hoped that the remaining 22 percent would be transferred to their full control (with minor modifications) and that 1948 issues, most notably the plight and property of the refugees, would be addressed. Hence the consensual stand expressed by Faisal Husseini, the late Palestinian leader in September 2000: "There can be no compromise on the compromise!"[98]

Although in recent years many Israelis have reluctantly accepted the existence of a Palestinian nation, they still perceived the Palestinian state-to-be as an entity to be shaped by the needs and concerns of Zionism. Israeli-Jews thus developed a convoluted debate about "how much land for peace?" Public discourse of the post-Oslo era was replete with arguments, agendas, and proposals of partial withdrawals, with Jews debating in their own exclusive "bubble," showing little concern to international law, or the historical-geographical dynamic of the conflict.[99]

This view led most Israelis, including the "leftist" Labor camp, to equate "going all the way for peace" (Barak's oft-used slogan) with the annexation of many Jewish settlements in the occupied territories, and a reticence to address the right of return for Palestinian refugees. In his recent memoirs of the Camp David peace talks, Israel's foreign minister at the time, Shlomo Ben-Ami boasts about the territorial achievements of his peace efforts:

> The Camp David summit was a major Israeli achievement: for the first time ... the Americans accepted ... and Clinton stressed the importance of annexing 80 per cent of the settlers to Israel ... and a large Jewish Jerusalem under Israeli sovereignty ... and we never, at any stage, agreed to the return of the Palestinian refugees.[100]

The breakdown of the peace negotiations caused the outbreak of the "al-Aqsa Intifada" in late September 2000.[101] Typically, this uprising began following a (very geographical!) provocation—a public visit of the then opposition leader, Ariel Sharon, to the heart of the imagined Palestinian homeland, the holy *Haram al-Sharif*, for a purpose as described in Sharon's own words: "To demonstrate Israel's undeniable sovereignty over the entire, united Jerusalem."[102] The visit was followed by Palestinian protest, Israeli strong-arm reaction, and a high number of casualties. This spawned mass Palestinian demonstrations, which confronted the main symbols of the occupation: road barriers, army camps, and Jewish settlements. The uprising began as popular action, but was quickly supported (often tacitly), by a widely condemned Palestinian leadership worried about its survival, and seeking new legitimacy. Significantly, the wave of mass protest was joined for over a week by large numbers of Palestinian-Arabs inside Israel. This resulted in the killing of 13 Arab citizens (and one Jew), and in a notable deterioration of Arab–Jewish relations inside Israel to one of their lowest ebbs ever.[103]

Unlike the first Intifada, this uprising developed quickly into an armed guerrilla struggle against the occupation, combined with escalating terrorism against Israeli civilians within the "Green Line." The escalation of violence toppled the Barak peace-leading government, who was replaced in landslide elections in February 2001 by the rightist Ariel Sharon. Under Sharon, Israel stepped up significantly its attempts to put down the uprising by military means, including repeated invasions into Palestinian cities and towns. This spawned a vicious cycle of violence and counter-violence.

The cost was predictably high: by the end of April 2002, some 1,292 Palestinians and 438 Jews (the vast majority civilians among both sides) were killed, the Palestinian economy shrunk by half, over 5,000 Palestinian homes and commercial properties, and over 10,000 dunams of fields and industries were destroyed.[104] The cycle of violence, which included continuing Israeli attacks on Palestinian leaders, institutions, and civilians, and a series of Palestinian suicide bombing in Israeli cities, brought the relations between the two peoples to one of their all-time nadirs.

REFLECTIONS

What do the details of the unfinished Zionist and Palestinian story tell us about the "when" and the "where" of the nation? Clearly, both time and space are crucial to the construction of the two national movements, and both are critical to one another. That is, perceptions of the "where" (the geographical homeland) both shape, and are also shaped by, the "when" (national origins and history), to create a *mutually constitutive time–space imagination*. But the makings of Zionism and Palestinian nationalism also highlight the dominance of the "where" over the "when" in conflictual "ethnocratic" settings, where the very process of nation-building is premised on the sanctification of place and territory.

National time, that is, the perceptions and recreation of collective pasts, is of course crucial, but it is generally transformed into a mythical, homogenous, and repeatedly recited backdrop, reaffirming the logic of the territorial project. Other ethnocratic societies, such as Sri Lanka, Northern Ireland, Cyprus, and Serbia display similar traits. The preoccupation with constructing a common national past as a cornerstone of "imagining" an inclusive and integrating territorial community—so typical to "normal" in situ societies[105]—gives way here to a focus on ethnic expansion, segregation, and the inevitability of violence.

Further, the exemplar case of Israel/Palestine highlights the centrality of "active space" and "diverse spatialities" to the making of nations and states. The relatively recent Zionist and Palestinian nations have been shaped through the geographical processes of immigration, eviction, exile, settlement, violent struggle, resistance, and development, or in short—through the Judaization of Palestine, pitting Jewish settlement versus Palestinian *sumud*. Further, the Israeli/Palestinian space has also been marked by *diversity and dynamism*, in which key groups were literally constituted by the creation of new spaces (e.g., Jewish West Bank settlers, development town-dwellers, landless Palestinian refugees, Bedouins in "unrecognized" village, or globalization-oriented Ashkenazi elites). The spatial agendas of these, and other groups, are now reshaping the territorial struggle, and with it the nature of national identities.

The Israel/Palestine case study highlights some shortcomings of the leading theories of nationalism reviewed above, as appropriate explanatory models for all types of nationalism. For example, the gaping chasm between the Jewish ethnocratic state and Palestinians generated much of the instability and conflict during that period. This runs counter to the observations of leading theories, moving Israel further away from the nation-state ideal. Further, the "flat" model of "the nation" which generally assumes "national territory" to be an unproblematic geographical backcloth, is also found wanting: it is impossible to understand the changing goals of Zionist nationalism, without accounting for the various discourses and interests of various ethno-classes. That is, the changing territorial agendas cannot be fathomed without "breathing life" into the making of "national" space and accounting for the competing geographical interests on the national (territorial) agenda.

Hence, there is a need to move the scholarly debate away from grand nationalism theories, which erroneously assume "flat," static and uniform national space, as well as a process of integration between nation and state. Israel/Palestine, like other ethnocratic settings, highlight several critical departures from these theories, most notably an aim to *exclude, not incorporate*, peripheral groups. This is performed with a certain duality: on the one hand, the ethnocratic state represents itself as a "normal" nation-state, with national histories leading to a point of "fulfilment" in building its "own" state. On this basis, it gains international and internal legitimacy. On the other hand, the project of ethnocratic expansion is often associated with *structural segregation,* ethno-class stratification and persisting links between state and hegemonic religion. As such, it violates major tenets of the nation-state model: the ideals of citizenship, territorial self-determination, and the desired fusion of nation and state.

Meta-theories describing and explaining nationalism as offered by the likes of Hobsbawm, Gellner, Anderson, and Smith, are bound to falter when faced with the enormous diversity of polities operating under the title of "nation." It may be more fruitful to treat "nationalism" as a broad shell—akin perhaps to the terms "society" or "state"—and explore in depth generalizable sub-types of collective movements, such as the ethnocratic case analyzed in this article. To do that, however, the analysis will have to "breathe life" into the dynamic geographies of ethno-national mobilizations, take seriously the mutual constitution of space and power, and the rich diversity of ethnic geographies. It will then be possible to examine comparatively other cases in which the "where" dominates the "when" as a centre of ethno-national politics, cultural production, and collective mobilization; that is, where *territory acts as the kernel of the nation*.

NOTES AND REFERENCES

1. The author is grateful for the useful comments received from Dr Haggay Ram, Dr Asad Ghanem, Prof. David Newman, Dr Amnon Raz-Krakotzkin and the journal's reviewers on earlier drafts, and to the Israeli Science Foundation for its generous support of the project "the Israeli land regime," which helped the writing of this paper.
2. http://www.israel.org/mfa/go.asp?MFAH00hb0.
3. http://208.55.122.96/politics/indep.html.
   (All translations from Hebrew and Arabic to English by the author).
4. Z. Bauman, *Society under Siege,* London, 2002.
5. The notion of priority as a legitimate claim to territorial sovereignty is outlined in A. Burghardt, "The Bases of Territorial Claims," *Geographical Review,* vol. 63, 1973, pp. 225–45.
6. O. Yiftachel, "Ethnocracy: The Politics of Judaizing Israel/Palestine," *Constellations,* vol. 6, no. 3, 1999, pp. 364–90.
7. S. Dellapergola, *Some Fundamentals of Jewish Demographic History.* Jerusalem, 2001.
8. B. Anderson, "Introduction," in G. Balakrishnan (ed.), *Mapping the Nation.* London, 1996, pp. 1–16.
9. See for instance, B. Anderson, *Imagined Communities: Reflections on the Origin and Spread of Nationalism.* London, 1991; R. Brubaker, *Nationalism Reframed: Nationhood and the National Question in the New Europe.* London, 1996; E. Gellner, "Do Nations Have Navels?" *Nations and Nationalism,* vol. 2, no. 3, 1996, pp. 366–71; E. Hobsbawm, *Nations and Nationalism since 1780.* Cambridge, 1990; A.D. Smith, *The Ethnic Origins of Nations.* London, 1986; ———, *Nations and Nationalism in a Global Era.* Cambridge, 1995.
10. E. Gellner, *Nations and Nationalism.* Oxford, 1983.
11. See Hobsbawm, *Nations and Nationalism since 1780.* Note 7. Cambridge, 1990; P.J. Taylor, "The State as a Container: Territoriality in the Modern World-System," *Progress in Human Geography,* vol. 18, no. 2, 1994, pp. 151–62; T. Nairn, *The Breakdown of Britain: Crisis and Neo-Nationalism,* London, 1977.
12. E. Gellner, "Do Nations Have Navels?" *Nations and Nationalism,* vol. 2, no. 3, 1996; Hobsbawm, *Nations and Nationalism since 1780.* Cambridge, 1990.

92 Oren Yiftachel

13. A.D. Smith, *Nations and Nationalism in the Global Era*, 1995; See also J. Hutchinson, "Ethnicity and the Modern Nation," *Ethnic and Racial Studies*. vol. 23, no. 3, 2000, pp. 651–69.
14. B. Anderson, *Imagined Communities: Reflections on the Origin and Spread of Nationalism*. London, 1991.
15. As mentioned earlier, referring to the works of Bhabha and Chatterjee.
16. B. Anderson, *Imagined Communities: Reflections on the Origin and Spread of Nationalism*. London, 1991; M. Anderson, "'Eastern' and 'Western' Nationalisms," *Arena Journal*, vol. 16, no. 1, 2001, pp. 121–32; R. Brubaker, *Nationalism Reframed: Nationhood and the National Question in the Europe*, London, 1996.
17. A. Gramsci, *Selections from Prison Notebook*. New York, 1971.
18. E. Lefevbre, *The Production of Space*. Oxford, 1991.
19. For important work on the link between social domination and space, see D. Massey, *Space, Place and Gender*. Oxford, 1994; A. Paasi, "Territorial Identities as Social Constructs," *Hagar: International Social Science Review*, vol. 1, no. 2, 2000, pp. 91–114. For further comprehensive critiques of nationalism theories along similar lines, see P. Chatterjee, *The Nation and its Fragments*. Princeton, New Jersey, 1983; P. Chatterjee, "Whose Imagined Community?" in G. Balakrishnan (ed.), *Mapping the Nation*. London, pp. 214–25.
20. For representative examples of this critique, see A. D. Smith, "Memory and Modernity: Reflections on Ernest Gellner's Theory of Nationalism," *Nations and Nationalism*, vol. 2, no. 3, 1995, pp. 371–88; E. Gellner, 1996, see Note 7.
21. M. Billig, *Banal Nationalism*. London, 1995.
22. See Note 17, P. Chatterjee, *The Nation and its Fragments*. Princeton, New Jersey, 1983; W. Connor, *Ethnonationalism: The Quest for Understanding*. Princeton, 1994; J. Penrose, "The Limitations of Nationalist Democracy: The Treatment of Marginal Groups as a Measure of State Legitimacy," *Hagar: International Social Science Review*, vol. 1, no. 2, 2000, pp. 33–62. Even recent studies of non-state concepts such as diaspora and immigration have generally reinforced the centrality of the nation-state. For a critique, see Y. Doysal, "Citizenship and Identity: Living in Diaspora in Post-War Europe?" in *Ethnic and Racial Studies*, vol. 23, no. 1, 2000, pp. 1–15.
23. See I. Lustick, *Unsettled States, Disputed Lands*. Ithaca, 1993; R. Samaddar, "Governing through Peace Accords," *Hagar: International Social Science*, vol. 1, no. 2, 2000, pp. 5–32.
24. Anderson, *Imagined Communities*, 1991.
25. J. Hakli, "In the Territory of Knowledge: State-Centred Discourses and the Construction of Society," *Progress in Human Geography*, vol. 25, no. 3, 2001, pp. 403–22.
26. J. Agnew, "Mapping Political Power Beyond State Boundaries: Territory, Identity and Movement in World Politics," *Millennium: Journal of International Studies*, vol. 28, no. 3, 1999, pp. 499–521.
27. See O. Yiftachel, "Ethnocracy: The Politics of Judaizing Israel/Palestine," *Constellations*, vol. 6, no. 3, 1999.

28. Lefebvre, *The Production of Space.* Oxford, 1991.
29. See G. Herb and D. Kaplan (eds), *Nested Identities: Nationalism, Territory and Scale.* Boulder, Rowman and Littlefield, New York, 1999; D. Newman and A. Paasi, "Fences and Neighbours in the Post-Modern World: Boundary Narratives in Political Geography," *Progress in Human Geography,* vol. 22, no. 2, 1998, pp. 186–207; J. Penrose, "The Limitation of Nationalist Democracy: The Treatment of Marginal Groups as a Measure of State Legitimacy," *Hagar International Social Science Review,* vol. 1, no. 2, 2000.
30. P. Jackson and J. Penrose (eds), *Constructions of Race, Place and Nation.* London, 1993.
31. A. Murphy, "The Territorial Underpinnings of National Identity." *Geopolitics*; R. Samaddar, "The Last Hurrah that Continues," *Transeuropeennes: Divided Countries, Separate Cities,* vol. 20, 2001, pp. 31–49.
32. M. Keith and S. Pile, "Introduction Part 1: The Politics of Place," in M. Keith and S. Pile. *Place and the Politics of Identity.* London, 1993, pp. 1–21.
33. R. Samaddar, "Governing through Peace Accords," *Hagar International Social Sciences,* vol. 1, no. 2, 2000.
34. Smith, *Nations and Nationalism in the Global Era,* 1995, p. 10.
35. B. Anderson, *Imagined Communities: Reflections on the Origin and Spread of Nationalism.* London, 1991, pp. 11–12.
36. See also L. Greenfield, *Nationalism: Five Roads to Modernity.* Cambridge, 1992; R. Brubaker, *Nationalism Reframed: Nationhood and the National Question in the New Europe.* London, 1996; J. Hutchinson, "Ethnicity and Modern Nation," *Ethnic and Racial Studies,* vol. 23, no. 3, 2000.
37. See O. Yiftachel, "Ethnocracy and Its Discontents: Minorities, Protest and the Israeli Polity," *Critical Inquiry,* vol. 26, no. 4, 2000, pp. 725–56.
38. J. Penrose, "The Limitation of Nationalist Democracy: The Treatment of Marginal Groups as a Measure of State Legitimacy," *Hagar International Social Science Review,* vol. 1, no. 2, 2000.
39. A. Burghardt, "The Bases of Territorial Claims," *Geographical Review,* vol. 63, 1973.
40. The territorial socialization process, through the use of biblical and historical narratives, is discussed in D. Newman, "Metaphysical and Concrete Landscapes: The Geopiety of Homeland Socialization in the Land of Israel," in H. Brodsky (ed.), *Land and Community: Geography in Jewish Studies.* Maryland, 1997, pp. 153–84.
41. Shor, N., *History of the Holy Land.* Hebrew. Tel-Aviv, Dvir, 1998, pp. 158–67.
42. Ibid.
43. See B.N. Al-Hout, *Palestine: The Cause, The People, the Civilizations.* Arabic Beirut, dar al-Istiqlal wal-nashar, 1991; J. Segal, S. Levy and E. Katz, *Negotiating Jerusalem,* Albany, 2001.
44. B. Doumani, *Rediscovering Palestine: Merchants and Peasants in Jabal Nablus, 1700–1900.* Berkeley, 1995.
45. R. Khalidi, *Palestinian Identity: The Construction of Modern National Consciousness.* New York, 1997.

46. S. Dellapergola, "Major Demographic Trends of World Jewry: The Last Hundred Years," in B. Bonne-Tamir and A. Adam (eds), *Genetic Diversity Among the Jews*. New York, 1992, pp. 3–30.

47. N. Abu al-Haj, *Facts on the Ground: Archaeological Practice and Territorial Self-Fashioning in Israeli Society*. Chicago, 2001.

48. Y. Zerubavel, *Recovered Roots: Collective Memory and the Making of Israeli National Tradition*. Chicago, 1995.

49. See B. Morris, *Righteous Victims: A History of the Zionist–Arab Conflict, 1881–1999*. New York, 1999.

50. G. Shafir, *Land, Labor, and the Origins of the Israeli–Palestinian Conflict 1882–1914*. Cambridge, 1989; B. Kimmerling, *Zionism and Territory*. Berkeley, 1983.

51. B. Doumani, *Rediscovering Palestine: Merchants and Peasants in Jabal Nablus, 1700–1900*, note 43, Berkeley, 1995.

52. See B. Abu-Manneh, "The Rise of the Sanjak of Jerusalem in the Late 19th Century," in G. Ben-Dor (ed.), *The Palestinians and the Middle East Conflict: Studies in Their History, Sociology and Politics*. Arabic, Ramat Gan, Turtledove, 1978, pp. 25–43; R. Khalidi, *Palestinian Identity: The Construction of Modern National Consciousness,* note 44. New York, 1997; M. Salih, *The Origins of Palestinian Nationalism*, New York, 1988.

53. M. Brawer, *Israel's Borders: Past, Present and Future*. Hebrew. Tel-Aviv, Yavne, 1988.

54. See D. Newman, "Metaphysical and Concrete Landscapes: The Geopiety of Homeland Socialization in the Land of Israel," in H. Brodsky (ed.), *Land and Community: Geography in Jewish Studies*. Maryland, 1997; A. Naor, *Greater Israel: Faith and Policy*. Hebrew Haifa, University of Haifa and Zmora Bittan, 2001.

55. B. Morris, *Righteous Victims: A History of the Zionist–Arab Conflict, 1881–1999*. New York, 1999.

56. See J. Haleli, "In the Territory of Knowledge: State-Centred Discourses and the Construction of Society," *Progress in Human Geography,* vol. 25, no. 3, 2001; T. Winichakul, *Siam Mapped: A History of a Geo-Body of a Nation*. Bangkok, 1994.

57. J. Portugali, *Implicate Relations: Society and Space in Israel*, The Hague, 1993.

58. See E. Shohat, *Forbidden Reminiscences*, Hebrew. Tel-Aviv, Bimat Kedem, 2001, pp. 237–38.

59. E. Said, *The Politics of Dispossession: The Struggle for Palestinian Self-Determination*. London, 1994.

60. R. Khalidi, *Palestinian Identity: The Construction of Modern National Consciousness*. New York, 1997.

61. E. Said, *The Politics of Dispossession*, 1994; E. Said, *Peace and Its Discontents: Essays on Palestine in the Middle East Peace Process*. New York, 1996.

62. G. Shafir, *Land, Labor and the Origins of the Israeli–Palstinian Conflict 1882–1914*. Cambridge, 1989.

63. B. Morris, *The Birth of the Palestinian Refugee Problem 1947–1949*. Cambridge, 1987; R. Khalidi, *Palestinian Identity: The Construction of Modern National Consciousness*. New York, 1997.
64. This does not imply, of course, that the *Shoah* and the *Nakbah* are comparable historical tragedies; clearly, the Jewish holocaust is a disaster of unmatched dimensions.
65. The concept of purification of space is discussed by D. Sibley, *Geographies of Exclusion*. In the Israel–Palestine context, it is used by G. Falah and D. Newman, "The Spatial Manifestation of Threat: Israelis and Palestinians Seek a 'Good' Border," *Political Geography*, vol. 14, no. 4, 1995, pp. 689–706.
66. See R. Khalidi, *Palestinian Identity: The Construction of Modern National Consciousness*. New York, 1997.
67. Dunam equals 1,000 square meter.
68. S. Kedar, "Minority Time, Majority Time: Land, Nation and the Law of Adverse Possession in Israel," *Iyyunei Mishpat*, vol. 21, no. 3, Hebrew. 1998, pp. 665–746.
69. See A. Shiblak, *The Lure of Zion: The Case of the Iraqi Jews*. London, 1986; E. Shohat, *Forbidden Reminisces*. Hebrew. Tel-Aviv, Bimat Kedem, 2001, pp. 237–38.
70. The scope of this paper limits discussion on another major consequence of the Judaization project: The reinforcement of ethno-class disparities within Jewish society, especially between Ashekanzim and Mizrahim; See O. Yiftachel, "Nation-Building and the Social Division of Space: Ashkenazi Dominance in the Israeli 'Ethnocracy'", *Nationalism and Ethnic Politics*, vol. 4, no. 3, 1998, pp. 33–58; M. Benvenisti, *Sacred Landscapes*, Los Angeles, 2001.
71. For details, see O. Yiftachel, "The Internal Frontier: The Territorial Control of Ethnic Minorities," *Regional Studies*, vol. 30, no. 5, 1996, pp. 493–508; O. Yiftachel, "Between Nation and State: 'Fractured' Regionalizm among Palestinian–Arabs in Israel," *Political Geography*, vol. 18, no. 2, 1999, pp. 85–307.
72. O. Almog, *The Sabra—A Profile*. Am Oved, Tel-Aviv, 1997.
73. A. Raz-Karkotzkin, "Diaspora within Sovereignty: Critique of 'Negation of the Diaspora' in Israeli Culture," *Teorya Uvikkoret (Theory and Critique)*, vol. 4, Hebrew. 1993, pp. 23–55. See also B. Kimmerling, *The Invention and Decline of Israeliness*. Los Angeles, 2001.
74. R. Khalidi, *Palestinian Identity: The Construction of Modern National Consciousness*. New York, 1997; S. Tamari, "Historical Reversals and the Uprising," in R. Brynen (ed.), *Echoes of the Intifada: Regional Repercussions of the Israeli–Palestinian Conflict*. Boulder, 1991.
75. N. Rouhana, *Palestinian Citizens in an Ethnic Jewish State: Identities and Conflict*. New Haven, 1997; E. Zureik, *Palestinians in Israel: A Study of Internal Colonialism*. London, 1979.
76. See B. Paramenter, *Giving Voice to Stones: Place and Identity in Palestinian Literature*. Austin, 1994.

77. See E. Said, *The Politics of Dispossession*, 1994; S. Tamari, "Historical Reversals and the Uprising," in R. Brynen (ed.), *Echoes of the Intifada: Regional Repercussions of the Israeli–Palestinian Conflict*. Boulder, 1991.
78. M. Budeiri, "On Palestine," *Journal of Palestine Studies*, 1998, pp. 39–49.
79. E. Said, *The Politics of Dispossession,* 1994.
80. D. Newman and T. Hermann, "A Comparative Study of Gush Emunim and Peace Now," *Middle Eastern Studies*, vol. 28, no. 3, 1992, pp. 509–30; N. Masalha, *Imperial Israel and the Palestinians*. London, 2000.
81. For an analysis of West Bank settlement policy, see D. Newman, "The Territorial Politics of Ex-urbanisation: Reflections on 25 Years of Jewish Settlement in the West Bank," *Israel Affairs*, vol. 3, no. 1, 1996, pp. 61–85.
82. Knesset Protocols, June 17, 1991.
83. I. Lustick, "The Fetish of Jerusalem: A Hegemonic Analysis," M. Barnett. *Israel in Comparative Perspective*. Albany, 1996, pp. 143–72; M. Klein, *Doves Over Jerusalem's Sky: The Peace Process and the City, 1977–1999*. Hebrew. Jerusalem, 1999. B. Wasserstein, *Divided Jerusalem: The Struggle for the Holy City*. London, 2001.
84. Klein, *Doves Over Jerusalem's Sky: The Peace Process and the City, 1977–1999*. Hebrew. Jerusalem, 1999.
85. M. Benveniste, *The West Bank Data Project*. Washington D.C., 1988; A. Ghanem, *The Palestinian Regime: A "Partial Democracy."* London, 2001; G. Usher, *Palestine in Crisis: The Struggle for Peace and Political Independence after Oslo*. London, 1995; R. Shehadeh, "Land and the Occupation: A Review," *Palestine–Israel Journal*, vol. 4, no. 2, 1997, pp. 25–31.
86. Benveniste, *The West Bank Data Project*. Washington D.C., 1988.
87. A. Ghanem, "The Palestinian Minority: Challenging the Jewish State and Its Implications," *Third World Quarterly*, vol. 21, no. 1, 2000, pp. 87–104.
88. E. Said, *Peace and its Discontents*, 1996.
89. The value has remained powerful to date; in 1998, for example, Yasser Arafat publicly stated that those selling Palestinian land deserve death.
90. R. Shehadeh, "Land and the Occupation: A Review," *Palestine–Israel Journal*, vol. 4, no. 2, 1997, pp. 25–31.
91. A local thorny cactus, adopted as a national symbol by Zionists.
92. A. Ghanem, *The Palestinian Regime: A "Partial Democracy."* London, 2001; K. Shekaki, *Old Guard, Young Guard: The Palestinian Authority and the Peace Process at Cross Roads*. Ramalla, 2001.
93. Portugali, *Implicate Relations: Society and Space in Israel, The Hague,* 1993.
94. Kimmerling, 2001, op. cit. Note 72.
95. S. Tamari and R. Hammami, "The Second Intifada," *MERIP*, vol. 30, no. 4, 2000, pp. 4–10.
96. *Maariv*, November 10, 1995.
97. For an analysis of the geographic outcome of the Oslo Accords, see D. Newman, "Creating the Fences of Territorial Separation: The Discourses of Israeli–Palestinian Conflict Resolution, *Geopolitics and International*

Boundaries, vol. 2, no. 2, 1997, pp. 1–35; D. Newman, "The Geopolitics of Peacemaking in Israel–Palestine," *Political Geography*, vol. 21, 2002.

98. *The Middle Eastern Times*, February 16, 2001.
99. Y. Beilin, *Guide for a Wounded Dove*. Hebrew. Tel-Aviv, Keter, 2001.
100. *Haaretz*, April 13, 2001.
101. Shekaki, *Old Guard, Young Guard: The Palestinian Authority and the Peace Process at Cross Roads*. Ramalla, 2001.
102. *Maariv*, September 30, 2000.
103. A. Ghanem and S. Ozacky-Lazar, *A Year after the October Events—What Has Changed?* Hebrew. Givat Haviva, 2001.
104. UNESCO. *The Impact on the Palestinian Economy of Confrontation, Border Closure and Mobility Restrictions*. New York, 2000; Batzelem, *Report on Casualties in Israeli–Palestinian Hostilities, September 2000–December 2000*. Jerusalem, Betzelem, 2002.
105. B. Anderson, *Imagined Communities: Reflections on the Origin and Spread of Nationalism*. London, 1991; A. Passi, "Territorial Identities as Social Constructs," *Hagar: International Social Science Review*, vol. 1, no. 2, 2000, pp. 91–114.

3

ANTHROPOLOGY OF RECONCILIATION: A CASE FOR LEGAL PLURALISM*

Pradip Kumar Bose

CONFLICT AND RECONCILIATION

Social science, including anthropology, has uncovered more knowledge about war and conflict than about peace and reconciliation, just as psychology, probably, has yielded more insights into negative deviance (such as, mental illness) than into positive deviance (such as, creativity). Unfortunately, studies tend to be focused on wars as units of analysis rather than on periods of peace, and there is a tendency to define peace simply as "non-war." Thus peace thinking has had a tendency to become utopian and to be oriented towards the future: it has been speculative and value-oriented rather than analytical and empirical. It is conceivable that this might change if research were to be focused more on peace than on war.

Anthropology of reconciliation generally comes as an appendage to the study of conflict and finds its relevance to an understanding of the functions of conflict, and its expression. The anthropologist studies conflict as a multi-dimensional social process that operates in many different contexts, and results in a variety of consequences. Although theoretical attention to social and cultural conflict is relatively new in anthropology, ethnographers have long been recording instances of conflict

*Originally published in Ranabir Samaddar and Helmut Reifeld (eds), *Peace as Process: Reconciliation and Conflict Resolution in South Asia*. Manohar, New Delhi, with the title "Anthropology of Reconciliation."

occurring under variety of guises. Such diverse phenomena as witchcraft practices, feuds, factionalism, warfare, competitive games, contradictory values, and discord between spouses have been viewed as conflict, or as the potential means of displacing conflict from one level of social grouping to another. In each of these instances, there are various reconciliation processes in operation governed by social and cultural matrix of the society. Conflict is discord; its opposite is harmony, reconciliation, which for many implies integration. Integration and conflict have often been discussed as opposites, and indeed, conflict has been equated with anomie—deviant, abnormal behavior which impedes successful integration of society. The absence of conflict and presence of co-operation and co-ordination are sometimes used as indexes of integration and social stability. Conflict is more readily observable than integration. As a result, much anthropological discussion of integration or stability is implicit rather than explicit.

Anthropologists for quite some time never paid much attention to the question of disputes and reconciliation; this field only developed in the last 50 years. It was from that time anthropologists began to publish detailed records of the course of disputes from their origin to their attempted settlement, and events that followed upon this attempt. However, anthropologists of these societies were handicapped by the fact that by the time they were undertaking their field work, colonizing powers had already suppressed indigenous modes of self-help. With the new rules, and by establishing systems of organized authority including own dominant powers, the colonial power made unnecessary full dependence on the reconciliation through public opinion and its cross-linkages towards settlement. Hence the cases on which these anthropologists had to rely were often partial records from the past by contemporary untrained observers, or the recollections of disputes by aged informants.

One of the crucial questions that emerged from the very beginning in the study of reconciliation process among indigenous population by anthropologists is the meaning of the word "law." In any language, most words, which refer to important social phenomena—as "law" obviously does—are likely to have several referents and to cover a wide range of meanings. We should therefore expect that the English word "law," and other related words, will not have a single precise meaning. If jurisprudence is full of controversy centring on how "law" should be defined, the terminological disputes are increased when tribal societies with their very different cultures, are investigated. Since our own words for "law" and related phenomena are already loaded with meaning, students of tribal societies run into difficulties as soon as they try to apply these words to activities of other cultures. Yet, on the other hand, how can we think or write outside our own language? Must the anthropologists develop a special technical language which some may confuse with jargon, or should they conclude that it is misleading to try to discuss tribal law in the principal concepts of Western jurisprudence, and instead, employ vernacular terms to describe the indigenous systems? This problem is not specific to anthropology but a general problem in all social science. In general terms, "law" is viewed as social control through the systematic application of the force of politically organized society. However, if "politically organized" implies the existence of courts, then there are societies without law. Thus Evans-Pritchard stated that "in the strict sense of the word, the Nuer have no law." Yet in another book on them published in the same year he spoke of Nuer law and of legal relations, and he described how people might recognize that justice lay on the other side in a dispute.[1] His pupil Howell followed him here in his *A Manual of Nuer Law* (1954), stating that "on this strict definition, the Nuer had no law." He adds immediately: "... but it is clear that in a less exact sense they were not lawless,"[2] and he states that he therefore uses the term "law" rather loosely. Such pronouncements give enough indications that the system of dispute settlements that anthropologists encountered, defied the standard format available in the West, and required a more flexible approach.

The analysis of the reasonings of reconciliation mechanisms involves considering the types of social relations out of which dispute has emerged. Gluckman points out that in some of the African tribes, where most transactions take place between closely related persons, usually kinsmen or in-laws, disputes in such societies are qualitatively different from those where persons are linked only by contract or tort, as we find in the modern societies.[3] In tribal societies, where closely related persons are involved, the adjudicator may well try to adjust their dispute so that they should be able to resume their friendly relationship, and it is a substantial advantage if all concur in the adjudication. In anthropological literature, those behaviors, which proceed from and are indicative of conflict, are also viewed as operating to resolve the conflict. If reconciliation is not achieved through routine procedures, the use of third party to achieve settlement by arbitration, mediation, compromise, or adjudication is also likely. Certain institutional forms of reconciliation, such as councils, courts, "go-betweens", or "crossers", perform these functions. For instance, among the Yurok of California, the parties to a dispute appointed unrelated persons from different communities, who took evidence from them and other available sources conferred among themselves and with the parties, and laid down a verdict. On the other hand, the role of Ifugao "go-between" is different. As Barton describes:

> To the end of peaceful settlement he exhausts every art of Ifugao diplomacy. He wheedles, coaxes, flatters, threatens, drives, scolds, insinuates. He beats down the demands of the plaintiff or prosecution, and bolsters up the proposals of the defendants until a point is reached at which the parties may compromise.[4]

He is more of a conciliator than an arbitrator. Among the Nuer, a person called "man of the earth" settles dispute by threatening to curse the disputing parties, and there is no suggestion that he listens to and weighs evidence. In fact, he can be best described as a ritual mediator. One can make a grade of authoritativeness among the intermediary, the mediator, the conciliator, and the arbitrator, and such a grade is related to the ranges of social pressure, which back their actions, ranges of relationships between parties which, in turn, determines the specific procedure that will be effective.

Anthropologists have made significant note of the fact that reconciliation and control of conflict need not be identified with specialized political offices. There are viable, stable societies which lack central government and specialized political roles, but which, nonetheless, have available other means of reconciling and regulating conflict. In such stateless societies a variety of institutions and personnel, such as diviner and shaman, may function as agents of reconciliation. Among the Dobu, sorcery is a socialized ritual that operates as the medium for a non-violent adjustment of opposing interests. The style of reconciliation derives from a society's structural principles of human association. Among the Nuer of Southern Sudan, as Evans-Pritchard has shown in his classic study, the political institution of the feud is regulated through the mechanism known as the "leopard-skin chief."[5] The person is one of those specialists who are concerned, in a ritual capacity, with various departments of Nuer social life and nature, and especially, with the reconciliation process. The chief settles the conflict in terms of a complex process of sanctions, compensation, and sacrifices for cleansing and atonement. If one gets the impression that the chief judges the case and compels the acceptance of his decision to the feuding parties, then nothing could be farther from facts. The chief is not asked to deliver a judgment; it would not occur to Nuer that one was required. He appears to force the aggrieved party (for instance, the kin of the dead man killed by others) to accept compensation by his insistence, even to the point of threatening to curse them, but it is an established convention that he shall do so, in order that the bereaved relatives may retain their prestige. What seems really to have counted was the acknowledgment of community ties between the parties concerned, and hence of the moral obligation to settle the affair by the acceptance of a traditional payment, and the wish on both sides, to avoid, for the time being at any rate, further hostilities. It is not difficult to comprehend that the smaller the group involved, the more easily feuds are resolved. When a feud occurs within a village, general opinion demands an early settlement, since it is obvious to everyone that were vengeance allowed, corporate life would be impossible. At the other end of the scale when conflict occurs between primary or secondary sections of a tribe, there is a little chance of an early reconciliation, and owing to distance reconciliation, process takes more time. Nevertheless, since the feuding parties, as a rule, have frequent social contacts, so eventually, the mechanism of the leopard-skin chief has to be employed to prevent their complete dislocation. The leopard-skin chief does not rule and judge, but acts as a mediator through whom communities desirous of ending open hostility can conclude an active state of feud. Evans-Pritchard writes that the feud, including the role played in it by the chief, is thus a mechanism by which the political structure maintains itself in the form known to us.

Gluckman points out that a man's prestige in his own group depends on his skill as an organizer of exchanges, on the number of partners he has in several directions and his ability to deal with them; and to manage these enterprises successfully, he also has to be able to manipulate his relationship with his own people in order to obtain means to exchange externally. He has to be able to direct the marriages in such a fashion that the group acquires in-laws in strategic positions. He has to be able to allocate his goods so as to put others in his debt, in order that he can mobilize resources to stage a feast. Only by showing skills in these enterprises can he become a big man and acquire prestige. Since a man's prestige in his own group depends on his relations with exchange partners, he as a big man has a great interest in the maintenance of sufficiently friendly relations with those partners who are big men in other groups. He is moved to oppose a state of all-out war. If war has broken out—over land, over theft, over vengeance for a killing—the big man needs in the end to bring about a resumption of peaceful relations, for, only if there is sufficient peace for the exchanges to go on, can he maintain his prestige. Therefore, there exists a mechanism which produces a peacemaker in the heart of each warring group.[6]

In a theoretical sense, disputes and their reconciliation provide a guide to the points of strain and contradiction in a social system, as well as, to the structures of power and authority, which are brought to bear on them. Disputes or episodes of conflict may be resolved or reconciled by means of a number of different procedural forms ranging from informal to the formal legal mode. Self-help, often violent in nature, is one kind of dispute management in which the parties handle the conflict by fighting, or feuding, or by other actions of offense or retribution. This often leads to the escalation of original conflict, and for this reason, many societies possess other kinds of mechanism which can be used to lead conflict toward a peaceful resolution. In some cases, disputes are settled by the process of ordeals or divination, and it is interesting to observe in such cases who is able to manipulate or define the outcome of such procedures.

In anthropological literature, divination means acquisition of information through the use of magic. There are a variety of means, from the interpretation of naturally occurring phenomena to a range of manipulative practices, which are performed in order to arrive at a verdict or decision. Divination is typically employed to discover the identity of a criminal, to resolve a dispute and effect reconciliation, or to predict the outcome of a future event. Evans-Pritchard's classic study of Azande witchcraft and divination established a tradition of structural-functionalist interpretations of religion and divinatory practices.[7] These studies focused on how oracles, divination, and the manner of interpreting their results, reflects the mechanism of fission, fusion, reconciliation, social control, and authority within the group.

Where a third party intervenes in the reconciliation process, we may distinguish several different modes of procedure, including mediation, adjudication, and arbitration. Arbitration is a more formalized mode of mediation, in which the conflicting parties agree to submit themselves to the decision of a qualified or appointed third party. Where there is no third party, we may distinguish the modes of negotiation or self-help as described earlier. In the anthropology of law, adjudication is the intervention in a dispute of a third person (or other persons) vested with special authority within a formal legal system. We may contrast mediation, where the third party is not vested with legal authority, and may be of high or low status in relation to disputing parties, and negotiation where the disputing parties or their representatives come to a direct agreement without intervention of a third party. Adjudication, or the formal legal mode of reconciliation and social control, is characteristic of societies with considerable specialization of roles. Anthropological analyses of conflict and reconciliation often focus on the manner in which situations of conflict reveal the structural alignments and divisions within the group. Differences and contradiction, which are masked in everyday interaction are generally laid bare in the conflicts, where persons are subject to pressure to define their loyalties. Disputes thus reveal important features of social and cultural organization, and the mechanisms, which exist for their settlement, likewise, indicate points of authority and cohesive power within social and political systems.

The conditions, which define the presence and use of reconciliation mechanism and controlling procedures, are various. Generally, anthropologists hold the view that greater density of population and the dissolution of family authority, and the power that accompanies the development of a centralized state system may strengthen the adjudication procedures in place of mediation or arbitration. In recent times, anthropologists have attempted a more comprehensive approach to the mechanism of reconciliation by examining the life cycles of particular conflicts. The process through which a conflict may pass may be found to be inherent in the type of conflict. Various mechanisms are employed within the same society to heal the breaches of peace. These actions range from informal arbitration to formal legal machinery, to the performance of public ritual. Anthropologists believe mystical beliefs and ritual action, rather than judicial machinery, are particularly effective in dealing with disturbances arising from process inherent in the life cycle of a group.

PROCESS OF RECONCILIATION

The process of reconciliation has been described in some detail by Bernard Cohn[8] in his study of anthropology of disputes in north India. As anthropologists shifted their attention from the study of primitive, isolated, pre-literate societies to that of social units which are part of great civilizations, they encountered a new range of problems which required description and analysis. Cohn in this study takes up the process of reconciliation in a local region in north India, and the effects that the establishment of British rule had on the indigenous dispute settlement process. One of the formal organizations of dispute settlement was the formally constituted caste councils, the membership of which was based on a regional division of various lineage segments. The principal basis of dispute settlement in such councils in the past had been arbitration and the balancing of power, so well analyzed by students of African political organizations.[9] The system of arbitration and power balance was reinforced by the expectation that internal strife in the dominant caste would be used by surrounding groups to destroy the suzerainty of the lineage over its little kingdom. In the case of a dominant caste like the Rajputs, the Thakurs also derived important status in their role as settlers of disputes and judges, from their claims to be kings in traditional social order.

If a dispute cannot be settled easily, then the contending parties can summon a meeting of the council to hear and settle the dispute. This meeting can be either formal or informal. An informal meeting generally includes the leaders of the council, heads of the households, and any interested person. In a formal meeting outside leaders are also called upon for advisory opinions. As they are not directly involved they can be less circumspect. Everyone who attends the meeting is aware of the facts and know that they can be affected by the chain of relations and dispute which lie behind it. The meeting after being opened by the leader is addressed by each side and the case stated in declamatory fashion, with no attempt at cross-examination or rebuttal. The other participants comment on the facts, they may also comment on human nature, the stress and strain of life, general morality, and so on. There is no systematic procedure to determine the facts of the situation. It is assumed that all participants are aware of facts. Participants can make general statements about the rules of behavior, and back up with cases and earlier decisions. Generally, there is no recourse to knowledge of sacred texts, law books, or current civil, or criminal law. The law, which is being used is the customary law. The general rule is that leaders of the respective contending units will act in some sense as mediators, because by going above the interests of the unit, the leader not only enhances his prestige, but demonstrates his ability to lead in the next larger unit and take a wider role and more active part in it. In fact, he would endanger his role of leader in the wider circle if he were to push the claim of his immediate followers too much. Cohn writes: "In essence, I judge, it is the role of the leader to bridge the gaps between the rings of the social 'onion,' by balancing between advocate of the rights of his immediate followers and the demands of the wider social group."[10]

One of the mechanisms of reconciliation is to settle the dispute through talking it out. The act of talking lets out the steam and takes out some of the aggression accumulated in the dispute. There is no time limit, and it is not expected that the dispute will be settled within a specified number of meetings. Often people talk and discuss for hours totally irrelevant issues. There is no expectation that the discussants will "stick to the point," and in the process, often a meeting held ostensibly to hear one dispute, goes beyond the dispute, and people will discuss and adjudicate another dispute, coming up as a side issue, which lies behind the antagonism. In such societies, life is not segmented so that issues can be compartmentalized easily, and hence they see no point in trying to decide matters only on the basis of immediate situation.

In a more general sense, we can say, that the principal task is to move towards social harmony and individual composure rather than away from them toward dissonance and vertigo. It is what disposition of issue is all about. It is the mechanism of decision-making, procedures of reconciliation, that occupy the centre of attention, rather than techniques of determining what actually happened. Such adjudications are also a matter of high etiquette, of patient, precise, and unexcited going through the elaborate forms of local consensus making. What matters finally is that unanimity of mind is demonstrated, not so much in the verdict itself, which is a mere denouement, but in the public process by which it has been generated. Propriety to be preserved must be seen to be preserved. As mentioned earlier, the processes involved are mainly discussion processes, the propriety mainly discursive propriety. Unanimity, or at least the appearance of it, is to be gained by talking through, in hard cases, over and over again in grand variety of contexts, in a set and settled manner. Reconciliation process, here, is truly a flow of admonitory proverbs, moral slogans, stereotyped speeches, recitations from didactic literature, fixed metaphors of vice and virtue—all delivered in a manner designed at once to soothe and persuade. Geertz quotes a passage, in which a mother instructs her son on how to behave when he is admitted to the various local councils:

> ... O my dear son
> if you are sent for by the council, you must answer;
> if invited you must come.
> If it happens you are sent for,
> invited to attend a council feast,

eat sufficiently before going,
and drink something too;
for at a feast or banquet
eating and drinking have a strict form,
sitting and standing have their place.
There you must use all your politeness,
never forgetting where you are.
Be polite in everything
and remember all the rules,
even in passing betel or cigarettes.

Then when it comes to the speeches,
always be careful what you say:
sweet speech is a quality of goodness.
Always speak truthfully
observing all the forms of politeness,
taking care to understand people's feelings.
When you speak, speak humbly,
always depreciating yourself.
Be sure you behave correctly
and control all your passions.
A council member should live by his principles,
his speech should be of the *adat*
following the line of the right path
—calm as a waveless sea,
settled as a plain without wind
his knowledge firm in his heart,
ever mindful of his elders' counsel.[11]

TRADITION AND RECONCILIATION

The kind of institutions through which the pre-colonial societies attempted reconciliation are diverse and multitudinous as the rules they sought to apply, the group they sought to apply them to, and justification they sought to give for them. But the principle that men of learning did the justifying and men of power did the applying seems to have been pervasive. In India, there was a vast hierarchy of caste and inter-caste councils, "dominant caste" mini-rajas of the so-called "little kingdoms", who served at various levels of dispute settlement and reconciliation. In Thailand, there was a tangle of 30 sorts of ministerial courts, as juridically ill-defined as the ministers themselves, advised by a consultative ministry of legal affairs, and manned, in this supposedly Buddhist country, by a dozen Brahmins. In Indonesia, there were hundreds of large experts of varying kinds, and competence under the immediate eye of the resident lord. However, everywhere the procedural norm was that the adjudicative process and reconciliation should follow the rules of *dharma*. In a schematic and simplified manner we can say that irrespective of the particular institutional shape of the process, the central evidentiary question to which it addressed itself pertained neither to the occasions of acts nor to their consequences, but to their type; that is, they were question of *dharma* and *adharma* brought down to a judiciable level. It become a matter of determining where in the local version of the grand taxonomy of dutiful behaviors, a particular behavior fell. The essence of traditional process of reconciliation was based not so much on the sifting through evidence of particular disputes, but rather on the aptness of the final judgments as to the total value of human existence.

Reconciliation mechanism in such societies is based on some notion of "law," not in the formal sense of the term, but in the sense of local knowledge; local not just as to place, time, class, and variety of issues, but as to accent—vernacular characterizations of what happens to vernacular imaginings of what can. Geertz calls this legal sensibility, by which he means this complex of characterizations and imaginings, stories about events cast in imagery about principles.[12] Srinivas points out that two terms that were heard frequently in the villagers' folk about disputes in Rampura were *nyaya* (according to law or rule, right, just, fair, moral) and *anyaya* (opposite of *nyaya*).[13] It was not simply the arguments or positions expressed by disputants, which were viewed as *nyaya* or *anyaya* but also the decisions of the arbitrators. The notion of *nyaya* is linked to morality and local practices, and expresses the local knowledge-based sensitivity to the subtler points of customary law and procedure.

In such a context, law is local knowledge and not placeless principle, which is constructive of social life. In the past, this social life was characterized in terms of accumulation of prestige than in terms of territory. The disagreements among various chiefdoms were rarely concerned with border problems, but with delicate question of mutual status and prestige. Korn relates an anecdote about South Celebes, which makes this point with grave irony of traditional wit. The Dutch, who wanted, for the usual administrative reasons, to get the boundary between two petty princedoms straight once for all, called the princes concerned and asked them where indeed the borders lay. Both agreed that border of princedom A lay at the farthest point from which a man could see the swamps, while the border of princedom B lay at the farthest point from which a man could still see the sea. Had they, then, never been fought over the land in between, from which one could neither see swamp nor sea? "Mijnheer," one of the old princes replied, "we had better reason to fight with one another than these shabby hills."

Even in contemporary times, the forms of legal sensibility, of which reconciliation process was only a minor part, persists in the Third World, because even if it has become modernized, it has not become placeless. In every Third World country, the tension between established notion of what justice ... *dharma* ...*adat*...is, and how it gets done, and imported ones more reflective of the forms and pressures of modern life, animates whatever there is of judicial process. For instance, in the Indian context, *Dharma* is understood not only as the code of conduct for an individual or a group, but also as an all-embracing system in which just relations are preserved between people and nature, between different social groups, and also between people and gods. *Dharma* is both a moment in the system, as well as the transcendental value of the system. Within the context of *Dharma*, law would not be a set of rules to be applied to all in a mechanistic fashion by a superior authority, but rather would embody a recognition that groups and individuals have a right to discover their own modes of being, and to devise the rules that are to govern their existence. Various terms have been invented to characterize the process, like "legal pluralism," "legal syncretism," and so on, but the central issue posed by the legal pluralism of the modern world that largely escapes the classroom formulation is, namely, that how ought are we to understand the office of the law now, and hence the process of reconciliation, when the varieties of "law" are so wildly intermingled?

Legal sensibility, in other words, draws its sustenance from the culturally given norms and practices of reconciliation. The modernist notion and practices of law often have an uneasy relationship with the "local knowledge"-based legal sensibility, and even when the varieties of law are intermingled, they acquire a specific character, depending on the social and cultural formation of that society. While the modern law is based on a detailed categorization of rules, offenses, punishments, etc., the legal sensibility is more unfocussed, it is a normative order with very broad parameters. This is also a reflection of distinct worldviews, spatial organization of people, and customary practices. In one sense, one can understand the instrumentality of legal sensibility as a counter-hegemonic strategy used by communities to protect their limited and conditional autonomy. In another sense, this overarching sensibility governs people's judgment about the reconciliation procedures of modern state systems. In many of the states such semi-autonomous local jurisdictions and reconciliation process have constituted, *de facto*, part of the apparatus of governance since the colonial period. In this sense, the incorporation of local difference into the institutionality of the state is not a new phenomenon: state power has long depended on complex negotiation with local interests (indigenous and non-indigenous), which have in turn, co-opted others by extending often highly coercive clientelist networks down to the village level.

However, it must be admitted that this conditional incorporation often was not premised on the basis of extending citizenship to the majority of population. In contrast, the underlying logic of incorporation of "local knowledge," local indigenous authorities, and legal practices into the national politico-legal systems has been to democratize the nation-state and construct pluralist practices of citizenship, which include indigenous people within state and society on the basis of equality and respect for cultural diversity. In many of the post-colonial states, a substantial section of the population continues to perceive modern state law and its institutions as arbitrary, distant, ineffective, and often, unjust on the grounds of prevalent normative order. In many cases, the judicial inefficiency, impunity, and corruption prevent the full exercise of rights or the enforcement of obligations, creating a situation, which has been termed as "low intensity citizenship." The highly deficient legal system, and consequently, its mechanism of reconciliation, along with the general culture of impunity, provide the context for constructing a more pluri-cultural rule of law, which is able to strengthen the local mechanism of conflict resolution, and the recuperation of what is being termed as "legal sensibilty," as a part of an overall strategy to reinforce the "other" identities, to achieve a more efficacious judicial system, and to promote greater justice. In the context of efforts to build a more culturally appropriate and responsive rule of law, what then becomes necessary is to make use of submerged signifiers, meaning, and practices of previous periods as a starting point for rethinking justice, reconciliation, and democracy.

NOTES AND REFERENCES

1. E.E. Evans-Pritchard, "The Nuer of the Southern Sudan" in *African Political Systems*. Oxford, 1940, pp. 293–96. For contrast see *The Nuer*. Oxford, 1940, pp. 160–65, 168.
2. P.P. Howel, *A Manual of Nuer Law*. Oxford, 1954, p. 95.
3. Max Gluckman, *Politics, Law and Ritual in Tribal Society*. Oxford, 1977, pp. 169–212.
4. R.F. Barton, *Ifugao Law,* California, 1919, p. 94.
5. E.E. Evans-Pritchard, *The Nuer: A Description of the Modes of Livelihood and Political Institution of a Nilotic People*. Oxford, 1940.
6. Max Gluckman, op. cit. pp. 59–63.
7. E.E. Evans-Pritchard, *Witchcraft, Magic and Oracles Among the Azande*. Oxford, 1937.
8. Bernard S. Cohn, "Some Notes on Law and Change in North India"; "Anthropological Notes on Law and Disputes in North India", in his *An Anthropologist Among the Historians and Other Essays*. New Delhi, 1990.
9. Max Gluckman, *Custom and Conflict in Africa*. Oxford, 1973, pp. 1–26.
10. Bernard S. Cohn, op. cit., p. 562.
11. Clifford Geertz, *Local Knowledge: Further Essays in Interpretive Anthropology*. London, 1993, p. 212.
12. Cited in Clifford Geertz, *The Interpretation of Culture*. London, 1993, pp. 336–37.
13. M.N. Srinivas, *The Remembered Village*. Bombay, 1976, p. 314.

SECTION II

PEACE AS PROCESS

INTRODUCTION

Paula Banerjee

The post cold war era is internationally marked by a series of state versus community conflicts, so much so that it is has been termed as a period of fragmentation. For want of an enemy outside, the states seemed to be looking inward and revaluating the "other." Not unusually then, for South Asia also, this phase is marked by enormous political violence and ethnic discord. Although most of South Asian conflicts have deep roots that go way back in history, yet the decade of the 90s is distinguishable as a period of escalating violence. Small wonder then that this was also a decade when efforts were made to fashion a process whereby violence from the rebels could be harnessed, and the states would be able to recover their initiatives of control. In this section of the Peace Studies, the reader is concerned with this dynamics, which has come to be known in recent history as "peace process."

What is known as the peace process in Kashmir, Northeast India, and Sri Lanka does not present before us a scenario of sanitized vacuum, but rather of acute contentions—a situation, where dialogue for peace continues, at the same time, violence looms large over the scene. Hence, conflict and dialogue for peace exist side by side in most of South Asia—a case of war–peace continuum. Interestingly enough, all four chapters in this section deal with internal or intra-state conflicts. But some of these chapters hint at what Kumar Rupesinghe has termed "the disappearing boundaries of internal and external conflicts."[1] For example, in the state versus community conflict in Kashmir, there is the third dimension in the form of Pakistan and several global factors. The author argues in the essay on Kashmir that for the peace process to succeed, some understanding with Pakistan is essential.

One expert has commented that the "most striking characteristic of internal conflict is its asymmetry: one party (government) is strong and the other (insurgents) is weak."[2] These
essays, however, contest such an unproblematic approach to
conflict. Sumantra Bose's essay on Kashmir makes out the case
that although there may be some difference in relative strengths
of the two sides, the difference in strength is more a matter of
perception—each side thinks it is the stronger side, while complexities on the ground abound. While discussing the civil defence system in Hindu majority areas in Jammu, he points out
to the discrepancy in the arms used—the *jehadis* using AK–
47s, and Village Defence Council (VDC) members—the GOI with
.303 rifles. Such a situation contradicts the understanding that
one party is always strong, and the other always weak. The
essays presented here point out that strengths and weaknesses
of the antagonists are both relative and location specific. In
fact, the essays point out that unless the rebels acquire enough
strength, the states will not negotiate with them. Indeed, the
fact that the state feels compelled to negotiate with the rebels,
indicates the strength of the adversary, which would have
otherwise remained unrecognized.

Also, the fact that the rebels often replicate the state structure
and become quasi state, indicates the strength of rebellion, and
something like an organic strength present in the process, which
at times, gives lie to the notion of power asymmetry. South Asian
experiences portray that states enter into the peace process
only with state-like organizations that can make claims of control at least in their own location. Therefore, according to Jehan
Perera, it was the "inability of the Sri Lankan state to wrest
back control over these areas over the past 15 years," that made
it imperative for them to enter into a peace process.

The peace processes under consideration in this section points
to the fact that none of the parties is a monolith. They have
fault lines within. This can be a source of strength as well as
weakness. The essay on Sri Lanka clearly states that it was the
fragmentation of opinion among the Sinhalese that made it
impossible for the government to negotiate with the Tamils for
peace. But the essay on Kashmir states that the *jehadis* are

but only one segment of the rebel group. There are others who steer clear from violence and would rather dialogue for peace than wage terrorist attacks. Also, discourses on peace processes often try to homogenize different voices into a meta-narrative. But it is essential to realize that there are multiple voices in this process, and a denial of space to these voices, which is done both by the state and the rebels, can result in jeopardizing the entire process. Therefore, by denying space to the Muslims in Sri Lanka, and the Gujjars in Kashmir, the antagonists have created a situation that at different times have jeopardized the process itself. Even the Communiqué of the Committee of Concerned Citizens makes a plea for bringing back peoples' voices to the peace process.

To be true, the Communiqué of the Committee of Concerned Citizens is unique in the South Asian literature on peace for several reasons. It deals with class issues, and hence addresses one of the many silences in the discourse on peace in South Asia. The Communiqué calls for a breakaway from a continuum of violence in the state versus peasant rebellion, popularly known as the Naxalite movement, and makes a plea for addressing larger issues of right to life and livelihood through a process of dialogue. It portrays how people losing their lives in this attrition in Andhra Pradesh are largely from economically oppressed sections of society. It questions the state's definition of the Naxalite movement as a law and order problem, and calls for recognition by the state that there is a necessity to restructure society in terms of access to resources. It deals with material problems in making peace, and rejects high moral grounds.

In fact, current usage of game theories in efforts to sustain peace processes portray that there is little scope in moralizing. Essays presented here also reflect this reality. No one side can be considered as universally black/white, good/bad. Both have legitimacy among its believers. It has to be realized that any peace process can be sustained largely through political dialogues. Yet either the government reduces intra-state conflicts to a law and order problem, or the rebels make it an emotional issue that justifies violence/sacrifice. Such developments deny space to dialogue. Therefore, although some observers feel that "force is not stopped, neutralized or contained, except by an equivalent or superior force," and often this is the argument used by both the rebels and the states, essays in this collection prove otherwise.[3] The collection reflects that force needs to be counterpoised by a just dialogue for sustaining a peace process. This brings us to the issue of dialogue in peace process, and in general, to the politics of peace.

Samir Das' essay evokes an interesting debate in this context. He tries to analyze how peace accords can be posited as a ground of contested meanings, and in this perspective challenges Ranabir Samaddar's concept of the term governmentality as a "technique of governance"[4] on the ground that Samaddar's use of the term smacks of instrumentalism that Foucault has distanced himself from. However, Samaddar's usage of the term as a basis for peace accords opens up another vista in the debate. By looking at peace accords as a system of governing and as a field of governing relations, Samaddar is able to bring out the limits built in peace accords. Although not unproblematic, such an analysis and deployment of the concept, at least, reflect possibilities of innovative ways of looking at peace accords. It portrays why rebel groups are cynical of accords and yet are compelled to participate in it, and how accords are but an ensemble of relations of rule and governance.

However, one has to acknowledge that there are some silences in this section that deals with discourses on peace process. Although in this volume in another section there is an essay on the gendered nature of accords, in this section, gender remains largely submerged in other issues. These essays discuss extensively how to bring back peoples' voices in peace-making exercises, and comment on the fractured nature of those voices. Gender is one of the most critical of those voices. There is an overriding need to bring gender on board in this perspective. Such silences as the one on gender also reflect the nature of the discourse where discussions on gender in peace processes are often kept outside the realm of the "mainstream," as if meant for specialized treatment by feminist scholars. Similar to categories of class and race current, events definitely indicate that it is essential to bring gender in the politics of peace. Probably future volumes of peace readers will address such silences.

Notes and References

1. Kumar Rupesinghe, "The Disappearing Boundaries of Internal and External Conflicts" in *Internal Conflicts and Governance*. New York, 1992, pp. 1–26.
2. William Zartman, ed., *Elusive Peace: Negotiating an End to Civil Wars*. Washington D.C., 1995, p. 7.
3. Pierre Hassner, *Violence and Peace: From the Atomic Bomb to Ethnic Cleansing*. Budapest/London, 1995, p. 39.
4. Ranabir Samaddar, "Those Accords: A Bunch of Documents," *SAFHR*, no. 4. Kathmandu, 1999, p. 7.

4

NOBODY'S COMMUNIQUÉ: ETHNIC ACCORDS IN NORTHEAST INDIA[*]

Samir Kumar Das

As the failures of ethnic accords in India, or in other parts of South Asia become increasingly apparent, peace audit exercises are gaining a certain currency amongst the socially minded scholars, as well as serious social activists. Such exercises seem to oscillate between politics of accusations, and what may for want of a better term be described as, non-politics of committing mistakes. While state counsellers and its protagonists have otherwise been highly self-critical, they often attribute the failures to a section of ethnic leaders whose wooden-headed intransigence is believed to have torpedoed the accords, one after another. Thus, while referring to the Shillong Accord of 1975, Subodh Chandra Dev, widely recognized as one of its principal architects, expresses his anxieties in these terms: "The biggest problem in the implementation of the accord is to make a section of (the China-trained) insurgents accept the Shillong Accord and to make them lay down their arms on the border itself."[1] Nari Rustomji and Ved Marwah, both having vast experience of serving in different parts of the region as members of the Indian Administrative Service (IAS) at different points of time, also find fault with all those whose apathy and lack of imagination have driven some ethnic communities to "extremes of

* Originally published in Ranabir Samaddar and Helmut Reifeld (eds), *Peace Process: Reconciliation and Conflict Resolution in South Asia*. Manohar, New Delhi, with the title "Nobody's Communiqué: Study of Ethnic Accords in Northeastern India."

paranoia,"[2] and their insensitive and irresponsible politics. But Rustomji, in particular, urges on the bulk of the tribal members to forget the past and forgive them, and most importantly, as a tribute to the value systems that they have evolved for themselves throughout the centuries. Writing in 1983, his observation on the Shillong Accord still betrays an optimism that is uncharacteristic of most of the run-of-the-mill social scientists: "... if they will cherish in their hearts with sincerity the Christian doctrine of forgiveness and atonement, the working out of the drama to its conclusion, but a happy and not a tragic conclusion, may yet prove a reality despite the bruises they have suffered."[3]

Others however, accuse the state of having turned accords into mere scraps of paper, or "those accords," as Samaddar puts it. Kumar Rupesinghe, for instance, argues that accords may simply be regarded as instruments through which a state "imposes its will" on the body politic.[4] Kumar Sanjay Singh draws our attention to the eternal paradox that the states per se face all over the world: while status quo necessarily works against the disadvantaged, any state assigns to itself the task of upholding and maintaining it. Accords, as Singh argues, may be likened to a "strategy" that the state deploys in order to "replicate the status quo and retain its legitimacy" in the eyes of the disadvantaged.[5] Although Samaddar invokes time and again, Foucauldian concept of "governmentality," his comment that accords are "a technique of governance" smacks of the traces of an otherwise instrumentalist view of power that Foucault has by his own admission taken pains of distancing himself from. By saying that accords are a means of "managing a set of norms" and their management is what enables "the rulers to rule," Samaddar brings in a logic that equates governmentality with "a technique of governance."[6] Governmentality for Foucault, is more a commitment on the state's part to the modernist framework of rationality than simply a tool or "technique of governance." Such a commitment is "peculiar" to the West for which it is more of a "passion" than anything else. As Barry Allen puts it: "There is something peculiar about the Western passion for government. It arises or at least is constantly reinforcing and reinforced by the idea we have cultivated as to what it means to be 'rational' in matters of political government."[7]

Commitment to rationality for him is an end in itself rather than a means to an end.

If one of the parties could secure its interests by making the accords, that it had itself entered into, fail, their success could have served their mutual interests better. Failure according to this argument is imputed to the mistakes that both parties commit much to the detriment of their interlocking interests. Horam, for instance, makes this comment on Shillong Accord: "There have been mistakes and blunders on both sides and the results of which were far from happy for either parties."[8] If politics is regarded as a rational pursuit of interests, then cumulative mistakes and blunders create, albeit unintentionally, a non-political domain in which parties involved are destined to lose because of the simple fact that they are not capable of pursuing their interests rationally. Both politics of accusations as well as non-politics of committing mistakes, revolve around the question of whether the failure of ethnic accords serves the interests of the rivalling parties better, or their success. Coupled with it, there is the somewhat tricky question of whether their interests are of common and interlocking nature to the extent that each has a vested interest in making it successful, or are they sufficiently isolated so much so that each can attain its interests only in exclusion of the other, thereby making accords fail. It is essentially the definition of their interests that sets these two positions apart.

In spite of all these differences, they both take what I have called, an instrumentalist view of accords. Accords are seen primarily as instruments that the contending parties seek to make use of, whether in isolation of, or in their combination in a bid to serve their respective interests. I propose to look upon the accords more as constructs that the rivalling parties have made for themselves, and once they are entered into, they seem not only to exist independently of whatever the signatories think about them, but shape and mould their thoughts and practices—"subjectifying" themselves as it were, by laying down the modalities on the basis of which their affairs are supposed to be conducted in future. Such an understanding of accords is predicated on two very closely interrelated assumptions: first, the Indian state has, by and large, been incapable of imposing its will on the larger body politic as much as none of the ethnic communities, howsoever sizeable it is, has been in a position to unilaterally and decisively influence it. The thesis of a highly "communalized" state spreading its tentacles throughout the length and breadth of India's body politic appears to be blown out of proportions. The state at present is far too weak to undergo such transformation. The assumption is grounded in one of Stanley Tambiah's arguments that the countries of South Asia have not yet been permeated by the moral economy of a coherent nation-state ideology:

> Modern South Asian ethnic conflicts take place in an environment that lacks a crystallized and coherent nation state ideology and a body of political norms and practices deriving from it that is acceptable to and shared by all (the majority of) the components and members of body politic. That there is crisis of the nation state in South Asia today is patently clear.[9]

In the absence of a crystallized and coherent moral economy, the actors seem to be engaged in what looks like an inordinately protracted and indecisive battle in which none is strong enough to assert its interests and wipe others out. Accords instead of putting an end to the battle that we are referring to, reflect its continuing nature. The battle, in other words, is embedded in the accords. On the one hand, they help in setting forth the rules within which the battle is sought to be carried out and conducted, and bringing about the semblance of an order in what otherwise could have degenerated into "a war of all against all." In simple terms, the signature of accords also results in certain transformations in the nature of subjects who made them. On the other hand, all accords being texts agreed upon by the contending parties, are bound to be open-ended and to use a term which is currently fashionable in linguistic circles, polysemic, and hence, leave ample scope for reading rather unforeseen, and may we say, even unforeseeable political practices into them. A good deal of these apparently enigmatic political practices turn the rules by their head, and produce new and hitherto unknown subjects working on the accords. Since the accords embody the battle that is protracted and indecisive, they pertain to nobody.

Second, all accords are necessarily preceded by ethnic discords while all discords do not necessarily culminate in accords. Within the scope of this brief paper, we propose to confine ourselves to an analysis of those ethnic discords in northeast India which have led to the signature of accords.[10] The distinction between discords that produce or are likely to produce accords, and those that do not or are unlikely to do so, however, should not be exaggerated. There are indeed many conjunctural factors, which contribute among other things, to the conversion of the latter into the former, and they need to be analyzed on a case-by-case basis. Of course that is much beside the point.

The present essay is organized into three very closely inter-related sections—the first focuses on the parties, more particularly, their nature, that are involved in the process of accord making. What is the nature of the ethnic communities, or more accurately, the organizations claiming to act on their behalf that the Indian state is interested in, in making peace with? Or similarly, what is the nature of the state itself that shows eagerness in making peace with the other? Both these questions are complementary and are discussed in the first section. The second section seeks to point out how the process of accord making, otherwise very long and tortuous, contributes to the reconstruction of subjects, and a re-negotiation of their relationships. Subjects do not create accords, accords create subjects. The third section reveals that accords also offer to the subjects the opportunity of reading their changing subjectivities into them, and working out a variety of subject positions within them. This section proposes to concentrate on the open and polysemic character of the texts of the accords in northeast India.

The Threshold within the Nation

The argument that the nation during the early years of Independence did not acquire a determinate form, and that the Indian state was, by and large, groping in the dark for it did not know for certain what the constituent elements of the nation would be, has to be taken with utmost caution. According to this argument, the state struck deals and signed accords, albeit implicitly, with whatever elements it had to encounter in the immediate aftermath of India's Independence. Such openness made the Constitution "an ensemble of accords."[11] While the argument draws our attention to the distinction between the nation and its "other," it hardly sensitizes us to an unacknowledged, albeit, very formidable threshold that divided the nation internally. Even if there were millions of unsigned accords encoded in the law of the land in the sense that they were undertaken after lots of debates and hard bargaining, the state knew how to make a distinction between those who were capable of making accords— the potential accord-makers, and those who were not. Indeed, their capability was so taken for granted that they did not have actually to sign off an accord to prove it. The nation was, to borrow a term coined by Mahmood Mamdani for describing the colonial world of African societies—"bi-furcated": "Citizenship would be a privilege of the uncivilized; the uncivilized would be subject of an all-round tutelage."[12] The threshold, in other words, split the nation into two asymmetrical spheres—those of the civilized and the uncivilized, of the citizens and the subjects, one on top of another. The spheres are also of uneven size.

The "civilized" sphere is precisely the society of potential accord-makers, for it consists of people who are both willing and able independently to enter into accords and contracts, are entitled to the security of their "life, liberty and pursuit of happiness" only in exchange of their acquiescence to the state. On the other hand, there is the "uncivilized" sphere of the subjects. By virtue of their being so, they are permanently kept outside the scope of contract. Since subjects do not deserve to enjoy the right to security of their life, liberty, and property, their acquiescence to the state is bound to precede their entitlement. There cannot be any equivalence between acquiescence and entitlement in their case. The notion of equivalence is otherwise considered as central to contractualism. Trust is what determines their relationship with the state, and the state is supposed to act as their trustee acting on their behalf and for their benefit. For them it is more a "moral duty" than a "rational practice."[13]

Accordingly, the state does not have any doubt about what the possible constituent elements of the nation would be, and embraced and encapsulated them as "natural" elements. The notion of the "natural" underlies the processes of integration of the princely states, as well as of reorganization of states on a linguistic basis since the early 1950s. It is interesting to note that the term "natural" figures over and over again in Sardar Patel's speeches on the integration of the princely states. The princely states, which have subsequently integrated themselves into India, are called "natural" because their integration not only facilitates the "secular" and "democratic" process that has already been set off within them, but are also compatible with the self-definition of the newly born Indian state. Patel did not find any difficulty in identifying either the states that can be regarded as "natural" elements of the Indian nation, or such states that are likely to accede to Pakistan.[14] Similarly, we know that the States' Reorganization Commission never recognized language as a rule-of-thumb principle of reorganization of states in India. While conceding to the demands of language-based communities for reorganizing the states, the Commission realized the importance of a threshold: "The problem is essentially one of determining how far the free play of provincial sentiment deriving from a consciousness of cultural and linguistic distinctiveness is a factor making for unity or diversity".[15] Thus Assam, for reasons spelt out in the report, was never recommended for any further reorganization. That the state was thereafter subjected to frequent surgical operations, is however a different story.

The state's policy towards the so-called, uncivilized sphere of the subject was basically three-fold. First, it did not hesitate to declare that they were not the "natural" parts of Indian nationhood. In fact, a certain celebration of their difference was considered to be strategic to their incorporation into the framework of Indian nation.[16] Second, the state's policy was not only to establish the difference but to hierarchize it, and to locate it within, what in classical development theory is called, "an evolutionary schemata." The state was imbued, as it were, with a modernist zeal, and the subjects were required to gradually follow without raising any question the rules that govern the civilized sphere, and be "benefited" by it. V. P. Menon—associated for long with the process of integration in India, for instance,— does not feel the necessity of granting to the subjects the right of signing accords: "With regard to the tribes located on the northeast frontier, there were no formal treaties and engagements; the Government of India's policy had been merely to extend gradually to those areas the benefits of settled administration."[17] Subjects only understand the language of "benefits", and not rights. Third, since the process of extension of settled administration is only too gradual, so much so that it does not adversely affect the already fragile balance of these societies, their acquiescence to the state and integration into nation are bound to predate the accrual of benefits to them. The implication is that they do not enjoy any right to be consulted, or taken into confidence. The Naga leaders initially were not averse to the idea of trusteeship. In a memorandum submitted to the British authorities on February 20, 1947, Naga National Council (NNC) for instance, made a strong plea for establishing an "interim government" for a period of 10 years at the end of which the Naga people should be left to choose any form of government they would think appropriate for them. The Council in the memorandum openly stated that a constitution drawn up by people having no knowledge of the Naga Hills and its people would be quite "unsuitable and unacceptable" to the Nagas. The fear of being boxed within the territorial confines of either of the two newly born Dominions in South Asia, without correspondingly enjoying any contractual right of voicing opinions and of being consulted, haunted the minds of not only the Nagas, but also many other communities including the plains' tribals of then undivided Assam.[18]

The so-called civilized sphere of the citizens is governed by what Mark Kingwell might call "socio-linguistics of politeness."[19] Let us see how. In order to illustrate the point, we may refer to the "talk" that took place on June 14, 1977—two years after the Shillong Accord was signed between Morarji Desai, the-then prime minister of India and A. Z. Phizo, the father of Naga insurgency in London. A detailed transcript of their talks is now available in M. Horam's book on *Naga Insurgency*, though of course there is a difference of opinion about the ontological status of these talks. As Horam writes: "Phizo claimed that he had tape-recorded the 'talk' at this meeting and the text of the

Phizoh–Desai talks was soon circulating in Nagaland. Mr Desai called it a 'garbled' version of his conversation with the Naga leaders".[20] Both of them, however, agreed that it was a non-official conversation. The reference to the Naga question and the state of the Naga people, as well as Phizo's claim of representing them, were two very crucial issues that virtually prevented the "talks" from taking off in the first place.

Phizo's first substantive remark, "I have come to meet the Prime Minister of India because my people have been suffering for a long time," invited strong rebuttal from Desai on two major counts.

First, Phizo's tacit claim of pushing the point as an uncontested representative of the Naga people was questioned by Desai primarily because he was a "foreigner" and "was staying in a foreign country." No modern state can acknowledge the right of the subjects to be represented by a foreigner—let alone, a foreign country. Hence, their dilemma is: while they have to remain as subjects, they cannot identify themselves as foreigners. They are an integral part of the nation, but very much outside its civilized sphere. Besides, there is difference between two representations of the Naga people offered by both Phizo and Desai, respectively. While making the claim of representing them, the Indian state actually keeps in mind only a section of the Nagas that has been invested with citizenship and contractual rights—thanks to the creation of the state of Nagaland within the Indian Union back in 1963. The creation of the state of Nagaland may be regarded as the first great step towards "the extension of settled administration." As Desai puts it: "It was the Nagas who came and asked for a state and it was given to them." In other words, the state felt obliged to respond to the demands of those who reportedly made it a point to raise the demand within the framework of the Indian state. Since acquiescence here is rewarded with rights, we may say that a section of the Nagas has nevertheless been inducted into the civilized sphere. Desai reiterates the state's commitment to "the protection of citizens": "By way of promising to exterminate the Naga rebels, we are protecting our citizens." His distinction between (Naga) citizens and "(a few) Nagas persisting on independence," in fact, sets forth the parameters of his talks whereby he remarks: "...if you want to talk only about Naga Independence, I won't talk to you." Phizo on the other hand, refers to the Nagas as a homogeneous collectivity and he says: "The Government of India may claim something on their part and the Nagas uphold something on their part and there may be a wide gap between us." In other words, it is only the Indian state that inflicts this so-called division on what Phizo holds to be a homogeneous community of Nagas. It simply means that unless the socio-linguistic rules of civilization, citizenship, and politeness are complied with, Phizo is unlikely to be heard. The only way to communicate the grievances is to observe these rules, and it is ironic that the observance of these rules, at the same time, makes the grievances incommunicable. For they are grievances, which cannot be communicated without breaking the rules.

Desai's second objection to Phizo's first substantive remark centres on the issue of the suffering of the Naga people. The issue is not so much whether the Nagas are suffering or not. It is on the contrary, hinged on the authority over the information of suffering. Desai claims that by virtue of his being the prime minister of India, he has a privileged access to this information and this is what authorizes him to say the last word: "You are a foreigner. You are staying in a foreign country. You receive reports and talk about it. I have all the reports and there is no problem. I know everything. I am the prime minister of India. Nobody needs to tell me that there is a problem." The state, in simple terms, arrogates to itself the invincible capacity for "knowing everything." Hence, the Nagas have "no problem" because the prime minister of India says so and only he is authorized to make a statement on this. It is power that invests knowledge with its "truthfulness." Thus it is no wonder that even within the brief span of three-and-half page talks, Phizo tried to raise the question of suffering not less than five times, and at each time, Desai had threatened to break off the talks. It points to a strange dilemma: You want to talk because there is a problem; but you are not allowed to talk if you bring in the problem. The rules of socio-linguistics lead to a metamorphosis of their agenda.

THE PROCESS OF SUBJECTIFICATION

To say that accords and discords are the poles of the same continuum, and that the former reflects the perpetuation of the
latter, is however not the same as saying that the same discords are reproduced through accords. An understanding of the
distinction between pre- and post-accord discords will enable
us to appreciate how the process of peacemaking through such
means as talks, dialogues, and confidence-building, etc., entails
a change not only in the agenda of ethnic communities or organizations staking the claim of representing them, but also in the
mutually contending subjects involved in the process. It may
be suggested that the discords that are likely to produce accords
involve a certain assertion of some degree of independence. The
term "independence" might at first sight appear to be a mis-
nomer, but for purposes of convenience we may use it in two
rather distinct senses.

First, we may come across communities that assert their identity as separate "nations", and by virtue of their being so, they
consider themselves to be entitled to complete self-determination
and full sovereign statehood. The United Liberation Front of
Assam (ULFA) has challenged the Indian state not because it
has subjected Assam to the "colonialism of New Delhi,' though
of course this question is secondary to its central critique, but
because it is the Indian state and hence, kept Assam constantly
out of the civilized sphere. ULFA's anti-statism springs from
the "truth" that the state is an "external agency" and hence,
has no authority to rule over Assam.[21] Assam, to ULFA, has
never been part of India before the British annexation. The
same view has been reiterated by the National Socialist Council
of Nagaland/Nagalim (I–M): "Nothing is more inalienable for a
nation, big or small, than her sovereignty.... The sovereign existence of Nagaland is more at peril than ever before."[22]

Independence, defined in this sense, hinges on a counter-
factual argument that, had the Indian state performed well and
not turned the fringe regions into its colonial hinterlands, the
fight for independence would have remained the same in essence.
Besides, communities engaged in discords may assert a very

different kind of independence. Here, independence is understood to mean a certain re-negotiation and re-adjustment of
their relationships within the Indian Union. What the communities do in this case is either to demand a share in the country's
power structure, or to make the state honor its commitment to
a free and thriving society, or even both. Almost all the accords
of northeast India focus on these two issues. They have led to
the formation of either new states as in the cases of the 16-point
Agreement of 1960, or the Mizo Accord of 1987—both resulting
in the birth of states of Nagaland and Mizoram respectively, or
new district councils as in the cases of Bodo Accord (1993),
Agartala Agreement (1993) signed with All-Tripura Tigers'
Force, Rabha–Hajong Accord (1995), Mishing (Tiwa) Accord
(1995), Karbi Tripartite Agreement (1995), etc. Some of the
accords have also made categorical provisions for the protection
of the language and culture of certain communities or peoples
living within the jurisdiction of states and councils who feel
threatened by the alarming influx from outside. Article six of
the Assam Accord for instance, declares: "Constitutional, legislative and administrative safeguards, as may be appropriate,
shall be provided to protect, preserve and promote the cultural,
social, linguistic identity of the Assamese people." On the other
hand, the Accord (1994) signed with the Hmar People's Convention leading to the formation of Sinlun Development Council,
proposes to give adequate autonomy to the Council for social,
economic, cultural, and educational advancement of the people
under the jurisdiction, and not only of the Hmars (Article Three).
Not all accords are equally exclusionary. Mizo insurgency viewed
in this light may be regarded as a case sui generis.

The memorandum submitted by Mizo National Front to the
prime minister of India on October 30, 1965 exudes a strain of
independence in the first sense: "Nationalism and patriotism
inspired by the political consciousness has now reached its
maturity and the cry for political self-determination is the only
will and the aspiration of the people, neplus ultra, the only final
and perfect embodiment of social being for them."[23] The Mizo
Declaration of Independence signed on March 1, 1966 is framed
in a manner that conveys the second sense. It is the state's

inability to respond to popular demands of the Mizos that is believed to have pushed them to the extreme course of independence. The text identifies as many as 12 areas including protections of human rights in which the state has failed miserably. Does it mean that a better performance by the Indian state could have saved Mizoram from the imbroglio?

It is the assertion of independence on the subjects' part that makes them eligible for making explicit and categorical accords with the state. For unless their demands are couched in ethnic–territorial terms, the state does not find any reason to respond to them. Being persistently denied of any access to so-called civilized sphere governed by the socio-linguistics of politeness, they are left with no other alternative but to make ethnic–territorial demands to attract state's attention. Even installation of an oil refinery requires two highly popular social movements in Assam. Although the movement demanding the recognition of Manipuri (Meithelon) as one of the scheduled languages of India is very old, unless it comes to a head, the state does not feel the necessity of responding to it. While the state refuses to apply rules of the civilized sphere to them, it has to evolve special rules or at least to make normal rules appear special or both by way of entering into accords with the subject ethnic communities. Almost every accord by rule includes what may be called, a cultural protection clause. The whole idea behind it is that the state or any of its authorized bodies promises to "take special care" or make "special attempts" for protecting the language and culture of some ethnic communities or peoples living under the jurisdiction of a state or a district council. The Hydari Agreement of 1947 sets forth the trend in this respect. The Agreement, among other things, made two very special provisions concerning adjudication of disputes and protection of tribal lands. Article 1 for instance announces:

> All cases whether civil or criminal, arising among the Nagas in the Naga Hills will be disposed of by duly constituted Naga customary law, or by such law as may be introduced with the consent of duly recognized Naga representative organizations, and where a sentence of death or transportation has been passed there by right of appeal to the Governor.

Article Four on the other hand seeks to protect the tribal land: "The land with all its resources in the Naga Hills should not be alienated to a non-Naga without the consent of the Naga Council." The provisions are special because the normal rules of the civilized sphere cannot be, or better say, allowed to be, extended to them. Conversely, sometimes accords also include provisions, which are otherwise governable by normal laws of the land so much so that they do not deserve attention in these documents. The accord signed with the Tribal National Volunteers in 1988 may serve as a case in point. It makes provisions for "skill formation of tribal youths of Tripura," "increasing the duration and content of All-India Radio Programmes in tribal languages or dialects of Tripura," "self-employment of tribal youths" and "subsidized distribution of rice, salt and kerosene." Interestingly, three odd articles have been added to the Assam Accord below the signatures as an appendix. These articles pledge for establishment of an oil refinery, and an IIT in Assam, and urges on the concerned governments to reopen Ashok Paper Mill and the Jute Mills. By way of incorporating them into accords, they are to look highly special. Pre-accord discords are characterized by a craving on the part of subject communities for recognition of this independence and speciality. Their status as independent and special subjects is a prerequisite for their role as accord-makers. This is not exactly the same kind of freedom and independence that classical liberal theory a la John Locke talks about. For one thing, while Lockean contractualism draws our attention to the irreducibility of the individual as the accord-maker, the claim of the ethnic organizations to act on behalf of certain communities is too serious to be brushed aside. For another, the craving for independence and speciality, according to Locke, is governed by special obligations enshrined in the contract. It is true that he grants to the individuals what he calls, "a right to rebellion." But even if it is a rebellion, it aims at making the state honour the obligations that it has committed itself to, while making the contract.[24] On the other hand, we have already pointed out that the state's claim to obedience from the subject communities is made free from any contractual obligations. We must keep in mind the crucial distinction between independence of the citizen and that of the subject. While the former is considered to be rational, the latter is not. That one is independent does not necessarily mean that one is rational too.[25]

What are the transformations that accords bring about in the nature of independent and special subjecthood of the concerned ethnic communities? First of all, the accords seek to disarm them, sever their connections with other armed organizations, and propose to restore the status quo ante of the supposedly pre-insurgent era. Usually, accords announce wholesome packages for the rehabilitation of the insurgents. All the four clauses of Article four of the Hmar Accord deal with the provisions for restoration of the order. While the first clause intends to disarm the armed cadres of Hmar People's Convention, the second one assigns to it the responsibility of taking immediate steps "to amend as may be necessary, its articles of Association Constitution so as to conform them to the provisions of law." Clause three vests the Governor of Mizoram with the responsibility of rehabilitating the rebels who have come over-ground before December 18, 1992. Clause four obtains the promise from HPC that it will not extend any support to such organizations as ULFA and NSCN (I–M). Articles two and three of the TNV Accord, mentioned earlier, have announced the same provisions. The accords of the northeast seem to be scripted on the same format.

Second, while the state helps a lot in organizing the subjects into closely knit communities by keeping them outside the civilized sphere, the process of peacemaking in general, and accords in particular, seem to disarticulate and disintegrate them. We have already seen that Desai's insistence on treating the Nagas as Indian citizens, in fact, strips them of their identity as Nagas. The division between the pacifists and the hostiles virtually cuts every community into at least two pieces. The formation of Nagaland as a separate state as per the Agreement of 1960 has been interpreted by a commentator as a ploy to divide the Nagas, and thereby to decimate them as a community:

The creation of Nagaland as a separate state has intended to take the sting out of the rebellion—it was to put in place a new moderate leadership which would accept the Indian Constitution and its control over Nagaland for substantial concessions in terms of autonomy.[26]

Considering that the Naga society is not a monolith, their prospects of being organized into a community are critically contingent on free exchange and circulation of opinions, on dialogues as a means of resolving their disagreements and differences, on what Craig Calhoun calls, "discourse about social arrangements." The members of a community need to engage themselves in discourse about social arrangements."[27] Luingam Luithui and Meredith Preston have critically reviewed the post-Shillong Accord scenario and shown how free circulation and exchange of opinions and views on it were censored and crippled.[28]

Third, accords also led to a certain fragmentation of the pre-accord agenda of ethnic communities. The packages offered through the accords under all normal circumstances do not pertain to the communities per se, but to Indian citizens who may just happen to be members of certain communities. Thus, the agenda of the community for its collective well-being always remain unaddressed. I have elsewhere shown how the signature of the Assam Accord amounted to a certain de-ethnicization of the demands underlying the movement (1979–85).[29] While the accords are made only when the demands are made in ethno-territorial terms, accords do not take care of the ethnic communities as subjects. An understanding of the pre-Shillong Accord scenario may be instructive in this connection. President's rule was clamped on March 25, 1975. This, according to S. C. Dev, then a Deputy Commissioner of Nagaland, "created for the bureaucrats opportunities to show their determination and commitment to principles, ideals and values."[30] They adopted what Subir Bhaumik calls, "a tribe-by-tribe approach" to what the Naga National Council construed as a pan–Naga problem. The whole idea was to depend on the intermediaries like, the *gaonburas* (the headmen), the village elders, the *dobhashis* (interpreters) the leaders of the public, and most importantly, the family members of the "hostiles", and to ask them to get in touch with the underground—failing which, unlimited state repression would be unleashed against them—sometimes, entire villages and family, to get them to surrender by way of accepting demands which are essentially of local nature, like construction of metalled roads, bridges, rural unemployment, etc.[31] The whole exercise is intended to fragment, and thereby decimate what was otherwise a comprehensive agenda of self-determination.

Accords certainly do not leave the state unaffected either. They lead to a transformation in its nature, in itself as a signatory to them. The state that puts its signature on the document and one that is supposed to implement its provisions are not exactly the same. The conclusion of both Assam Accord and Mizo Accord was complemented by a change of regimes. The implication was that in both cases, those who had hitherto been on the wrong side of the fence were called upon to share the responsibility of implementing the accords. The Assam Accord, in particular, set forth the parameters within which the Asom Gana Parishad-led government especially during 1985–1990 was supposed to operate. We all know how the Accord proved to be a stumbling bloc to its functioning, and how the party took pains to distance itself from it.[32] We also know that the Accord was supposed to address itself to the foreigners' issue, and the crisis that the government faced, and of course continues to face, is: To the extent it pushes the issue, to that extent it alienates the ethnic minorities especially Bengali Muslims—already a sizeable vote bank, who are afraid of being called "foreigners", and facing all the consequences that will follow upon it. But to the extent it distances itself from the issue, it alienates the Assamese-speaking Varna–Hindus who actually harbour the fear of being swamped by them.

Accords, in short, are sites where parties meet together as friends and "take up" their roles as friends.[33] Accords, in other words, subjectify them as friends, and hence subject them to the tangled web of friendship.

THE CONTESTATION

It is sometimes argued that since accords have a character of their own—existing independently of what the actors otherwise would have thought and practised, serving in the process nobody's (pre-accord) interests, the only way to get out of this tangled web is to do away with them. Hostility to accords is as much rampant today as the euphoria with them. Collective emancipation, in other words, is defined as an assertion on the people's right to transgress and break accords. This argument views emancipation and accords as not only different, but opposed to each other. By citing resistance and emancipation beyond the purview of accords, this argument denies the latter of what may be called, their textuality. That the accords being over and above texts, account for a variety of subject positions including the more radical and subversive ones, and allow them to be worked out and played around with, within their corpus is a point hardly understood by this argument. On the other hand, subjectification by its very nature generates resistance. Indeed, Foucault's notion of social dialogue is sensitive to this duality.

> Foucault's human beings are active bodies that exist in the midst of the world, and to be in the world in this way is to be wholly and inescapably open to transformation by other forces, to be "totally imprinted by history," as Foucault puts it. At the same time because forces are always imposed on other forces, this imposition requires the overcoming of those other forces, a subduing or taming of them; and there is also resistance, struggle against the limits such overcoming imposes, and the ever-present possibility of reversal."[34]

It is the notion of textuality that, on the other hand, shows how "such struggle against the limits", may be conducted within the "limits," and how it can be read into the texts of accords. Accords in other words, embody what Roland Barthes might call, "stereographic plurality."

> The text is plural. This does not mean just that it has several meanings, but rather it achieves plurality of meanings, an irreducible plurality. The text is not coexistence of meanings but passage, traversal, thus it answers not to an interpretation, liberal though it may be, but to an explosion, a dissemination. The text's plurality does not depend on the ambiguity of its contents, but rather on what could be called the stereographic plurality of the signifiers that weave it.[35]

By way of concluding this paper, we may just refer to two kinds of examples showing how the "limits" set forth by the accords are sought to be transcended without necessarily doing away with them: First, once an accord is signed, representatives of the ethnic communities have invariably expressed their resentments against its non-implementation or maybe, its half-hearted implementation. The struggle for implementation, or in some cases adequate and proper implementation has been as much strong as those that characterized the pre-accord era. While doing all this, they may tend to retain the prerogative of defining what implementation involves, or the propriety and adequacy of it. The leaders of the Assam movement could not realize that the Illegal Migrants (Detection by Tribunals) Act of 1983 would prove to be an insurmountable obstacle to the process of detection, disenfranchizement and deportation of foreigners promised by the Assam Accord. Their experience in government led them to realize the gravity of the situation and suggest some amendments to it. The AGP-government finally called for repealing the Act altogether for a proper implementation of the Accord.[36] The present AGP-government during 1996–2001 has conveniently forgotten its early stand on the Act, and simply stopped referring to it any longer. Sometimes, leaders press for completing the obligations left incomplete by the accords. The excruciating brevity of the Shillong Accord became an object of fierce resentments. It comprises only three articles of which the first two spell out the obligations to be fulfilled by the underground organizations, i.e., "acceptance of the Constitution of India by their own volition" and their disarmament. The concluding article keeps the other issues for "discussion and final settlement" under suspended animation without fixing a deadline. The issue was revived by a number of Naga leaders who wanted "the other issues" to be thrashed out, discussed, and settled. However, the level of disillusionment was so high that the struggle did not cut much ice among the Nagas.

Second, the accords may sometimes be observed in a way that turns them by their head. Ironically, the very perverse observance of their provisions amounts to their violation. The Bodo Accord (1993) provides a classic illustration of this point. When the Assam government refused to entrust the Bodo Autonomous Council with a jurisdiction of over a little more than

1000 villages that the Bodos claimed for themselves back in 1993 on the ground that the Bodos do not constitute a numerical majority in those areas (nor are these areas contiguous with the proposed Bodoland), the leaders got the message, went deep inside the disputed villages, and cleansed them of the non-Bodos—particularly, the Muslims and the Santhals in a bid to tilt the demographic balance in their favour. Observance of this so-called democratic–majoritarian principle in fact made a mockery of the principle itself and deprived it of what was hitherto construed as its essence. Liberal democracy's insensitivity to the cultural rights of the ethnic communities, or what Carl Schmidt calls, their "way of life" turned out to be only too expensive in this case.[37]

All these subversive political practices can however be referred back to the accords. The accords give credence to all such political practices. The foes within the friends are never allowed to come into the open and indulge in a free for all.

NOTES AND REFERENCES

1. S. C. Dev, *Nagaland: The Untold Story.* Calcutta, 1988, p. 124.
2. See Nari Rustomji, *Imperilled Frontiers: India's Northeastern Borderlands.* Delhi, 1983, p. 71. Also, Ved Marwah, *Uncivil Wars: Pathology of Terrorism in India.* New Delhi, 1995, pp. 303–5, passim.
3. Rustomji, ibid., p. 71.
4. Kumar Rupesinghe, "Strategies of Conflict Resolution: The Case of South Asia," in Kumar Rupesinghe and Kumar David (eds), *Internal Conflicts in South Asia.* London, 1996, p. 180.
5. Kumar Sanjay Singh, "Naga Accords: An Instance of Domination Through Negotiation," 1999, *mimeo.*
6. Ranabir Samaddar, "'Those Accords': A Bunch of Documents," SAFHR Paper Series, vol. 4, Kathmandu, 1999, p. 7.
7. Barry Allen, "Foucault and Modern Political Philosophy" in Jeremy Moss (ed.), *The Later Foucault.* London, 1998, p. 188.
8. M. Horam, *Naga Insurgency: The Last Thirty Years.* New Delhi, 1980, p. 205.
9. Stanley Tambiah, *Levelling Crowds: Ethnonational Conflicts and Collective Violence in South Asia,* New Delhi, 1996, p. 322.
10. For the texts of these accords, I have depended on P.S. Datta, *Ethnic Peace Accords in North-East India.* Delhi, 1995.
11. Such an argument has been advanced by many of whom Rajni Kothari seems to be the pioneering spokesman. See, Rajni Kothari, "Integration and Performance: Two Pivots of India's Model of Nation-Building" in

Rajni Kothari (ed.), *State and Nation-Building: A Third World Perspective.* Bombay, 1976.

12. Mahmood Mamdani, *Citizen and Subject: Decentralized Despotism and the Legacy of Late Colonialism.* Delhi, 1997, p. 17.

13. For a theoretical exploration of this point, see, John Dunn, *The History of Political Theory and Other Essays.* Cambridge, 1996, Chap. 5.

14. See *For a United India: Speeches of Sardar Patel 1947–1950.* New Delhi, 1949, passim.

15. *Report of the States Reorganisation Commission.* New Delhi, 1955, p. 30.

16. See Samir Kumar Das, "Tribes as the Other: A Critique of Political Anthropology of Northeastern India," in *Journal of Politics.* vol. 3, Dibrugarh, 1996.

17. V. P. Menon, *The Transfer of Power in India.* New Delhi, 1957, p. 407.

18. For an understanding of the problem of the Plains tribals, see Girin Phukon, *Assam: Attitude to Federalism.* Delhi, 1984. Also, Girin Phukon, *Politics of Regionalism in Northeastern India.* Guwahati, 1996, pp. 9–10. Also, Girin Phukon, "Politics of Ahom Identity," in *The Calcutta Journal of Political Studies,* special no. 1999, pp. 52–61.

19. Mark Kingwell, *A Civil Tongue: Justice, Dialogue and the Politics of Pluralism.* Pennsylvania, 1995, p. 198. His analysis though commendable in many respects, is seemingly oblivious to the relations of power.

20. M. Horam, *Naga Insurgency: The Last Thirty Years.* New Delhi, 1980, p. 188.

21. For an elaboration of this argument, see Samir Kumar Das, *ULFA: A Political Analysis.* Delhi, 1994, p. 97.

22. Manifesto of the National Socialist Council of Nagaland (I-M) dated January 31, 1980. Quoted in Luingam Luithui and Nandita Haksar (eds), *Nagaland File: Violation of Human Rights.* Delhi, 1984, p. 112.

23. Quoted in S. N. Singh, *Mizoram.* New Delhi, 1994, p. 258.

24. See John Locke, "An Essay Concerning the True Original Extent and End of Civil Government" in Sir Ernest Barker (ed.), *Social Contract: Essays by Locke, Hume, Rousseau.* London, 1958.

25. See John Elster, "Rational Choice Theory" in *The Polity Reader in Social Theory.* London, 1994, pp. 121–25.

26. Subir Bhaumik, "The Accord that Never Was: A Critique of the 1975 Shillong Accord," 1999, in this volume.

27. Craig Calhoun, "Nationalism and Civil Society" in Craig Calhoun (ed.), *Social Theory and the Politics of Identity.* Cambridge, 1994, p. 327.

28. Luingam Luithui and Meredith Preston, "The Politics of Peace in Nagaland Today," 1999, *mimeo.*

29. Samir Kumar Das, "On Institutionalization: A Reconsideration of the Assam Movement (1983–1985)" in *Journal of Politics,* vol. 4, 1998, pp. 68–72.

30. S. C. Dev, *Nagaland: The Untold Story.* Calcutta, 1988, p. 137.

31. Ibid., pp. 98–114.

32. For a detailed analysis, see Samir Kumar Das, *Regionalism in Power: The Case of Asom Gana Parishad (1985–1990).* New Delhi, 1998, Chap. 6.

33. The words "take up" are borrowed from Derrida and are used in the same Derridean sense. See Jacques Derrida, *Politics of Friendship*, George Collins (trans), London, 1997.

34. Christopher Falzon, *Foucault and the Social Dialogue: Beyond Fragmentation.* London, 1998, p. 45.

35. Roland Barthes, "From Work to Text," in Josue V. Harari (ed.), *Textual Strategies: Perspectives in Post-Structuralist Criticism.* London, 1980, p. 76.

36. Das, *Regionalism in Power*, pp. 124–26.

37. Andrew Norris, "Carl Schmidt on Friends, Enemies and the Political," in *Telos*, vol. 112, 1998. For an excellent analysis of liberal democracy's incompatibility with cultural particularism, see Bhikhu Parekh, "The Cultural Particularities of Liberal Democracy," in David Held (ed.), *Prospects of Democracy: North, South, East and West.* Stanford, California, 1993, pp. 165–75.

5

KASHMIR AT THE CROSSROADS: PROBLEMS AND POSSIBILITIES*

Sumantra Bose

A TALE OF TWO SHAHS

March 1987. Elections are being held for the legislative assembly of Indian-controlled Jammu & Kashmir (J&K). Two men are competing to win a seat in this assembly for Amirakadal, a district in the heart of Srinagar, capital city of the Valley of Kashmir. One, Ghulam Mohiuddin Shah, is sponsored by the National Conference (NC), the party of Kashmir's political establishment allied with the Congress, India's powerful ruling party, at the time of these elections. The other, Mohammad Yusuf Shah, has been put forward by the Muslim United Front (MUF), an ad hoc coalition of anti-establishment groups of grassroots movements that have joined together to challenge the traditional elite of Kashmir, and its sponsor in New Delhi. The MUF has managed to attract a large number of Kashmiri youth by harping on the corruption of the NC establishment, and the history of manipulation of politics in J&K by rulers in New Delhi. As the MUF campaign draws an increasingly favorable response from the public, it seems that for the first time in J&K's politics, a mass-based electoral opposition to traditional ruling cliques may be taking shape in the Kashmir Valley.

As counting begins, it becomes clear that Mohammad Yusuf Shah, the underdog candidate, is heading for massive victory.

* Originally published in *Security Dialogue*, vol. 32, no. 1, 2001.

According to observers present at the scene, the dejected establishments candidate had left the counting centre when, to his amazement, he heard the counting authorities declare him winner of the contest over loudspeakers installed at the site. At the same time, Indian police swooped on the counting centre, and arrested his rival, who was to be imprisoned for the next nine months without any formal charge, let alone trial. The pattern was repeated throughout the Valley and some other areas of J&K, *as an* attempt by a cross-section of non-elite, non-establishment Kashmiris to participate in the Indian-sponsored political process, which was rudely snuffed out.

Fourteen years later, much has happened, and much has changed in India-controlled J&K. But both Shahs are still in business. Ghulam Mohiuddin Shah, loser-turned-victor in 1987, is a senior minister in J&K's latest Indian-sponsored government, revived by Delhi in 1996 to provide a civilian façade to its military control of the territory. But it is his defeated challenger who has really moved up in the world since then, except that he is no longer known as Yusuf Shah. Since 1990, he has been known by his nom de guerre, Syed Salahuddin—commander-in-chief of Hizbul Mujahideen (HM), the Kashmiri guerrilla movement that hit the international headlines during the summer of 2000 by first declaring, and then revoking, a unilateral cease-fire against Indian forces in J&K.

UNDERSTANDING KASHMIR

There are two sides to the Kashmir story. The first is captured in sensational headlines and soundbites reporting killings, bomb attacks, massacres, and assassinations. It is also reflected in the verbal war between the parties to the dispute, an endlessly repetitive cacophony of competing slogans. Thus a complex conflict is reduced to "cross-border terrorism," and lately, *jehad* in certain understandings (popular in New Delhi and Washington D.C., among other places). The second interpretation sees this as a simple case of occupation and oppression of Muslim people by an armed alien state since 1947 (popular in Islamabad and, in a more sophisticated version, in Srinagar). Neither interpretation is entirely spurious; both contain significant elements of truth. Yet they also propagate and reinforce distortions, stereotypes, and caricatured images, which cumulatively produce gross misunderstandings of the conflict in and over J&K. The human denizens of this contested land remain in the shadows, abstractions at best, and caricatured stereotypes of their real selves at worst.

Then there is the other, usually untold, story of the war in J&K. This story relates to the actual, everyday experiences of real people, as well as to the multiple layers and dimensions of a complicated conflict involving interlinked issues of religion, ethnicity, and intense inter-state rivalry over the identity and allegiance of J&K's diverse spectrum of communities. Unpacking the Kashmir "problem" involves acknowledging a level of complexity that the commonly prevalent interpretations of the crisis simply cannot handle. We already know that the struggle over Kashmir makes this subcontinent one of the world's few regions where a nuclear conflict cannot be ruled out, and that J&K has lately become the destination for some radical Islamists seeking to liberate fellow-Muslims from oppression. What are much less known, and even more poorly understood, are the mundane specifics—how this dangerous conflict plays out at the local level, what variations exist and why, in the wishes of the diverse communities that inhabit J&K, and what motivates the men with guns on all sides.[1]

Yet these are hardly trivial issues. The devil of the Kashmir conflict is very much in the detail, and the stakes are high. The second half of 2000 saw an unprecedented development—two initiatives in a space of months designed to de-escalate armed hostilities in J&K. The summer cease-fire between the HM and Indian security forces failed to last beyond two weeks. But hopes were revived when, in November, Indian Prime Minister Atal Behari Vajpayee personally announced that all Indian forces in J&K had been instructed "not to initiate combat operations against militants" for the duration of the Muslim holy month of Ramzan, from late November to late December.[2] After initially expressing scepticism about Indian intentions, Pakistan responded in early December by announcing that its armed forces deployed along the volatile Line of Control (LoC) between the Indian and Pakistani parts of J&K—the scene of daily cross-border firing and shelling—would "observe maximum restraint in order to strengthen and stabilize the cease-fire."[3]

At the time of writing, the ultimate fate of the "Ramzan initiative"—extended on 20 December by the Indian government for another month—remains very much in the balance. There is cause for cautious optimism. Pakistan reacted to India's extension with an announcement that it would "move back" some troops from the LoC, although absolutely no indication was given of how many troops would he involved, or where. But gestures aside, the basic positions of India and Pakistan on the Kashmir dispute are very far apart, and major disagreements exist on the modalities of initiating a process of dialogue. The tentative opening to a dialogue-based approach after 11 years of continual strife makes it ever more urgent and essential that the Kashmir conflict be unclouded, as far as possible, by rhetoric and propaganda. Without a serious attempt to come to grips with complexities and nuances that exist on the ground, it is likely that any "peace process" will fail or, worse still, perhaps even aggravate a very volatile situation.

This (essay) seeks to contribute to such an understanding. The next section presents a condensed narrative of how life is lived, and how the war is fought on a daily basis in Poonch and Rajouri, two violence-wrecked districts in J&K. From this local narrative, I then try to tease out some general trends and factors, which help explain recent efforts to de-escalate armed confrontation, and embark on a path of dialogue. The subsequent section goes on to discuss the forbidding obstacles to finding a solution to the conflict that would be acceptable to both countries, and to all factions in J&K; yet, I will also try to provide pointers on how to deal (and, equally important, how *not* to deal) with this slew of complications, and best capitalize on the prospects for building a sustainable peace.

FRONTIERS OF CONFLICT

J&K consists of three distinct geographical regions. When armed insurgency erupted in the territory in 1990, it was initially confined largely to the Kashmir Valley[4] a compact area centred on the capital, Srinagar. The Valley is overwhelmingly

Muslim (primarily Sunni Muslim, although there is a sizeable Shia minority) and, barring a few enclaves, Kashmiri-speaking. Its population in 2001 was about 4.5 million.[5]

Jammu, the considerably larger (but with a population of approximately 4 million), and socially much more heterogeneous region to the south of the Valley, was by and large unaffected by any armed insurgency. By 1992, however, guerrilla operations had spilled over from the Valley into an adjoining district in the Jammu region, Doda, which has a Kashmiri-speaking Muslim majority, and is often regarded as a political and socio-cultural extension of the Valley (although Hindus constitute 40 percent of Doda's population, a fact that makes this district especially interesting). By contrast, two other districts in the Jammu region with solidly Muslim majority populations, Rajouri (65 percent) and Poonch (85 percent), remained fairly quiet, even though both are border districts adjoining the LoC with Pakistan-controlled Kashmir, known as Azad ("Free") Jammu & Kashmir (AJK). The key to this apparent puzzle lies in the fact that the Muslim majorities in Rajouri and Poonch, unlike those in the Kashmir Valley and Doda, are largely not Kashmiris, and mostly belong to other communities such as Gujjars and Bakerwals (traditionally nomadic pastoralists), Rajputs and other smaller ethnic groups. The predominant language in the mountain tracts of Poonch and Rajouri is neither Kashmiri nor Dogri, which is spoken in the Jammu lowlands, but Pahadi, a dialect of Punjabi. The failure of the armed struggle to put down solid roots in Muslim-dominated (but mostly non-Kashmiri) border areas of Poonch and Rajouri, as opposed to its influence in the (Kashmiri-dominated) Valley and Doda, is illustrative of a very important fact: the core base of the movement for *azaadi* ("freedom") in J&K is defined by a shared ethno-linguistic heritage[6] and not by pan-Muslim solidarity cutting across different ethnic and linguistic communities.[7]

J&K's third constituent region, a vast but sparsely populated high-altitude area called Ladakh with a mixed population of Buddhists and Muslims, also remained largely peaceful until the summer of 1999, when a localized war between Indian and Pakistani forces erupted along the LoC in one of its two districts, Kargil.

Since 1998, however, the sleepy hills and forests of Poonch and Rajouri have been transformed into the most active zone of insurgency and counterinsurgency in J&K. I had toured the Kashmir Valley and Doda district extensively in 1995 and 1996,[8] but had neglected to visit the non-happening districts of Poonch and Rajouri. Their apparent transformation into the new frontier of the Kashmir conflict, however, is no accident, coincidence, or aberration. This remote, mountainous border belt, where religion, ethnicity, and inter-state rivalry over territory, and the allegiance of people come together in an incendiary mix, is a microcosm of the complex and fluid character of the war in J&K.

A trip to the battle zone, located in the plains to the south undertaken by this author in September 2000, involves hard drive from the city of Jammu. The Jammu–Rajouri–Poonch road, going in a northwesterly direction, traverses 250 km in all, running just alongside the de jure and de facto borders between India and Pakistan, one of the most disturbed borders in the world, where small-arms exchanges, as well as artillery duels between the two opposing armies are a daily occurrence. It takes five hours to reach the district headquarters in the town of Rajouri, another three hours to the town of Poonch. For the first 50 or so kilometres, the road runs parallel to the international border (IB) between the Indian Jammu province and Pakistani Punjab. Near the Indian town of Akhnur, the IB gives way to the LoC, which demarcates the de facto frontier between India's J&K and Pakistani-controlled AJK (the entire LoC is 740 km long). The road here is crossed by numerous infiltration routes used by insurgents arriving from the Pakistani side to fight on the Indian side, although plenty of west-to-east infiltration also takes place to the south, across the IB. Beyond Akhnur, the road begins to climb in sharp twists and turns; the especially treacherous stretch from Rajouri to Poonch is dotted with milestones put up by the Indian army's Border Roads Organization which entreat drivers to "be gentle on my curves." There are also signs, written in Hindi-speaking North India's Devnagari script, which proclaim *"Kashmir se Kanyakumari tak – mera Bharat mahann!"* ("From Kashmir to Kanyakumari, My India is Great"—Kanyakumari being the southernmost tip of the subcontinent).

The reality, of course, is far less sanguine. This is a classic borderland, where no magnitude of manpower and firepower can assure secure control, and where the allegiances of much of the local population are at least slightly suspect. Before the division of J&K into Indian and Pakistani portions in 1947–48, Rajouri and Poonch formed part of a common linguistic-cultural and economic zone with the Azad Kashmir districts of Mirpur and Muzaffarabad, the western (Pakistani) Punjab districts of Rawalpindi, Jhelum, Campbellpur, and Mianwali, and the North-West Frontier Province (NWFP) districts of Abbottabad and Mansehra. Many Muslim families living in the border villages of Poonch and Rajouri still have relations on the Pakistani side. Indeed, there are villages which are neatly bisected by the LoC, an arbitrary line drawn in Indian and Pakistani blood, a half century ago.[9] While Rajouri and Poonch are both Muslim-majority districts, the towns of Rajouri and Poonch—which serve as the districts' centres of administration, trade and commerce, and education—both have a majority of Hindu and Sikh residents. Most of the Hindus and Sikhs settled in the townships of Rajouri and Poonch are refugees, or descendants of refugees from Pakistani Kashmir. It is quite common, to find Hindus or Sikhs in the town of Rajouri whose origins are in Kotli, an immediately adjacent AJK district to the west. Many Hindus and Sikhs in the town of Poonch are, likewise, from Rawalakot, a town directly across the LoC in AJK. The historical district of Poonch, which formed an autonomous principality within the kingdom of J&K but has been divided between J&K and AJK since the end of the first Indo-Pakistani war over Kashmir in January 1949, and contested in subsequent wars in 1965 and 1971, has a reputation for producing hardline nationalists on both sides of the dividing line. For example, General Muhammad Aziz, a hardline army officer, whose support was crucial to General Pervez Musharraf's seizure of power in Pakistan in October 1999, is from a well-known *biradari* (clan-based kinship network) in the AJK's portion of Poonch.

The Hindu and Sikh minorities of Rajouri and Poonch feel deeply threatened by the upsurge, or guerrilla activity in their immediate neighborhood. In the southern hills of Rajouri district (closer to the Hindu dominated areas of the Jammu plains), where the population is evenly balanced between Hindus and

Muslims and includes a strong sprinkling of Sikhs, I met a group of about 20 Hindu villagers who have been organized by the government into a Village Defence Committee (VDC). A network of these VDCs—"self-defence" militia—exists throughout the communally mixed, insurgency-prone areas of the Jammu region, and usually comprises only Hindus, as well as local Sikhs. Muslims either do not wish to join, or are regarded as unreliable by the organizers, so practically no operational VDCs exist in Muslim-populated rural areas of Poonch. The VDCs are frequently valorized in the Indian media as the vanguard of patriotic resistance to Pakistan and its agents, and vilified by pro-Pakistan and pro-independence elements in J&K as unsavoury auxiliaries of a repressive Indian occupation.

The VDC members I met matched neither of the two carica-tures. They were poor, simple villagers, dressed in soiled, tat-tered clothes and scuffed shoes, clutching antiquated .303 rifles with a self-consciousness that bordered on the comical. They had many complaints—poor and irregular pay for their services from the authorities, a strictly rationed supply of bullets and, above all, the ridiculously inadequate calibre of their weapons. The .303 rifle, they explained, can fire only one bullet at a time, and it takes quite a bit of time to reload and fire again. The standard firearm of the "militants" (as the guerrillas are known in J&K) is, of course, the AK-47 assault rifle. The VDC members had nothing but contempt for the authorities who had equipped them with such substandard weaponry, and they were visibly apprehensive about the dangerous conditions in the area. I asked what motivated them to enroll as VDC members at all if the terms were so poor and the treatment of the authorities so callous. "We have to be prepared to defend our village to the best of our ability if the need arises," they replied. In other words, a minimum guarantee of survival and security, rather than a patriotic resolve to defend India's frontiers against ex-ternal and internal foes, was what motivated these ragged-looking but curiously gallant grassroots warriors.

They are not the only reluctant warriors in J&K today. Be-yond a small tense town called Surankote, the Rajouri–Poonch road no longer has a paved surface. It becomes a glorified dirt-track, barely motorable even by jeep-type vehicles. These 30 or so kilometres from Surankote to Poonch, running through meandering mountains, and across decrepit bridges over dried-up streams with occasional deserted hamlets along the way, constitute perhaps the most dangerous stretch of road in J&K. Not even the military moves on this road after dusk. As we drove to Poonch along this road early one evening, my driver joked: "Sir, whenever I travel on this road I never know whether I'm going straight to Poonch or straight to heaven." This was a reference not just to the harsh terrain: the road is pitted with craters—of varying sizes—from landmine and IED (Improvized Explosive Device) blasts, necessitating some truly skilful use of the steering wheel.

The faceless adversaries who keep the ...(counterforce) Force in a permanent state of jitters are the feared *jehadi* fighters—transnational Islamist militants—whose activities have aroused anxiety from New Delhi to Washington. However, according to the estimates of both counterinsurgency sources and local community leaders and journalists, the number of active "foreign militants" is surprisingly small. For example, only 250–300 "foreigners," operating in small groups, are estimated to be active in Poonch, whose population is about 350,000. In this district alone, they face five brigades (at least 15,000 soldiers) deployed for internal counterinsurgency, in addition to heavy Indian troop deployment along the LoC itself. These small numbers have, according to these well-informed local sources, remained constant over the last four or five years. While infiltration from across the LoC is a regular phenomenon, the infiltrators suffer high casualty rates at the hands of the army during and after infiltration. Most of the *jehadis* killed in action have been Pakistanis, many from Azad Kashmir districts across the border, some from provincial towns in Pakistani Punjab. There is a sprinkling of ethnic Pathans as well, mainly from Pakistan's NWFP but also from Afghanistan, and the occasional fighter from further afield. All the prominent Pakistan-based *jehadi* groups (Lashkar-e-Tayyaba, Jaish-e-Mohammad or JeM, Al-Badr, Harkat-ul-Jehad-I-Islami) have fighters in the area, and they often pool their resources for operations against military targets. In addition, there is the more indigenously based Hizbul Mujahideen's fighting force, which in the Poonch–Rajouri belt is known as HMPPR (Hizbul Mujahideen Pir Panjal Regiment), a reference to the Pir Panjal massif that cuts through the region in an east–west arc.

How is it possible for such small numbers of insurgents to sustain effective operations across a large area, and transform Poonch and Rajouri into the most happening theatre of war in J&K?

One part of the answer was provided by a young police officer fighting against the guerrillas, and with whom I had a long and candid conversation. A Kashmiri-speaking Muslim from Doda district, he spoke with frustration of what he regards as the Indian state's unsympathetic attitude towards the rights and grievances of Kashmiris, and he recounted how the army frequently mistreats local people and mishandles local situations. But he also spoke with pride of how his special police unit had "eliminated" eight infiltrated JeM[10] fighters in a fierce encounter in August 2000, after receiving a tip-off about their presence from local villagers. Clearly, he had chosen to make his career with the side he regards as the lesser devil. "I have a lot of admiration for them (the infiltrators)," he told me. "They are incredibly well-organized, rigorously trained, superbly equipped and, above all, highly determined and motivated. Very brave, very tough people." He showed me an inventory of weapons and equipment seized from guerrillas since the beginning of the year: RPG-7 grenade launchers, a PIKA long-range light machine-gun, AK-47 assault rifles, Dragunov sniper rifles, BC-IS rifle-mounted grenade launchers, Chinese pistols, Chinese anti-tank rockets, 82 mm mortar bombs and other ammunition, high-explosive hand grenades, anti-tank and anti-personnel mines, IEDs of various types, remote controls for detonating mines and LEDs, huge quantities of RDX explosive, flame-throwers, night-vision devices, binoculars, the latest Kenwood and Yaesu radio sets for communication with other units and with bases across the LoC, and decoding sheets for coded communications. As I inspected this arsenal and listened on the officer's own radio to two nearby guerrilla units bantering with each other in Punjabi, I realized that this *jehad* is a full-fledged military operation run by professionals.

Advanced equipment, greater mobility, and grit and determination are obviously factors crucial to the guerrillas' success in pinning down entire brigades and divisions of the Indian army. But what of local fighters in the militants' ranks? At the least, was it possible for a relative handful of "foreigners" to generate this level of disturbance without various forms of support and assistance from elements of the local population? At these questions, my informant turned taciturn. When I asked him whether the Hizbul Mujahideen's PPR, active in the area, was composed mainly of foreigners or local fighters, he became visibly uncomfortable.

I found tentative answers to my unresolved questions elsewhere. In a village called Lassana, I met Chaudhary Mohammad Aslam, a prominent local "pro-India" politician, in his heavily fortified hilltop home. Over the past 20 years, Aslam has had a distinguished career in J&K's Indian-sponsored political establishment: at various times he was education minister, agriculture minister, speaker of the Jammu & Kashmir legislative assembly and president of the Congress party in J&K. He is also the traditional leader of the Gujjar community in Rajouri and Poonch. The Gujjars, a nomadic people, are usually herdsmen living in remote mountain areas and suffer from above-average levels of poverty and illiteracy. However, they constitute the single largest ethnic group in many areas of Rajouri and Poonch, and their loyalty is a crucial determinant of who has the upper hand in these contested borderlands.

"Nobody wants Pakistan here," Chaudhary Aslam assured me confidently. If any Gujjars provide food, shelter, or intelligence to insurgents, or act as their guides and couriers, it is, he claimed, "*majboori se*" ("because they are threatened into doing so") or else "*garibi se*" ("because of acute poverty, they give some assistance in exchange for money"). This was plausible, but not entirely convincing. Is it not a fact, I asked, that some local Gujjar youth have actually joined the insurgents. "Yes," he admitted, with such a pained look on his face that I felt like a dentist extracting a rotten tooth; "the rhetoric of *jehad* has had some effect unfortunately." It was only after the interview was over that I found out that Chaudhary Aslam's own antecedents are much more fluid than he would like to acknowledge. During the fighting between Indian and Pakistani forces in Poonch and Rajouri in 1947–48, Aslam's father, Chaudhary Ghulam Hussein, had sided with Pakistan, and he migrated to the Pakistani side of the cease-fire line in January 1949. Ghulam Hussein returned only in 1954, after which his son embarked on his career as an Indian politician. But the allegiances of the next generation of Gujjars had, apparently, again become indeterminate. Aslam's own nephew, I later learned, was a leading guerrilla in the area.

Master Majid Khan, an influential trade union leader in the Surankote area, helped me to fill out the conspicuous missing elements in Chaudhary Aslam's account. "People here have suffered a lot in the India–Pakistan conflicts of 1947–1949, 1965 and 1971," he said. "So when trouble erupted again in 1990, the reflexive instinct of most people was to try and stay out of it, to avoid bringing more suffering on themselves." "But," he explained, "there is a socio-economic basis for militancy here. Most people are very poor, they lack the basics of life like drinking water, educational facilities, and health care. The local administration and India-backed politicians are totally callous to their needs and grievances, and renowned for corruption. They seem to have no sense of accountability to the people at all. In certain provinces of India, like Bihar and Andhra Pradesh, such feelings of marginalization and neglect have provided fertile ground for the rise of Naxalite (ultra-leftist Maoist) insurgencies. Here, in a border area of a disputed territory, resistance has taken a different form. Many people feel so deprived that it only takes one or two humiliating experiences at the hands of the army to turn them into militant sympathizers and even, in some cases, active militants."

Nonetheless, Majid Khan maintained that the loyalties of the Gujjars and Bakerwals, Rajputs, Pathans, and other non-Kashmiri Muslim groups are fluid compared with those of the Kashmiri Muslims, who form the core ethnolinguistic base of the struggle against India. While these groups may not be enthusiastic about India, the *azaadi* slogan is still widely regarded as primarily a "Kashmiri" cause. Srinagar remains distant not just literally, but also figuratively, and the local base of insurgency is still relatively weak in these areas. It is necessary to inject infiltrators to escalate the violence. Hence the above-average concentration of "foreign" *mujahideen* in areas of Rajouri and Poonch that are predominantly populated by non-Kashmiri Muslim communities. This view seemed corroborated when I later encountered a group of HMPPR fighters further north, in a Kashmiri-speaking pocket of Poonch district adjoining the Kashmir Valley. Of the 30 men in the unit, I was able to verify that 27 were locals, while the other three were from Azad Kashmir. The composition of this unit was typical: approximately 90 percent of the Hizbul Mujahideen rank-and-file in J&K are composed of local recruits, according to local journalists as well as Indian intelligence sources.

THE CONVOLUTED REALITIES OF KASHMIR

There are significant variations in patterns of politics across different communities and regional locales of J&K. Overlapping layers of group identity—ethnic, confessional, local—come together in a fluid mix in a context of intense inter-state rivalry over territory, and the allegiance of people. A cacophony of competing tunes, rather than a single melody, emerges from the texture of this richly diverse, plural society. Recognition of these multiple layers of ambiguity, fluidity, and complexity is essential to any informed understanding of the Kashmir problem, and to any policy designed to address this complicated crisis.

Two conclusions follow from this multi-layered and nuanced conception of the Kashmir problem. First, the importance of non-local Islamist radical groups in this crisis is being exaggerated by at least three different sources: the *jehadi* spokesmen, Indian spokesmen and officials, and, most recently, official and some non-official quarters in the United States. Statistics released by Indian counterinsurgency authorities clearly reveal that the Kashmir insurgency is mostly composed of local militants. In the first eight months of 1999, for example, 617 guerrillas are said to have died at the hands of Indian security forces; of these, 167 (27 percent) were identified as "foreigners." During the corresponding period in 2000, 941 militants were killed, of whom 261 (28 percent) were foreigners. In both 1999 and 2000, then, local cadres comprised more than 70 percent of slain insurgent in J&K,[11] although non-local elements have been responsible for some of the most publicized attacks, such as *fidayeen* (suicide squad) raids on Indian military camps. Recent reports from Doda and Udhampur also indicate that local participation and support, rather than an influx of outsiders, are the main factors sustaining insurgency.[12] In Rajouri and Poonch, the concentration of foreign fighters is relatively higher because of specific local conditions. Even so, the Pir Panjal range has provided infiltration routes for fighters crossing the LoC from AJK ever since 1990, and the late spread of insurgency in these two districts has only been enabled by a moderate build-up of local support since 1996. According to the commander of Romeo Force, his men eliminated 166 guerrillas in the six months between March 15 and September 15, 2000, of whom 89 (54 percent) were foreigners.[13] This means that even in this foreigner-infested area, almost half of the insurgent casualties consisted of local people.

Eleven years after the war began, the conflict in Kashmir retains a distinctly specific character. It has not been reduced to an epiphenomenon of an allegedly global problem of transnational Islamist militancy, although the zeal of the *jehadis* has further complicated a troubled situation. But the "guest militants" active in J&K are potentially vulnerable. Their activities are sustained by two crucial sources of support: the Pakistani military and its agencies in AJK, and the networks of local militants inside India-controlled territory. If official patronage were to be curtailed by the Pakistanis, according to one senior radical, "it will be a tragedy. We could still operate ... but the movement will soon die out."[14] In the Kashmir Valley, where I travelled after visiting Rajouri and Poonch, there is a consensus of opinion that should a lasting cease-fire between the Hizbul Mujahideen—the only indigenous guerrilla organization in the field—and the Indian forces come into effect, the more radical groups composed primarily of Pakistanis would find it increasingly difficult to maintain operations on their own. Organized in hard-to-crack underground cells of two or three militants each, they would still be capable of spectacular strikes for a time, but their future prospects would be severely diminished.

The second conclusion is that many of those involved in fighting are exhausted by a violent, mutually hurting stalemate. This could "be an important window of opportunity for a de-escalation of violence, and the initiation of a serious, multi-channel process of dialogue, which is the only way to make any cease-fire sustainable." My conversations with the Romeo Force soldiers were not misleading. In September 2000, a confidential

assessment circulated among top Indian military officers con-
firmed that the army is overburdened with counterinsurgency
in Kashmir, leading to serious problems of morale, discipline,
and effectiveness in many field units. The assessment emphasized the need for a coherent political strategy to deal with the
Kashmir problem.[15] After 11 years, Indian counterinsurgency
forces know that without a political breakthrough, their long-
haul battle will continue indefinitely. Only the location of the
most intense firefighting will fluctuate—back and forth between
Doda–Udhampur, Rajouri–Poonch, and various parts of the
Kashmir Valley. Viewed in this context, the Indian government's decision in November 2000 to call a unilateral, albeit
temporary, halt to offensive anti-guerrilla operations is not
surprising.

Two weeks after the breakdown of the summer 2000 cease-
fire between the HM and Indian security forces, HM's operational commander in J&K, Abdul Majid Dar, reiterated that
"even if this bloodshed continues for another 10 years, ultimately the concerned parties will have to sit around a table and
find a solution through talks." So it is better that a serious and
meaningful dialogue begin now so that further bloodshed is
stopped.[16] In Kashmir, Dar has a reputation for ruthlessness
equalled by few guerrilla commanders, but he too sounds exhausted. Since the cease-fire ended on 8 August, the HM and
the Indian forces reverted to taking a heavy toll on each other's
fighters. Yet, as one Indian commentary noted about the two-
week cease-fire, "the remarkable aspect of the whole episode is
not that it proved infructuous, but that it occurred at all."[17] It is
not impossible, especially in the light of developments during
November–December, that the short-lived cease-fire declared
unilaterally by Hizbul Mujahideen on 24 July and reciprocated
by the Indians on 28 July will go down retrospectively as the
beginning of a long process of winding down the war in J&K.

PROBLEMS AND POSSIBILITIES

In September 1999, just after the end of the Kargil war, I wrote
that "there is a powerful faction within the most pro-Pakistan
groups in J&K, the Jama'at-Islami and its affiliated armed
organization, Hizbul Mujahideen—which genuinely wants an

end to the present stalemate and would welcome a new approach to the Kashmir problem." I also noted that "even then, a cessation of fighting may not prove easy to achieve given the doubtful degree of control of any Pakistani agency over some of the more radical groups that have become active in Kashmir over the last few years, not to mention the likely opposition of hardline elements within the Pakistani military, intelligence and state-security apparatus to a more cooperative approach."[18]

At the end of 2000, radical Islamist groups based in Pakistan, proved to be the greatest impediment to the Indian leadership's bid to de-escalate hostilities in J&K. During the first three and a half weeks of the month of Ramzan, militants, belonging in most cases to the Lashkar-e-Tayyaba, carried out at least five frontal assaults on Indian military encampments in the Kashmir Valley and Poonch, killing over a dozen soldiers. The Jaish-e-Mohammad and Hizbul Mujahideen targeted security force patrols and convoys with IEDS in Srinagar, and in the country-side. The Indian announcement was also greeted with execution-style killings of Hindu and Sikh civilians in Doda and Udhampur districts. But these predictable attacks appear to have failed to wreck the moves towards de-escalation. After the Pakistani military regime declared its "maximum restraint" policy on 2 December, reciprocal shelling and firing ceased along most sectors of the LoC, and declined to negligible levels particularly along volatile stretches, such as Rajouri–Poonch. Inside J&K, there was a relative yet definite reduction in violent incidents during Ramzan, and a relaxation in the level of tension in many areas.[19]

Although it seems premature to talk as yet of any "peace process" in the meaningful, substantive sense, some encouraging signs do exist.[20] One is the cautious welcome given to the Indian government's overtures by the All-Party Hurriyat Conference (APHC), the umbrella co-ordination body of a large number of disparate anti-India factions. As the month of Ramzan drew to a close, efforts were also being made to persuade the largest guerrilla faction, Hizbul Mujahideen, whose Pakistan-based leaders continued to express scepticism about the Indian offer, and threaten violence (even as many field units appeared to be observing significant restraint), to respond in a much more constructive manner.

An Essential Building Block: Improving Everyday Life

The HM is numerically the strongest of the insurgent formations operating in J&K. Its cadre consists mainly of local recruits; it has an armed presence throughout the Kashmir Valley and four of Jammu's six districts, and the back-up support provided by its organizational network is key to the ability of outsider-dominated *jehadi* groups to execute operations against Indian targets. It is thus in a position to help deliver a very significant de-escalation of violence, leading to a degree of normalization of the ground situation. This would be an essential intermediate step before any substantive process of dialogue can be seriously contemplated.

It is not possible to ascertain exactly how many people have died violently in J&K during the last 11 years. Indian official sources typically cite a figure in the vicinity of 35,000–40,000, while the APHC claims a toll as high as 70,000–80,000. In either case, several hundred thousand people in J&K, mostly concentrated in the Kashmir Valley and the disturbed zones of the Jammu region, have experienced the death of a close family member, torture, or imprisonment in the last decade.

But almost all the 6–7 million people who live in the war-zone have experienced at least some form of abuse or humiliation at the hands of the forces of law and order during this time. It is this type of abuse—relatively minor, but routinized forms of harassment and humiliation at checkpoints on the streets, and during patrols, and house-to-house searches in neighbourhoods—that has produced the deepest resentment against India and kept armed militancy alive in J&K. Srinagar, for example, is less a city under siege today than when I visited in 1995 and 1996. Sandbag bunkers, checkpoints, and patrols are all significantly reduced. In contrast to experiences several years ago, it was possible for me to drive from one end of Srinagar to the other late in the evening without being stopped once, even though I was riding pillion on a motorbike, the fa-voured mode of transportation of *fidayeen* on suicide-attack missions against police and military installations. Nonetheless, Kashmir still has a prison-like atmosphere for those who live there permanently, and people deeply resent that they often cannot walk, or travel in their own neighborhood, town, and homeland without being subject to questioning and searches by gun-toting outsiders.

During the two-week cease-fire period between the HM and Indian forces in July–August 2000, the security forces were relatively relaxed, and citizens appreciated the reduction in routine forms of harassment and humiliation. In September 1999, I pointed out that "following a more or less stable cease-fire, the Indian security presence would need to become as unoffensive and unobtrusive as possible towards the civilian population."[21] Indian initiatives during November and December 2000 to dismantle bunkers in heavily populated areas of Srinagar reflect this imperative. A lasting cease-fire would "lock in" such apparently mundane but vital improvements to everyday civilian life as an end to cordon-and-search operations, and a further reduction in checkpoints. Such a broadening and deepening of the "Ramzan initiative" requires a formal cease-fire declaration by the HM to consolidate a de facto policy of restraint observed by most HM units. A mitigation of the oppressive environment of the war-zones would, in turn, enable progress in implementing more tangible normalization measures:

- more effective monitoring and enforcement of human rights standards of the security forces;
- restructuring of policing arrangements so that the role of outside forces[22] is reduced, and that of local J&K police, which has already been revived to some extent, further enhanced;
- a quick beginning to phased release of most political prisoners being held in Indian jails;
- psychological and material assistance to thousands of widows, orphans, and the families of an estimated 2,500 disappeared persons.[23]

THE FRAGMENTATION OF J&K's SOCIAL AND POLITICAL LANDSCAPE: IMPLICATIONS

It is commonplace for United States officials to say that "the wishes of the Kashmiri people" must be taken into account in any settlement,[24] or for Pakistani officials to say, as they did after the HM's declaration of cease-fire in July 2000, that "any solution acceptable to the Kashmiris is acceptable to us." As of December 2000, the Pakistani military government's foreign minister continued to speak in terms of a non-existent monolith called "the Kashmiri people."[25] References to "the Kashmiri people" or "the Kashmiris" obscure very important reality: the extraordinary degree of fragmentation of society and politics in J&K. The probable wishes of certain sections of the population in J&K (e.g., the majority of the Valley's population) are in conflict with the wishes of certain other sections of citizens (e.g., the overall Hindu majority in the Jammu region), while the wishes of yet other sections (e.g., non-Kashmiri Muslims in the Jammu region or Muslims in the Kargil district of Ladakh) are unclear. The existence of this medley of competing voices is a key political fact that needs to be appreciated by all interested in resolving the Kashmir problem.

The differences between the three regions are only the most obvious form of international, social, and political cleavage in J&K. Further divisions and tensions exist within the regions. For example, in the largely pro-*azaadi* Valley of Kashmir, a basic disagreement exists between a large segment that defines *azaadi* as independence from both India and Pakistan, and a much smaller but not insignificant segment that sees *azaadi* as synonymous with incorporation into Pakistan. There is also a third segment in the Valley. This is made up of many Kashmiri-speaking Shia Muslims, many Gujjars and some members of the dominant Kashmiri-speaking Sunni group, in addition to the small minority of Hindu Kashmiri Pandits, and the allegiance of this segment is ultimately with India (for the Muslim groups, only because they view Pakistan with suspicion and think that independence is an unrealizable political agenda). In the Jammu region, confessional Hindus (65 percent of the population) almost invariably identify with India, but there are schisms among these Hindus as well. Divisions exist on the basis of ethno-linguistic particularity (whether people are Dogras, Rajputs, or Punjabis), caste (upper castes vs lower "scheduled" castes), rural–urban and class divides (poor cultivators vs professional middle-class urbanites), location of residence (hillfolk vs plainspeople), political ideology (liberals vs Hindu nationalists), or some combination of these markers of differentiation.

These have further complications. Although the Jammu region has an overall Hindu majority of close to two-thirds, three of its six districts actually have Muslim majorities. Non-Muslims (Hindus and Sikhs) comprise significant minorities in each of these three districts: over 40 percent in Doda, 35 percent in Rajouri, and 41.5 percent in Poonch (including, as I have noted, majorities in the towns of Rajouri and Poonch). Among the Muslim-majority districts, Doda's Kashmiri-speaking Muslim majority is by and large—although by no means invariably—pro-*azaadi* (with the predictable split between pro-independence and pro-Pakistan elements), as is the Kashmiri-speaking Muslim belt in the northeastern reaches of Poonch district, adjoining the Valley. Meanwhile, one can only speculate about the preferences of Gujjars and Bakerwals, Rajptus and others who form the bulk of the Muslim populations in Rajouri and Poonch districts. Moreover, one of the Jammu region's three Hindu-dominated districts, Udhampur, has a Muslim minority of almost 30 percent including both Kashmiris and Gujjars. Even the solidly "Hindu" city of Jammu in the south of J&K has a Muslim population of several tens of thousands who have lived there for generations.

The internal social and political picture of J&K thus resembles a Russian *matryoshka-doll*—beneath one layer of complexity there is always another one. Partitionist proposals are an easy temptation for those who do not want to deal with these layers of social diversity and plurality, and the political challenges they pose. Numerous proposals to carve up the territory of J&K in an effort to dilute diversity and engineer greater homogeneity are in circulation. Some upper-caste urban Hindu elites in the Jammu region want to "trifurcate" J&K into three separate units—"Hindu-majority" Jammu, "Muslim-majority" Kashmir, and "Buddhist" Ladakh.[26] Some Kashmiri Muslim elites in the Kashmir Valley have responded to this proposal with a counter-proposal to trifurcate the Jammu region instead, effectively separating its Muslim-majority areas from the Hindu-majority areas. One US-based group, which is financed by an expatriate

Kashmiri-American businessman and includes retired US diplo-
mats, has carried the dubious logic of partition further.[27] It proposes the creation of a "sovereign Kashmiri entity, but without
an international personality" (which is possibly a contradiction
in terms) encompassing the Kashmir Valley and some of the
Muslim-majority as well as confessionally mixed areas in
the Jammu region. These proposals are utterly insensitive to
the "Russian doll" situation, and fluidity of identities that
are the reality of social and political life in J&K. All would create
"stranded" minorities, and the last, more ambitious scheme, could
trigger a spiral of sectarian violence and reciprocal expulsions
in numerous locales, which could lead to a general conflict between India and Pakistan. Partition is not only no solution to
the internal complexity of J&K, it is a positively dangerous idea.[28]

The multiple forms of fragmentation of society in J&K are
mirrored in its fragmented political spectrum of diverse parties,
groups, and movements. The All-Party Hurriyat Conference is
a grab-bag of disparate ideologies, factions, and personalities,
ranging from the revolutionary independentists of the J&K
Liberation Front (JKLF), who want an independent state of
J&K encompassing both Indian- and Pakistani-controlled areas,
to the Pakistan-oriented religious conservatives of the Jama'at-
i-Islami. These disparate tendencies are gathered under one
roof only by a shared aversion to Indian repression. The Indian
government's Ramzan cease-fire, and apparent willingness to
engage in dialogue with "domestic" dissident groups has served
to bring into sharp relief the deep divisions within the Hurriyat.
Of the seven members of the body's executive committee (before
the split of APHC, editor), three—Yasin Malik, Mirwaiz Umer
Farooq, and Abdul Ghani Lone—are relative moderates genuinely interested in a constructive dialogue with the Indian government. However, another three—Syed Ali Shah Geelani,
Maulana Abbas Ansari, and Sheikh Abdul Aziz—are relative
hardliners who represent a more sceptical stance. (The seventh
member, Abdul Ghani Butt, is also a pro-Pakistan hardliner
who is currently walking a tightrope between the two feuding
factions.) Although the APHC harbours ambitions of being the
pivotal player in talks involving India, Pakistan, and "representatives of Kashmir," its ability to act as a cohesive group is in

serious doubt because of clashing personal egos, factional rivalries, and ideological disagreements. In addition, it is important
to remember that the popular sentiment the APHC symbolizes—
the aspiration to *azaadi* (freedom) and *khudmukhtari* (self-
rule)—is limited to the Kashmir Valley and a few zones inhabited by Kashmiri-speaking Muslims in the Jammu region.

The "pro-India" stream of politics is represented by some
"regional" parties, such as the National Conference, which runs
a corrupt and unpopular civilian regime, and is the local surrogate of New Delhi, as well as a rising opposition party called
the People's Democratic Party (PDP). The PDP, led by a one-
time senior Congress party leader from the Kashmir Valley, is
loyal to India, but tries to capitalize on popular discontent with
the NC regime.[29] Both the NC and the PDP have some influence
in various parts of J&K. In addition, "national" (i.e., all-India)
parties like the BJP and Congress have some following in pockets
of the three constituent regions. There are also various smaller
groupings.

BUILDING A PEACE PROCESS: LESSONS
FROM THE PAST AND POINTERS TO THE FUTURE

It will obviously be difficult, at best, to reconcile this multitude
of competing tendencies and aspirations. However, certain
costly follies of the past should not be repeated. Ever since 1947,
successive Indian governments have made a habit of striking
deals with particular factions and personalities in J&K as a
means of maintaining Indian control over the region. These
local client groups have then been given a certain authority to
govern J&K—although always subject to New Delhi's overriding veto—while the rest of the political spectrum has been
denied recognition and rights to effective participation, and even
criminalized in some cases. The result has been an absolute
retardation of democratic institutionalization in J&K. J&K's
government has, with few exceptions, been the preserve of a
series of corrupt cliques whose composition has fluctuated constantly over the last 50 years, depending on New Delhi's changing assessments about which groups among Kashmir's political class have been most willing and able to run surrogate

governments. The cliques, in turn, have had little sense of accountability to the public because they have judged, correctly, that their political fate is ultimately dependent not on the will of the people of J&K but on the whims of those in power in New Delhi. They have thus concentrated their energies not on governance, but on accumulating wealth and victimizing political opponents. On occasions when the favored cliques have shown signs of independent behavior, New Delhi has arranged for their removal and replacement by less popular, and hence, more compliant cliques. This is what happened to the relatively representative governments led by Sheikh Abdullah in 1953 and his son Farooq Abdullah in 1984.

Throughout, political oppositions to the ruling cliques have been repressed and stigmatized as "anti-national." The most infamous example is that of the MUF in 1987. As a result, political opposition—indispensable to the functioning of a competitive system of representative democracy—has also remained uninstitutionalized. This bizarre puppet theatre, with New Delhi playing the puppeteer, eventually collapsed in 1990, as Yusuf Shah metamorphosed into Salahuddin. The essence of the tragedy is an absolute disjuncture between the pluralism of J&K's society and politics, and the anti-plural institutional space promoted by the Indian authorities.[30]

J&K's political landscape has changed radically in the last 11 years. But the past still holds one vital lesson for the present and future: any process of dialogue to address the conflict must be as inclusive and broadly based as possible. It must actively seek to involve the rainbow spectrum of political activism and opinion in J&K, ranging from the HM and the APHC to the major pro-India parties. This would be quite difficult given the deep disagreements on fundamental questions of allegiance and identity, but it is also essential. Both the acute difficulties and the acute necessity of such an inclusive framework are demonstrated by the experience of the Northern Ireland peace process.

THE INTERNATIONAL DIMENSION: PAKISTAN AS A FACTOR

Compulsions of history, geography, culture, and politics all point to the conclusion that any meaningful dialogue on Kashmir requires the involvement of Pakistan in some capacity. This may not be fully appreciated in Delhi, but it is fairly obvious on the frontlines of conflict in Rajouri, Poonch, or Srinagar. In the Kashmir Valley, there is unanimity cutting across political fault-lines on the need for Pakistan's involvement.[31]

However, exactly *how* to get Pakistan involved has emerged as the most troublesome issue of the incipient Kashmir peace process. In August 2000, the HM abruptly terminated its cease-fire when the Indian government rejected the group's ultimatum to acknowledge Kashmir as a trilateral dispute necessitating immediate tripartite talks between India, Pakistan, and repre-sentatives of J&K's population. The Indian government, for its part, has stayed firm in its refusal to countenance such a set-up for dialogue on Kashmir even after Pakistan responded to its Ramzan initiative. Even while admitting that the LoC has gone largely quiet since late November (even before the formal Pakistani announcement), Indian officials have ruled out sitting around the same table, at the same time, to discuss Kashmir with Pakistanis, and representatives of disaffected J&K citizens. The Indians say that Pakistan has still not expressly undertaken to stop infiltration of militants from its side of the border into Indian-controlled territory, and that Pakistani duplicity in laun-ching the Kargil operation in 1999 within months of the Indian prime minister's goodwill journey to Lahore cannot be forgotten. It is unlikely that Delhi will shift from this position and agree to an explicitly tripartite set-up for a Kashmir peace process.[32]

However, it is possible to devise a working solution to the bilateral–trilateral conundrum that should be acceptable to all sides. As early as mid-September, HM chief Salahuddin, who is based in Pakistan, stated that his organization saw nothing wrong with bilateral dialogue between New Delhi and repre-sentatives of pro-*azaadi* groups in J&K, as long as there was a guarantee that Pakistan would be included "during the decisive phase of the dialogue ... at the second or third stage."[33] In early December, following the unequivocal Indian rejection of an ex-plicitly tripartite set-up, Pakistan's foreign office ventured a very similar suggestion that such bilateral contacts could pro-ceed with the caveat that they "should be followed by three-way dialogue involving Islamabad immediately afterwards."[34] New Delhi then called for "an early resumption of the composite dia-logue process" with Islamabad on all issues of mutual concern, but not limited to Kashmir (the Pakistanis would ideally like a process that is not only explicitly three-cornered, but also exclusively focused on the Kashmir problem). The Indian statement, while apparently unyielding, actually marked a subtle but significant shift from India's refusal, since the Kargil episode, to engage with Pakistan at all. On 20 December, while announcing the decision to extend the Ramzan moratorium on offensive anti-guerrilla operations in J&K for another month, Vajpayee again spoke of his government's intent to "initiate exploratory steps" towards "renewal of the composite dialogue process with Pakistan."[35]

The working solution to the bilateral, or trilateral obstacle may thus lie in two formally separate, but related and parallel tracks of engagement. The Indian government, as well as the moderate elements in the Hurriyat Conference, have no qualms about the first track—New Delhi–Srinagar. Indian leaders have repeatedly emphasized their readiness in principle to talk to representatives of their "own" citizens, while Hurriyat moderates are so eager to get a dialogue off the ground that they are willing to be flexible on the "modalities." The second axis of dialogue—New Delhi–Islamabad—would probably have to begin more or less on India's terms (as a "composite" process) if it were to begin at all in the near future. This may not be liked by Pakistan, but pragmatic Pakistanis should know that their unstable country, in the throes of economic and institutional crisis, is more isolated in the world community on the Kashmir question than ever in the past. The net result of the Pakistan army's Kargil misadventure was to produce an international consensus (among the United States, China, Russia, and Britain) on the urgency of respecting the Line of Control if regional security were not to be completely jeopardized. Eighteen months later, the Pakistani authorities appear to have finally conceded to the principle of restraint, even if belatedly and reluctantly. But with similarly broad-based international support for the peace moves in Kashmir initiated by the Indian side towards the end of 2000, the Pakistanis have limited room for maneuver. Given Pakistan's infelicitous circumstances of internal turmoil and international isolation, an implicit, somewhat indirect, three-way dialogue on Kashmir, which can with time and progress be converted into a direct and explicit three-way process, may not be such a bad starting-point at all.

In any event, an agreed solution to the Kashmir dispute remains a very remote prospect. India and Pakistan have both chosen to make possession of Kashmir central to their national ideologies of, respectively, "secular" and Muslim nationalism. These polarized positions make any substantive settlement—which must necessarily be a compromise—inherently difficult, even without the complication of J&K's internal socio-political diversity.

Once a process of substantive dialogue between the two countries and the different sections of opinion in J&K becomes a real possibility, its systematic development will benefit from a conceptual framework, a strategic "road-map." I have elsewhere tried to define the basic principles and clarify the essential dimensions of such a framework for building peace, extrapolating key elements and principles from the peacebuilding model used in Northern Ireland.[36] The main leader of the pro-independence JKLF in Srinagar, Yasin Malik, has welcomed the Indians' Ramzan initiative as a "bold step" and called on Vajpayee to emulate Yitzhak Rabin's peacemaking role. However, he has also warned that "peace cannot be built in a vacuum," and that unless a serious political process unfolds, the momentum towards peace can easily dissipate.[37] He is right. But at the same time, peace can only be built step by step, through a gradual, incremental process. Following the Indian government's extension of its de facto cease-fire against guerrillas in J&K until late January 2001, the next logical step in the unfolding peace drama in Kashmir is a formal cease-fire announcement by the Hizbul Mujahideen.

THE RETURN OF *INSANIYAT*?

In Srinagar in autumn 2000, I met Dr M., a prominent medical practitioner in the city, whom I had first met in New York in 1994, shortly after he had been forced to flee Kashmir after repeated threats to his life by the Hizbul Mujahideen, which saw him as an enemy because of his affiliation with the pro-independence JKLF. The HM's gunmen by 1994 had murdered a number of figures from the Kashmiri intelligentsia, known for their pro-independence sympathies, in addition to scores of JKLF cadres and ordinary supporters. Dr M. was a prime target since he had been involved with the JKLF since 1988, when the uprising that erupted in 1990 was beginning to crystallize. He returned to Srinagar only in late 1999.

Six years ago, Dr M. would not openly tell me who exactly had forced him to leave Kashmir for exile. He spoke only about the brutal behavior of the "Indian occupation forces," responsible for massacres of civilians, summary executions of countless Kashmiri youths, rapes of Kashmir's women, and gruesome torture of suspects. Sitting in the garden of his Srinagar home, I asked him to reflect on the 12 years since 1988. He still spoke with revulsion of the custodial killings and murders of civilians committed by Indian forces, and their sponsorship of gangs of turncoat ex-guerrillas who have become auxiliaries of the Indian security apparatus operating under the J&K police's Special Operations Group (SOG), which is notorious for corruption and brutality. But he also told me, for the first time directly, who had forced him to leave Kashmir, and squarely blamed the HM and other Pakistan-sponsored groups for the atrocities that drove some civilians and members of other guerrilla formations to seek refuge in the arms of the Indian security apparatus. I told him that on my way to his house in the suburbs, I had passed through a place in downtown Srinagar where a grenade attack on a security force vehicle had taken place only a couple of hours earlier. Two soldiers had been killed on the spot and three others critically wounded, but I had been struck by how blasé people in the neighborhood seemed about the incident. He agreed that it was troubling how desensitized society seemed to have become to everyday violence.

As I was leaving, we discussed the *fidayeen* attack on an army camp in central Kashmir that had happened the previous day. An Indian major and 13 soldiers had been killed in the attack; the two *fidayeens* responsible (one local Kashmiri and one *jehadi* from Pakistan) had also died. There had been a further development, however, that I did not know about. Dr M. had just heard that the wife of the slain major had committed suicide after hearing about her husband's death. "It sickens me," Dr M. said, "this senseless loss of young lives." He paused for a moment and then added: "On both sides."

In his more generous moments, India's Prime Minister Vajpayee, who is also a poet, likes to say that the best framework for talks on Kashmir would be the framework of *insaniyat* (humanity). The JKLF, the organization that launched the armed struggle in Kashmir, abandoned the gun in 1994; the HM, a considerably more hardline force, may also be willing to give peace a chance. Whether New Delhi and Islamabad (perhaps with the aid of some discreet facilitation and encouragement from Washington) will also realize the virtues of *insaniyat* over war, remains to be seen. J&K has been a pawn of conflicting nationalist positions and ruthless power-games for over 50 years.

Consequently, its own people, including the local elites in Srinagar, have little control over the unfolding of events. The prospects of a durable peace in Kashmir will be decided in the corridors of power in the two metropolitan capitals.

NOTES AND REFERENCES

1. Accounts which seek to contest simplified understandings of the Kashmir conflict and present an alternative perspective include: Sumantra Bose, *The Challenge in Kashmir: Democracy, Self-Determination and a Just Peace.* New Delhi, 1997; Tavleen Singh, *Kashmir: A Tragedy of Errors.* Delhi, 1995; Victoria Schofield, *Kashmir—in the Crossfire.* London, 2000; and Balraj Puri, *Kashmir: Towards Insurgency.* Delhi, 1993. See also Robert Wirsing, *India, Pakistan and the Kashmir Dispute.* New York, 1994 and Raju Thomas (ed.), *Perspectives on Kashmir.* Boulder, Colorado, 1992.
2. Vajpayee made his statement on November 19, 2000, and the Indians' moratorium on offensive combat operations came into effect on 28 November. The full text of Vajpayee's statement can be found at http://pmindia.nic.in/infocentre/press.htm.
3. See "Ramzan Truce: Pakistan Responds with 'Restraint' on the LoC," *The Hindustan Times,* December 3, 2000, p. 1.
4. The Kashmir Valley is divided administratively into six districts: Baramulla and Kupwara in north Kashmir, Srinagar and Badgam in central Kashmir, and Anantnag and Pulwama in south Kashmir.
5. All statistics relating to population figures cited in this article are estimates based on the Government of India census conducted in Jammu & Kashmir in 1981. Since that time, no official census results have been available. See *Population Atlas of India.* Delhi, 1999.

6. Of course, this ethno-linguistic identity is inevitably infused with a religious dimension because the vast majority of the Valley's population is Muslim. The Muslim element of Kashmiri regional identity, centred historically and geographically on the Valley, has also been somewhat accentuated since 1989 because of the radicalization induced by the protracted violent confrontation with the Indian state.

7. The Jammu region has six districts: three in the northern and western parts of the region have overall Muslim majorities (Poonch, Rajouri, and Doda) while the other three, located to the south and east, are predominantly Hindu (Jammu, Udhampur, and Kathua). Significant religious minorities are, however, present in each of these districts. Moreover, the confessional Hindus of the Jammu region are, like their Muslim compatriots, internally divided along faultlines of language, ethnicity, caste, and party affiliation.

8. Sumantra Bose, op. cit.

9. The ceasefire line of January 1949 was renamed the LoC by the Indo-Pakistani agreement of 1972.

10. The JeM is led by Maulana Masood Azhar, a radical Pakistani cleric. He formed the group in early 2000 as a breakaway group from its parent organization, Harkat-ul-Jehad-i-lslami, after his followers forced his release from an Indian prison by hijacking an Indian Airlines civilian airliner to Kandahar—the Taliban stronghold in southern Afghanistan.

11. *The Statesman*, September 7, 2000, p. 1.

12. "Militancy Gains Momentum in Doda, Udhampur: Local Ultras Outnumber Foreigners," *Kashmir Times*, September 8, 2000, p. 1.

13. *Daily Excelsior*, September 19, 2000, p. 1.

14. "Inside the Jehad Factory," *Outlook*, September 25, 2000, p. 38.

15. *The Indian Express*, September 25, 2000, p. 1.

16. *Kashmir Times*, August 23, 2000, p. 1.

17. "Immediate Tasks in Kashmir," editorial in *Economic and Political Weekly*, August 12, 2000, pp. 2883–84.

18. Sumantra Bose, "Kashmir: Sources of Conflict, Dimensions of Peace," *Survival*, vol. 41, no. 3, 1999, pp. 149–71.

19. Muzamil Jaleel, "The Ramzan Thaw," *The Indian Express*, December 20, 2000, p. 8.

20. After the Indian prime minister's announcement, the Pakistan-based leaders of HM kept insisting that India acknowledge the need for a tripartite conference on the Kashmir dispute—meaning, essentially, that it concede a central and integral role for Pakistan in any talks. However, the group's operational commander inside J&K, Abdul Majid Dar (the key figure in the HM's cease-fire declaration in summer 2000), maintained total silence. "Hizb Threat to Intensify Attacks," *Kashmir Times*, December 5, 2000, p. 1.

21. Sumantra Bose, op. cit. p. 165.

22. The vast majority of Indian army personnel deployed in J&K (as well as the Border Security Force and the Central Reserve Police Force) are non-Muslims from outside J&K.

23. These steps to normalization are described in greater detail in Sumantra Bose, op. cit., pp. 165–66.

24. However, in a departure from its standard language, the state department commented in December 2000 that India, Pakistan, and "all residents of the Kashmir region" need to be involved in any meaningful peace process. *Hindustan Times,* December 6, 2000, p. 1.

25. Abdul Sattar, interview with CNN International, December 3, 2000.

26. This "trifurcation" proposal was publicly rejected by Indian home (interior) minister L.K. Advani in November 2000.

27. See Kashmir Study Group, *Kashmir: A Way Forward,* February 2000. The Kashmir Study Group is sponsored by businessman Farooq Kathwari.

28. For a critique of partitionist "solutions" to the Kashmir tangle, see Amitabh Mattoo, "Divide and Rule: Towards Polarisation in Jammu & Kashmir," *The Times of India,* October 6, 2000 (op-ed page).

29. Mufti Mohammed Sayeed, former home (interior) minister in the Indian government.

30. This argument is developed by Sumantra Bose in *The Challenge in Kashmir: Democracy, Self-Determination and a Just Peace.* New Delhi, 1997.

31. "Valley's Left and Right, All Say Talk to Pakistan: You Have To Involve Them, Say Parties from National Conference to Congress, even BJP," *The Indian Express,* December 9, 2000, p. 1.

32. See "Delhi Plays Cool to Pak Border Truce Offer," *The Times of India,* December 3, 2000, p. 1; "India Says No to Tripartite Talks with Pakistan," *The Hindustan Times,* December 5, 2000, p. 1.

33. See interview with Salahuddin in *India Today,* September 18, 2000, p. 32.

34. "India-Militant Talks Fine: Pakistan," *The Hindustan Times,* December 5, 2000, p. 1.

35. Prime Minister's statement in the Indian Parliament, December 20, 2000.

36. Sumantra Bose, op. cit., pp. 149–71.

37. Author's personal conversation with Yasin Malik in Delhi, December 12, 2000.

6

ARMED CONFLICT IN ANDHRA PRADESH AND THE SEARCH OF DEMOCRATIC SPACE[*]

Committee of Concerned Citizens

BACKGROUND

Agrarian movements are not a new phenomenon in Andhra Pradesh. Land-based struggles of the poor, especially the tribals, have taken place several times in the region's history. These struggles are undoubtedly political in nature, and have a distinct social and economic base.

The present phase of the Naxalite movement is three decades old. The movement as a part of the people's struggle has taken different forms, and adopted a variety of strategies and instruments during its long course. There has been a corresponding series of actions on the part of the state, and its agencies. As a result, there is presently a situation, particularly in the north Telangana districts, in which the right to normal and peaceful living of the common people is severely curtailed by a continuing spiral of violence and all-round suffering. This is a matter of concern for all right thinking people.

This was the backdrop against which a group of citizens came together early in 1997. The group which came to be known as the Committee of Concerned Citizens (Paura Spandana Vedika), in Hyderabad, was not formed at the instance of any authority or organization. It emerged, on its own, hoping to reflect the voice of a large democratic section of the society, which is tired at being reduced to a mute spectator in the game with peoples'

[*] Originally published as a report of the Committee of Concerned Citizens, entitled "In Search of Democratic Space," August 5, 1998.

lives played by the state and the revolutionary parties. The Committee of Concerned Citizens (CCC) is essentially an independent collective of individuals sharing a common concern on the climate of violence, brutalization, insensitivity, and suffering that is prevailing in the state, particularly in the Telangana districts, in the context of the three-decade-old Naxalite movement, and the states approach in dealing with the issues.

ANALYSIS ON THE DEMOCRATIC PARADIGM

The Committee considered that there was a need to analyze the problem in terms other than violence and counter-violence, and to pose it mainly as a question of people's aspirations. The purpose was to bring "people" back to the centre stage of the policies of the state, or the revolutionary program of the Naxalite groups. A meaningful search for a permanent solution had to be launched by breaking away from the "chicken or egg" kind of arguments on "violence to deal with violence," and create a new set of terms for a democratic debate. The object was to bring back on the agenda the issues of people—the right to livelihood, the right to life, and in a sense, staying alive in a dignified and honourable existence.

Even a cursory look at the regional newspapers gives the strong impression of a daily tragedy being played out in the rural areas of Telangana, which the masses are silently suffering. The violence seems to be self-perpetuating, and neither the state nor the revolutionary parties are able to control it. There is hardly a day without reports of deaths or destruction at the hands of the police, or the Naxalite political parties in the Telangana districts. While on the one hand there is little respect for law and life on the part of the state and its agencies, on the other, ruthless violence regardless of people's will, aspirations, and sufferings seems to have overtaken the revolutionary parties as well.

While one death is as tragic and as meaningless as another; over a thousand persons were killed by the Naxalites in different incidents in Andhra Pradesh during the current decade, and almost as many have been killed by the state in police encounters during the same period. It goes without saying that the majority of those who lost their lives were poor, and from the backward castes, scheduled castes, and scheduled tribes. As reports of violent deaths occur with nauseating frequency, people seem to have become increasingly insensitive, and the society is getting progressively brutalized.

It is becoming evident that one must break away from the prevailing viewpoints and look into the social, economic, and political context and consequences of the happenings, to analyze and discuss the issues in a broader democratic framework. The situation calls for, what may be termed, as citizens' intervention on behalf of the people and in favor of the people, and to explore ways of putting an end to such wanton wastage of human potential.

The Committee believes that it is possible to find a long-term direction for a democratic restructuring of the society, which alone can completely address any of the questions, which are being faced today. The Committee seeks to take a people-centred view of the situation, and locates itself in a transformatory paradigm. Primarily, the Committee is committed to the democratic and human rights, and humane objectives, which inspired our freedom struggle, and were inscribed in the preamble, the fundamental rights, and directive principles in the constitution. These provide the basic minimum structure and the starting point for the political and institutional processes to work continuously for social transformation. The Committee is of the opinion that a "right-people" perspective should inform our understanding and interpretation of movements, events, and instruments.

The constitution also mandates that every citizen should so order his life that he cherishes and promotes the ideals that inspired our freedom struggle. The independence struggle used the Rule of Law in an insurgent manner. In the context of the preamble, the Rule of Law has to work for human dignity with social, economic, and political justice as the objective, while in that of the fundamental rights, it should have a rights-perspective, and social transformation should work towards an egalitarian society. The Committee feels that it is in this regard that the state has failed in its obligation.

The Committee is of the firm view that the state has to adhere strictly to the Rule of Law. Indeed, the state has no other moral authority to rule. Clearly, Rule of Law is not just a weapon in the hands of the state but also a restraint on its behavior. Quite the contrary, the government continues to portray the Naxalite movement as a law and order problem, and does not wish to acknowledge the fact that the movement is essentially an expression of the people's aspirations to a life of dignity and self-respect. ...

The Committee is conscious of the structural violence, or violence built into the social system such as inequality, exploitation or lack of freedom, and the need for contextualization of the tensions in terms of social, economic, and political factors, as well as the immediacy of the circumstances of physical violence. The Committee recognizes that "inequitable land relations" are central to any debate on the emergence of violence in rural Andhra Pradesh, and that attempts to mitigate the degree of violence are unlikely to yield results unless the land question is fully addressed. Along with the land issue, the issues of human dignity and life struggle have to be addressed.

OBJECTIVES

The Committee's intervention has a fourfold objective of arriving at a vantage point to understand the Naxalite movement with a focus on people's aspirations: intervening to solve some of the persistent problems, effecting policy shifts, halt killings, and prevent further brutalization of society. The Committee intends to pursue its endeavors through consultations with all sections of people. The Committee is anxious that the available democratic space, to the extent guaranteed by the Constitution, should be fully explored. This will become possible only if the government on the one hand and the various CPI–ML (Communist Party of India–Marxist–Leninist) groups on the other observed restraint and reordered their approach.

The Committee has abiding faith in the common people who have the highest stake in the move forward to a just and humane society. While the Committee is concerned with measures to democratize the system and increasing the democratic space, it is not the intention of the Committee to thwart the revolutionary efforts of any political movement. The concern of the Committee is to humanize the society, the political movements and the governments.

The deliberations of the Committee so far have been confined to discussions with a limited section of the people, and to a dialogue with the CPI–ML Peoples War, and with the government. The Committee has not yet reached out to the other Naxalite parties. The Committee has no doubt that there is a large section in the society which wishes to participate in this debate, wants equity and justice through democratic resolution of conflicts, and is interested in strict implementation of Rule of Law. This section is presently silent perhaps as it feels inhibited by the pervasive "gun versus gun" culture and an atmosphere of fear. The Committee considers that the time has come to address the large majority of people who are equally concerned, and to appeal them. In the ultimate analysis, Governments and the movements are accountable to the people. The Committee is accordingly publishing all these deliberations to initiate and facilitate an informed and wide public debate in order to promote conditions for an atmosphere in which common people can live without fear, and with dignity.

7

THE PEACE PROCESS IN SRI LANKA: FROM CONFRONTATION TO ACCOMMODATION

Jehan Perera

When Sri Lanka gets into the international media, it is usually on account of its ethnic-related violence. This has included mob riots, in which there has been government complicity, the loss of a thousand soldiers in a single day with the fall of major army bases, and the destruction of half of the country's fleet of international airplanes at its international airport. The major part of this violence has pitted the Sri Lankan government against the Liberation Tigers of Tamil Eelam (LTTE), which has been fighting for an independent Tamil homeland. The LTTE is an organization that has its own army, and has laid claim to be the sole representative of the Tamil people on whose behalf it is fighting a war of independence. It has a leader of cult status, and an army of over 10,000 each of whom has sworn to commit suicide by swallowing a cyanide capsule rather than surrender.

However, after the dramatic signing of a cease-fire agreement between the Sri Lankan government and LTTE in February 2002 that followed nearly three months of an unofficial cease-fire, Sri Lanka is being looked upon as a possible model of peace-making. The South Asian region, which includes Afghanistan and nuclear rivals—India and Pakistan, is amongst the most unstable in the world. Sri Lanka offers a beacon of hope that textbook approaches in peacemaking, with third party mediation, can be successful.

The question is whether a stable negotiated peace that entails mutual compromise is possible in Sri Lanka. On the one hand, the LTTE's highly military nature, a fragmented Sinhalese polity, and vested economic interests put roadblocks on the path to political reforms and compromise. On the other hand, a general war-weariness among the general population, economic debilitation, and the threat of the US led war against terrorism puts pressure on the conflicting parties to compromise and resolve their disputes through political negotiations. In February 2002, the Sri Lankan government and LTTE signed a cease-fire agreement under the auspices of the Norwegian government that appears to offer the real prospect of a final end to violence, as a means of conflict resolution.

However, even a month later, demonstrating the fragility of the cease-fire, the US embassy in Sri Lanka under the hand of its ambassador, Ashley Wills, felt impelled to issue a statement. It said:

> We have heard credible reports that the Liberation Tigers of Tamil Eelam are engaged in activities that could jeopardize the recent indefinite cease-fire accord reached with the Sri Lankan government. These reports recount increased LTTE recruitment in Sri Lanka's north and east, including of children, as well as kidnapping and extortion, especially of Muslims. To be fair, we understand that incidents of recruitment, kidnapping and extortion have apparently decreased in recent days, a trend that we hope will continue. There also have been credible reports of LTTE resupply operations since the ceasefire. Continued smuggling of weapons by the LTTE could undermine the trust needed to move from a cessation of hostilities to a lasting peace.[1]

The reference in the US statement to the Muslims brings to the fore one of the submerged aspects of Sri Lanka's ethnic conflict. The Muslims who are mainly Tamil-speaking nevertheless consider themselves to be a distinct ethnic community. Although they constitute 8 percent of the Sri Lankan population, yet they are spread throughout the country, which has weakened their bargaining strength for regional autonomy, unlike the 12 percent of Tamils who are regionally concentrated in the north and the east. But the Muslims are a majority in significant pockets of the east. Along with the Tamils, they have been victims of government-sponsored land settlement schemes that settled Sinhalese in areas of the east where they once predominated. However, they have also suffered grievously at the hands of the LTTE, the most striking occasion being when nearly 100,000 Muslims were expelled from Jaffna and other parts of the north in 1990 with just two hours' notice. The Muslims were forced to leave without even being able to take along their movable property, such as jewellery. During the period of armed conflict they were reluctant to voice their sentiments, but now with the advent of the cease-fire and increased international attention, they have been demanding the same rights and privileges to be accorded to the Tamils.

While Tamil politicians and media reacted negatively to the US statement, it is likely that many other sectors among the Tamil community felt otherwise. There is no doubt that the offences identified by the US ambassador have been taking place, with even independent human rights organizations such as Amnesty International calling on the LTTE to stop them. It is not only Muslims who have been feeling the heavy taxation of the LTTE, but also Tamils, in areas newly accessible to the LTTE, on account of the cease-fire agreement. Although Tamil politicians and media reacted negatively to the US allegations, the immediate response of the LTTE itself was much milder. The LTTE's chief negotiator, Dr Anton Balasingham, pledged that the LTTE was committed to the peace process. Subsequently, it was reported that the LTTE leader Velupillai Prabakaran was himself much concerned about the allegations, and would take action against any LTTE violations of the cease-fire agreement. These are promising signs that the LTTE is making in the transition to a political organization, and one that is prepared to deal with the rest of the world on the basis of give and take, and accountability on the basis of international norms of human rights.[2]

TRACING ORIGINS

Sri Lanka has a plural society of several different ethnic communities—numbering 18 million. The Sinhalese form the main ethnic group with 74 percent of the population. The majority of the Sinhalese are Buddhists by religion and are mainly concentrated in the south, west, and central parts of the country. The Sri Lanka Tamils with 12 percent of the population form the next major ethnic group. They are a majority in the north-east of the country. The Muslims form the third major ethnic group with 8 percent of the population with a concentration in the east. The up-country Tamils, who are of recent Indian origins, form the fourth major community with about 5 percent of the population. They live in the central hills of the country and have not been involved in the separatist conflict. Most of the Tamils are Hindu by religion. While a minority of both Sinhalese and Tamils comprising about 7 percent are Christian by religion, they are not considered to be a separate ethnic group. The population census of 2001 carried out after an interval of 20 years was not conducted in most of the northeast province, which is a contested territory, and claimed by Tamil nationalists as the "traditional Tamil homeland." However, estimates indicate that the Sri Lanka Tamil population has dropped to a little under 11 percent of the population in the intervening period.[3] Among the salient points brought out by the census is the intermingling of the Sri Lankan population, with Colombo, the main city located in the southwest of the country, registering a Sinhalese population of only 41 percent, with a majority being from Tamil-speaking communities.

Sri Lanka's ongoing ethnic conflict, and the separatist war it has given rise to, can be described as the country's most intractable and destructive problem. The war that steadily escalated between the Sri Lankan government and the Liberation Tigers of Tamil Eelam is generally counted as having started in 1983. It has caused around 65,000 deaths, and major damage to personal and public property with the total loss between 1993–98 estimated at 1.27 times the GDP as at 1998.[4] A total of some 1 million persons have been uprooted and displaced internally as a result at some time or the other, with another half million leaving the country to claim refugee status abroad.

Ironically, Sri Lanka has had a relatively long tradition of modern democracy, stretching back to the British colonial period. The country was one of the first countries in the world to enjoy universal suffrage in 1931. But the inability of the political elites belonging to the different ethnic communities to share power equitably among them led to a series of broken agreements, and to acute mistrust between the communities. The difficulty of protecting minority interests in a parliamentary system in which majority–minority relations are strained is exemplified by Sri Lanka's modern political history. In Sri Lanka, the centralized state bequeathed to the newly independent country in 1948 effectively transferred political power into the hands of the Sinhalese majority. This power was immediately used to restrict the membership of the polity by denying citizenship rights to the "Indian Tamil," or up country Tamil population, and by seeking to correct "historical wrongs" done to the majority. This followed a pattern in which the politicization of ethnicity has occurred in contemporary plural societies, and the claims to group entitlements in current mass politics provide the initial basis for collective identity, mobilization, and action. The skewed distribution of political power in Parliament also led to economic disparities emerging between the Sinhalese, and Tamil majority parts of the country. While social welfare benefits, such as health and education were relatively equitably distributed throughout the country, the same did not hold true for large-scale economic investments. With few exceptions, these prized projects, which provided opportunities for political patronage and development, were located in the Sinhalese majority parts of the country. Ruling party politicians engaged themselves in tussles to obtain these projects for their own electorates. As the Tamils from the north, in particular, were rarely represented in the higher rungs of the government, their case went by default. The situation of deprivation of the Tamil majority areas has continued and escalated due to the war situation that has been prevailing over the past 18 years. A recent study has shown that the output of the northeast is a mere 60 percent of what it used to be in 1983, when the war commenced.[5]

Several serious efforts made by government leaders to work out a solution with the Tamil political leaderships failed due to the inability of the government leadership to obtain the backing of their own party, let alone the opposition. The most outstanding instance was the agreement reached in 1957 between the prime minister at that time, S.W.R.D. Bandaranaike, and the leader to the largest Tamil party. The prime minister unilaterally abrogated the agreement when it proved generally unpopular in the country. Buddhist monks even demonstrated in numbers against the agreement, which gave autonomy to the

Tamil areas. A similar agreement arrived at in 1965 by Prime Minister Dudley Senanayake suffered the same fate, but this time due to strong internal divisions within the ruling party itself.[6] The main objective of both these agreements was to provide a degree of autonomy to the northern and eastern provinces, and to permit them to merge, or work together, if they so desired. The issue of self-rule, regional autonomy, and merger of the two provinces remain the key issues dividing Sinhalese, and Tamil sentiment to this day.

The 13th Amendment to the constitution, which gave effect to the devolution provisions of the Indo-Lanka Peace Accord of July 1987, sought to devolve power to provincial councils throughout Sri Lanka. It contained three lists, which enumerated areas of power devolved to the provinces, retained at the centre, and a concurrent list of shared functions, which were ultimately controlled by Parliament at the centre. However, continued centralization of power was represented by the executive presidency. According to Rohan Edrisinha, "Perhaps the greatest obstacle to practical devolution was the first phrase of the Reserved List, which provided for 'National Policy on all Subjects and Functions' to be determined by Parliament. This phrase completely undermined powers apparently devolved to the provinces. Since the inauguration of the 13th Amendment, Parliament has used this rubric often to encroach into the provincial sphere."[7]

So far the most radical proposals for ending the ethnic conflict through a constitutional arrangement has been the "Devolution Package" of August 1995, proposed by the government as a draft document. This sought to redefine "the constitutional foundation of a plural society." The provincial councils of the 13th Amendment were renamed as Regional Councils with added powers. According to Edrisinha:

> the deletion of Articles Two and 76 of the constitution, which entrenched the unitary character of Sri Lanka, removed an unnecessary obstacle to substantial devolution. The abolition of the Concurrent List was another positive feature, as were other attempts to remove ambiguity in the division of powers. These included the clarification of the role of provincial governors and the awarding of greater revenue raising powers to the regional council.[8]

However, a major weakness in the proposed regional councils would have been the ability of the executive president to dissolve a council in case of emergency. Further, its framers failed to respond to the larger issues, such as those of self-determination and nationhood, and obtaining the concurrence of the LTTE, which rejected the devolution package as being insufficient.

OBSTACLES TO PEACE

Despite the progress in the peace process since the election of a new government in December 2001, there remain concerns about the sustainability of the peace process. Sections of the opposition are vigorously opposing the cease-fire agreement on various grounds as being unconstitutional, a "sell-out," and as paving the ground for a renewed LTTE military campaign for separation. Spearheading the opposition to the cease-fire agreement is the JVP (People's Liberation Front), a Marxist-oriented political party that attempted to violently overthrow the government in 1971 and again in 1988–89. On both occasions, the JVP was militarily suppressed at the cost of tens of thousands of lives, estimated at around 15,000 and 30,000, respectively.

The JVP's position draws upon a perception shared by many Sinhalese that the devolution of power is a means of dividing the country along ethnic lines. The fears of the division of the country in the minds of a sizeable proportion of the Sinhalese constitutes a major obstacle to a negotiated solution with the LTTE. Clearly, the preferred option of this section of the population is a military solution that could eliminate the LTTE, and thereby end the threat to the country's unity.

A second obstacle is the continued rivalry between the government and opposition parties in the Sri Lankan political mainstream, in which the ethnic conflict becomes yet another means of one side embarrassing the other for narrow political gain. Godfrey Goonatilleke has written:

A clear lesson emerging from past failures is that no effort at resolving the conflict will succeed unless there is a broad-based consensus within each community, Sinhala and Tamil, around a solution that is perceived by both as equitable. The internal power struggles within both the communities—Sinhala and Tamil—have continuously thwarted such a process of consensus building. The negotiations took place in a changing configuration of political power with the constant prospect of changes of government, in which the ethnic issue was perceived as being a crucial factor. The history of negotiations up to 1990 shows that each of the two major Sinhala-dominated political parties, SLFP and UNP, have endeavoured to reach a political settlement when they have been in power and have opposed or thwarted a settlement when are in opposition. The party in power then opts for an easy way out of the dilemma by withdrawing its proposal. It justifies its action on the ground that they cannot obtain the support of the people.[9]

Gunatilleke continues,

The other feature in the Sinhala–Tamil relations was the incapacity or unwillingness of the Sinhala leadership to resist the well organized, highly vocal pressure groups within their own constituency. This became a recurring characteristic of Sinhala–Tamil negotiations.[10]

As for Bandaranaike himself, his

convictions were not deep enough to oppose the Sinhala leaders who would not concede that the Tamils had genuine grievances or that their aspirations for a share of power were reasonable. Above all, the Tamil issue seemed to be at the periphery of the political agenda, and largely for demographic reasons the dissatisfaction of the Tamils seemed manageable. What pre-occupied Bandaranaike and other Sinhala leaders was the socio-economic socialist agenda and its impact upon the population as a whole.[11]

For many years now those who are community leaders and political analysts have been calling for a consensus between the two major political parties for a solution to the long drawn out ethnic conflict to emerge. But in doing so, they may have glossed over the political realities that have kept the two dominant parties apart on the issue. The hard fact is that the Sinhalese community, which by far forms the largest segment of the electorate, is still more or less evenly divided on the question of political reforms that could lead to a political settlement of the ethnic conflict.

A public opinion poll commissioned by the National Peace Council in 1999 and carried out by Research International

showed that up to 48 percent of the Sinhalese polled did not
favor using the government's devolution package in negotiations with the LTTE, with only 41 percent in favor. Although
48 percent of Sinhalese were in favor of government–LTTE
negotiations, another 48 percent were not in favor, and 37 percent favored an outright military solution.[12] More recent opinion
polls carried out show that upwards of 80 percent of those sur-
veyed approve of the present cease-fire, and believe that peace
talks are the way to resolve the conflict.[13] But the hard reality
of a Sinhalese population that is not united in meeting Tamil
negotiating positions cannot be glossed over. A significant proportion of these also express their disquiet about the concessions
being made on the ground. They are clearly divided though perhaps with those willing to accept a political solution and compromise, enjoying the upper hand at this time.

While it has long been believed that at various levels the
defence establishment has been a beneficiary of the ethnic conflict and the associated war, it is noticeable that these vested
interests have not been able to pose any sort of open challenge
to the present cease-fire agreement. The military appears to
be co-operating with the government in the cease-fire at the
present time, suggesting that the strength of the military's
vested interest in the continuation of the war has been overesti-
mated. Certainly, the conditions of war have permitted rentseek-
ing behavior at all levels of the military, such as at checkpoints,
where an unofficial tax can be extracted from the traders and
civilians. Massive military procurements have led to allegations
of commissions determining the nature of such purposes. But
the manner in which the military has been co-operating with
the new government in the cease-fire also suggests that the
military is unable to resist a political leadership that is determined to engage in non-violent conflict resolution.

A further obstacle to a peace settlement would be the difficulty
that the LTTE is likely to encounter in adjusting to a non-
military lifestyle in conformity with democratic practices. Since
its inception in the early 1970s, the LTTE has been a highly
centralized and militarized organization without an effective
political wing. At present due to the Norwegian-facilitated peace
process, an LTTE political wing appears to be emerging, but

unlike the Sinn Fein–IRA arrangement in Northern Ireland, the LTTE's political wing is completely under the domination of the military leadership, and the LTTE's undisputed leader Velupillai Prabakaran. Further, the LTTE leader has an Indian arrest warrant against him due to the Indian judiciary's finding that the LTTE was responsible for the assassination of former Indian Prime Minister Rajiv Gandhi in 1991. These circumstances will make it more difficult for the LTTE to enter the mainstream of civil and political life.

Two Lessons

The new government's strategy is a complete shift from that of the previous government, which was to confront the LTTE at every level. The government's strategy appears to be based on an assessment of the former government's failure to succeed through confrontation. After the collapse of the peace talks with the LTTE at the very beginning of its term of office in April 1995, the former government declared a full-scale war for peace. The two-pronged military and political strategy aimed to weaken, and sideline the LTTE. But both types of confrontation failed. Initially, the retaking of Jaffna by the Sri Lankan Army, through Operation Riviresa in November 1995, seemed to indicate that the military strategy of full-scale confrontation would succeed. But thereafter, poorly executed military campaigns, such as the two-and-a-half year Operation Jayasikuru to retake the A9 main road to Jaffna failed at very high cost. Instead of being militarily weakened, the LTTE emerged militarily strengthened from these major confrontations. The former government's political prong against the LTTE in the form of the devolution package, which offered much hope in its initial manifestation of August 1995, could also not be sustained. The government fiercely confronted all political opponents of its devolution package, even incurring the curses of religious prelates upon it. But ultimately, the government's bid to transmute the devolution package into constitutional law proved unsuccessful. In a replay of partisan politics that has dogged all political efforts down the decades to end the ethnic conflict through negotiations, the opposition led by Ranil Wickremesinghe simply refused to co-operate.

It seems that the new government under Prime Minister Wickremesinghe has absorbed two important lessons from the former government's failure. The first is that head-on confrontation will not bring a solution to the ethnic conflict. Accordingly, political and structural reforms might have to be de facto rather than de jure, to be acquiesced in by the general population with whom as little information as possible is shared. The alternative of explaining everything in detail to the people in order to get them to vote in favor of the settlement is likely to get into too much controversy. There is deep-rooted resistance in the Sinhalese community to fundamental constitutional reform that would lead to power sharing across the ethnic and regional lines. Further, the LTTE too thrives on confrontation, by its astuteness in ensuring that the costs of any confrontational situation are piled onto the Tamil civilian population, creating in them alienation towards the government, which is made to appear as the source of the problem.

The second lesson evidently learnt by the new government is that all outstanding problems cannot be resolved in one go, but require a stage by stage approach. The two-pronged approach of the former government aimed at knock-out victories, such as by the Jaffna victory, and the devolution package. But even when the task was accomplished, as in the retaking and successful holding of Jaffna, the resilience of the LTTE ensured that the victory was incomplete. It is likely that even if the devolution package had been passed with the bipartisan support of the opposition, its implementation would have been impossible due to resistance by the LTTE. Having witnessed, and contributed to, the failure of the former government's confrontational strategy, the new government appears to have opted for a non-confrontational strategy for at least the time being.

Two Scenarios

The inability of the Sri Lankan state to wrest back control over these areas over the past 15 years is a key feature of the current situation. A viable strategy for the government would be to accept the situation of dual military power, so long as there is no major fighting between the two armies, one controlled by the government, the other by the LTTE. However, recognizing the fact that the LTTE is unlikely to be content with remaining confined in its political power to the areas currently under its direct military control, they will have to be given a greater scope for such power in northeast areas under government control as well. It is likely that both the government and LTTE will see this arrangement to be an indefinitely extendable one in which the major military contests between the two sides are put to an end. With the onset of peace there is likely to be enhanced economic growth and activity leading to incremental political changes that introduce more democratic practices as business prospers. Whether the LTTE will be satisfied with ruling the northeast by proxy, and for how long the Sri Lankan government will wish to continue this arrangement where it effectively cedes de jure sovereignty over a part of its territory, will be a matter of uncertainty.

The alternative course of straightforward political negotiations between the government and LTTE leading to a new constitutional order and permanent political settlement is superficially more attractive, but is unlikely to be feasible for two key reasons. The first is the unlikelihood of the government being able to obtain the bipartisan support of the opposition for this purpose. The Sri Lankan constitution requires a two-third majority in Parliament for any constitutional amendment, followed by a referendum at which the people have to give their consent to changes in any entrenched constitutional provision. Changes in the political structure that would satisfy the LTTE and Tamil aspirations would undoubtedly require an uprooting of Article Two of the constitution that specifies that the state shall be unitary, which means that far-reaching devolution of powers is not possible so long as it is in existence. As Article Two is an entrenched provision of the constitution, it would require popular approval at a referendum. However, the unvarying pattern of the past is that the political parties in opposition do not lend their support to the parties in government when it comes to addressing the ethnic conflict. Instead, they use the occasion of an anticipated political reform to oppose the government on the grounds that it is endangering the unity of the country.

From its inception, the LTTE has had an ideological commitment to an independent state of Tamil Eelam, with its letterhead having the motto—"The thirst of the Tigers is Tamil Eelam." Motivated by this vision of independence, several hundred LTTE cadres have died in combat or assassination bids as suicide bombers. The LTTE has killed the leadership of every other Tamil political party, including other guerrilla groups, and many leading members of the Sri Lankan government. Ever since its inception, the LTTE has had only one leader, Velupillai Prabakaran, who enjoys a cult status within the organization, and is believed to be a virtual superman outside. For such an autocratic, ruthless, and committed organization to join the democratic mainstream within the framework of a united Sri Lanka, in which there is a Sinhalese majority, and be subjected to the checks and balances of democracy, is difficult to envisage at this time.

At present, the LTTE appears to be satisfied with the government's willingness not to push them too soon into discussing the political issues, and appears to be co-operating with the government. However, the danger exists of the government permitting the cease-fire to continue indefinitely without addressing the hard political issues that underlie the ethnic conflict. The government must be prepared to acknowledge the hard political issues and make a commitment that it is prepared to deal with them after a stable cease-fire has been reached. Clearly, what is appropriate at this time is not a full-fledged negotiation on political issues. The time is still premature for such a political solution. What the LTTE wants, and must ask for, at this time, is too much for the government to concede. These would include an autonomous arrangement that includes the Thimpu principles of Tamil nationhood, self-determination, and homelands. Likewise, what the government will want of the LTTE is too much for the LTTE to concede at this time, particularly, the renunciation of a separate state, and the decommissioning of arms. While the gap between the government and LTTE on the political issues is too wide to be bridged at this time, there is a likelihood that a successful cease-fire that lasts a further year, and is accompanied by rapid economic growth, would serve as a confidence-building measure. It could make the gap in the positions of the government and LTTE more bridgeable in the years ahead. The prospect of resolving the hard political issues by negotiating a durable and just political solution could also become the motivation to maintain the cease-fire.

The building blocks of a negotiated solution would be the non-negotiables of the two sides. On the government side, it would be the unity and territorial integrity of the country. On the LTTE side it would be the Thimpu principles, which lay claim to the Tamils being a nation, with a homeland, and the right of self-determination. The LTTE would also wish to keep their arms for the foreseeable future. The constitutional and political arrangements suggested by these determinants would be a variant of federalism and confederalism. Asymmetric federalism, that provides the Tamil-dominated region more powers than other regions of the country, was suggested by Prime Minister Ranil Wickremesinghe when he was leader of the opposition. It is likely that the devolution of powers to the Tamil-dominated region would be more substantial in areas that have been contested ones, such as education, land, industry, and security. Provision would also have to be made for the protection of the rights of the Tamil-speaking Muslim minority, and Sinhalese in the north and east that will come under Tamil majority rule. Further, given the ethnic mix outside of the northeast, and the large numbers of Tamils and Muslims outside of the north and the east, mechanisms to ensure power-sharing at the centre and the rights of ethnic minorities countrywide would also need to be found.

Where questions of political power and constitutional reforms are concerned, there is likely to be a high degree of contestation regarding the way forward to a mutually acceptable solution. There will undoubtedly be differences between the government, opposition, and LTTE. These differences pertaining to issues of governance will be reflected among the people at large. A more democratic and consultative type of decision-making will be required at this later stage than what the new government appears to be contemplating. Civil society organizations need to be preparing the people for the restructuring of the polity in the longer term. The international community will have to play an important and effective role. The past experience with the LTTE has been one of disengagement once discussions reach substantive issues. This is on account of the wide gap between

LTTE demands and what Sri Lankan governments have hitherto been prepared to offer. The success of the peace talks would
depend largely on international pressure that would keep the
government and LTTE at the negotiations table, and compel
them towards compromise.

The latest breakthrough in Oslo in November 2002 was in
keeping with the record set by the government and LTTE following the general election of December 2001. The statement
issued by the Norwegian facilitators at the close of the third
session of peace talks in Oslo stated that

> Responding to a proposal by the leadership of the LTTE, the parties
> agreed to explore a solution founded on the principle of internal self-
> determination in areas of historical habitation of the Tamil-speaking
> people based on a federal structure within a united Sri Lanka. The
> parties acknowledged that the solution has to be acceptable to all
> communities.[14]

Just as the lifting of the security barriers in Colombo in February
caught most people by surprise, so was the latest announcement
regarding the acceptability of a federal model of government
by the two parties. Until that announcement, the LTTE had never
categorically stated what type of concrete political solution it
would be prepared to accept.

Viable Alternative

For the past several years the LTTE had been saying it was
prepared to accept a viable alternative to Tamil Eelam. But it
never specified what this might mean. The farthest it would go
was to say that this viable alternative should be in accordance
with the principles worked out jointly by all Tamil parties par-
ticipating at the Thimpu peace talks in 1985. The relevant principles being Tamil nationhood, Tamil self-determination, and
Tamil traditional homelands, it was not surprising that they
were construed both by successive governments, and by Sinhalese
nationalists to mean nothing short of independence. However,
in the context of the mutual inability of the government and
LTTE to militarily defeat each other in the territory demarcated
as the traditional homeland, some analysts believed that the

LTTE would settle for nothing less than a confederation. In broad terms, a confederation is a political system in which two or more separate states, with their own prime ministers, parliaments, and armies, are loosely tied to each other for specific purposes. The Commonwealth of Independent States, which was formed in the aftermath of the collapse of the Soviet Union would be one example.

During the years of war, sections of Tamil opinion held fast to the confederal model. This may have included the LTTE as well, to the extent that those who were fighting a war could think in terms of constitutional concepts. But inasmuch as the present peace process has opened the closed roads of the north and east, so has it opened the Tamil nationalist movement to the mainstream currents of international thinking on governance in multi-ethnic societies. It is likely that in the engagement and dialogue taking place due to the peace process, the reality of federalism as the only viable alternative will make its presence felt. However, the difficulties likely to be faced by the LTTE leadership in accepting a federal model need to be appreciated. After all, federalism was the slogan of half a century ago. In a sense the acceptance of a federal model is to go back in order to go forward to the future. Sections of Tamil nationalist opinion residing abroad, and in Colombo away from the battlegrounds of the northeast may prefer a harder bargaining position. Besides the LTTE military cadre itself has been inculcated with a deep yearning for an independent state of Tamil Eelam epitomized in the standard LTTE cry—"The thirst of the Tigers is Tamil Eelam."

It is ironic that the LTTE negotiators will be charged with not bargaining hard enough in the same way that the government negotiators are being criticized by sections of the political opposition. The answer to the charge is that the two sides are not negotiating in a spirit of bargaining. Those who pride themselves on being hard bargainers are often too insensitive to realize that their so-called success is at the cost of long-term building of relationships. They might get themselves a good bargain on one occasion. But the relationship is unlikely to survive. Usually hard bargaining is most effective in a one-off negotiation, such as when bargaining on the street with a

pavement hawker. However, when it comes to long-term relationships, those who engage in hard bargaining are likely to
fail. Sustaining long-term relationships requires a different type
of negotiations in which the interests of each side are met in a
fair and reasonable manner. It seems that the government and
LTTE negotiators have engaged in such interest-based negotiations with one another. They have not tried to defeat each
other at the negotiating table, but have instead sought to engage
in joint problem-solving. In short, they appear to have sat together on the same side of the table to solve a common problem
that was ruining the country and its entire people.

Federalism is a standard constitutional system that exists in
many countries of the world. It is particularly effective in permitting power sharing between ethnic communities in multi-
ethnic societies. Federalism permits national minorities who
are regional majorities to enjoy the right of self-determination,
and thereby, wield political power at the regional level. But 50
years ago when the Tamil-dominated Federal Party launched
its campaign for a federal state in the north and east of Sri Lanka,
Sinhalese nationalists opposed it as a stepping-stone to a separate state. Federalism was bitterly opposed by Sinhalese nationalists to the extent that it became a bad word to mainstream
political parties. But after two decades of war, the reality of virtual
separation has dawned upon most people. Most of the north
and east was inaccessible to the people living in the rest of the
country. Federalism has now become the stepping-stone in re-
uniting a divided country and bringing long-term prosperity
and peace to all its inhabitants. Shortly, before the Oslo peace
talks in October 2002, the Presidential Secretariat issued a
statement in which President Chandrika Kumaratunga said
that "the PA was the only political party to spell out its devolution of power proposal as a draft constitution in 1997 and still
upheld the devolution of power along a federalist or Indian
model within a united Sri Lanka."[15] Accordingly, the government
and main opposition party stand on common ground with respect to a political solution based on federal principles. They
need to put their personal and political rivalries aside and find
a means to collaborate to make a permanent and a just peace a
reality for all communities inhabiting Sri Lanka.

NOTES AND REFERENCES

1. Embassy of the United States, Colombo, Press Release, March 11, 2002.
2. *Sunday Leader*, March 17, 2002.
3. S. Kohobanwickrema, "A Lost Referendum," *Island*, December 15, 2001.
4. National Peace Council, *Cost of the War*, Colombo, 2001.
5. Ibid. p. 28.
6. A.J. Wilson, S.J.V. Chelvanayakam, *The Crisis of Sri Lankan Tamil Nationalism, 1947–77: A Political Biography*. London, 1994, p. 86, 105.
7. Rohan Edrisinha, "Trying Times: Constitutional Efforts to Resolve Armed Conflict in Sri Lanka," in Jeremy Armon and Liz Philipson (ed.), *Accord, Demanding Sacrifice: War and Negotiation in Sri Lanka*. Issue 4, 1993, Conciliation Resources, London, in association with Social Services Association, Colombo, p. 29.
8. Ibid. p. 33.
9. Godfrey Gunatilleke, p. 51.
10. Godfrey Gunatilleke, *Negotiations for the Resolution of the Ethnic Conflict*. Marga: Monograph Series on Ethnic Reconciliation, no. 1, 2001, p. 11.
11. Godfrey Gunatilleke, ibid., p. 12.
12. National Peace Council, *What the People Think About the Ethnic Conflict—Results of Opinion Polls*, Colombo, 2000.
13. *Social Indicator*, October 2002.
14. *Daily Mirror*, November 3, 2002.
15. *Daily Mirror*, October 30, 2002.

Section III

Peace Accords

INTRODUCTION

Parimal Ghosh

The tragedy of decolonization is that it frequently brings in its wake a rude awakening to the harsh realities of nation building. During the freedom struggles, often an overtly idealistic homogeneity is projected while imagining the nation, and the fissures and fragments are either ignored, or plastered over. This may even be seen as a necessary tactic for creating a united front against foreign rulers. The post-colonial rulers soon become trapped in their own rhetoric, and are unable to reconsider their options once power devolves upon them. What once was a merely tactical projection of "national" unity in the face of foreign domination, soon assumes the status of a sacrosanct identity—immutable, and often divine, in its proportions. Any attempt at interrogating, or even revising the format on the part of the marginalized communities within the body politic of a newly independent state is then seen as a betrayal of nationhood. The tragedy further deepened when the British Indian territories were partitioned into two, and subsequently three separate states. The event as we are painfully aware, gave rise to enormous mutual suspicion, resulting in the spectre of ever increasing military spending, three bloodsoaked wars, and now the unthinkable, the possibility of a nuclear confrontation. Accords viewed in this light may be seen as the instruments through which states in this region try to come to terms with their own fractured nations.

Of the four papers, three deal directly with this fairly common syndrome of newly independent states, whereas the fifth is concerned with another equally typical facet of the internal working of underdeveloped states—its inability to chart out an independent policy for developing its natural resources.

Subir Bhaumik weaves a more cynical account of how the Indian state sought to overwhelm both politically and militarily the Naga resistance. In the early years after independence, when the Indian state was not sufficiently confident, or by a different reading, some elements of idealism from the Indian freedom struggle were still alive in the minds of the leaders ruling the country, substantial concessions were made to the Nagas. But over time as the state gained in strength and became more sure of itself, it strove for splitting the Naga leaders creating thereby a moderate faction, with which it could make a deal. Relentless counterinsurgency military operations, coupled with the circumstances leading to the dismemberment of Pakistan and the emergence of Bangladesh, immensely strengthened the position of the Indian state in the northeast. This was the background to the "sell-out" recorded in the Shillong Accord of 1975. The insurgent Nagas, fighting for about 25 years, for the right to develop in their own way, were now forced to submit. In exchange, as Bhaumik puts it, they received absolutely nothing.

Amena Mohsin tells a similar tale from a feminist perspective with regard to the struggle in Chittagong Hill Tracts in Bangladesh. The liberation war in Bangladesh was fought to establish the right of self-determination of the Bengali-speaking people. But once the state of Bangladesh was born, it chose to forget its own travails under Pakistani rule when the right of the Bengali people to their own language and culture was consistently trampled upon. In its turn, after achieving independence, the state of Bangladesh took up a policy which aimed at creating a homogenous nation. From the very beginning, the declared aim of the newly born republic was to establish the domination of the language and culture of the Bengali people, in the process ignoring the rights of the various minorities. A particularly unfortunate instance of this was the fate of the Chakmas in Chittagong Hill Tracts. Almost immediately after independence, Sheikh Mujib, the first premier of Bangladesh, made it clear that there was going to be one nation in Bangladesh, the Bengali nation, and no claim to any separate identity would be entertained. The constitution adopted a unitary structure, even though under Pakistani rule the Awami League had struggled for a federal system to safeguard Bengali language and culture. Besides, Mohsin draws our attention to another well-known dimension of this familiar story—that of patriarchy, the manner in which the state machinery wiped out the memories of sacrifice of women in the freedom struggle. It is difficult to avoid the impression that, in this regard, more than the intentions of the state what counted was the attitude of the society at large. It appears from evidence that some 200,000 women were raped by Pakistani soldiers. The nation too chose to forget them as well as the war babies. Amena Mohsin's paper points out how the nation-building project in newly independent states of South Asia involved marginalization of both ethnic minorities and women, and how these two are complementary to each other.

The paper by Dipak Gyawali and Ajaya Dixit on the Indo-Nepal conflict over the utilization of the Mahakali River waters illustrates another facet of the behavior pattern of a big state in relation to its smaller neighbor, and the way in which this is perceived by various elements within the political establishment of the latter. As the authors point out, there are important lessons to be learnt on both sides. That India, as the predominant economic power in the subcontinent, may in the short run persuade somehow or the other the political leadership of a smaller neighbor to accept its will. And that in the longer run, this does not produce the desirable results. A wiser policy should be to try and achieve a genuine agreement in which the interests of the two sides are protected. For the smaller neighbor, instead of depending on foreign experts and consultants, the goal should be to achieve self-reliance by unleashing the true potentiality of its people.

Mubashir Hasan's paper on India–Pakistan relations is almost like the anguished cry of someone on the "other" side, anxious to reach out across the national divide. Some of the observations may sound a little one-sided to the Indian ear, but the points the author makes remain valid in the discourse of peace. Too often we are plagued by uncertainties about the unknown, and when the governments of the two countries are averse to taking risk, the only way to serve the peace movement is to increase contacts at all levels of the civil society.

8

THE ACCORD THAT NEVER WAS: SHILLONG ACCORD, 1975

Subir Bhaumik

Since 1947, the Indian government has signed three accords with various strands of Naga leadership. The Nine-point agreement was signed between the Governor of Assam Sir Akbar Hydari, and the Naga National Council (NNC) in June that year. The 16-point agreement between the Indian government, and the Naga Peoples' Convention, made up of moderates opposed to the NNC, was signed in July 1960. The Shillong Accord was signed on November 11, 1975 between the Government of India and the "Underground Nagas," a term used to denote those elements within the NNC that were willing to surrender their weapons, and accept the Indian Constitution as the basis for "future settlement."

I

These three accords reflect as many distinct phases in Indo-Naga relations. In 1947, the Indian state was still uncertain about its ability to handle intransigent princely states or freedom-loving peoples, such as the Nagas. Gandhi was still alive and was said to be unwilling to use force to bring the Nagas into India. Hence, the Nine-point agreement provided the NNC, which was already demanding self-determination, a lot of powers in running the administration of the Naga Hills. These powers were arbitrarily withdrawn as independent India successfully incorporated the princely states, and then turned to deal with the Naga movement for self-determination with a heavy hand.

As the rebellion in the Naga Hills developed into a fierce armed separatist movement, the Indian government unleashed a counterinsurgency campaign, and simultaneously started a dialogue with the moderates in Naga politics. That culminated in the 16-point agreement with the Naga Peoples' Convention in 1960, which paved the way for the creation of a separate state of Nagaland, but one that was within the Indian Union. This marks the first real Indian effort to divide the Naga society between moderates and hardliners, and the concessions accruing from the agreement were intended to create a political space for the moderates to the exclusion of the believers in armed struggle. The Shillong Accord sealed the fate of the NNC. But instead of bringing the Naga armed insurrection to an end, it ended up splitting the NNC into pro-accord and no-accord factions that led to the emergence of the breakaway National Socialist Council of Nagaland, or the NSCN. In a matter of four years, the NSCN had pushed the NNC into complete oblivion.

On the eve of the British withdrawal from the sub-continent, the NNC's predominance in the Naga Hills stood at its peak. The Nine-point agreement recognized it. The Nine-point agreement laid down nine areas where the NNC could exercise its authority ranging from the judicial to the executive, and the legislative. The NNC was left in control of the resources and land in the Naga Hills, and a mechanism to impose, collect, and spend land revenue was detailed under the agreement. The Accord made it clear that the "Nagas had the right to develop according to their own wishes," and expressed the desirability to "bring under one unified administrative unit, so far as possible, all the Nagas." Fifty years hence, the terms of the Nine-point agreement would appear to be a distant dream for any Naga aspiring for self-determination. If the Nine-point agreement marked the peak of the NNC's predominance in Naga politics, the Shillong Accord marked its nadir because it denied the NNC any recognition as the legitimate representative of the Naga rebel movement, and merely dismissed it off as "Underground Nagas." In between, the 1960 agreement is believed to be the most substantive in terms of political concessions made to the Nagas, because it led to the creation of a separate state of Nagaland within the Indian union.

Detailing the other accords, except the one signed at Shillong in 1975, is beyond the scope of his paper. But this writer believes that it was no mistake on the part of the detractors of the Shillong Accord to describe it as a "sell-out" because the Nagas got nothing out of it after 20 years of bloody fighting. A series of only four rounds of discussions preceded the signing of the Shillong Accord—some alone with the Governor for the Northeast states, L.P. Singh, others with the Governor and two of his advisers on Nagaland, Murkot Ramunny and Pu Zopianga. All five members of the Liaison Committee, who mediated between the Naga rebel leaders and the Governor, participated in the final round of the discussions.

The most redeeming feature of the Shillong Accord was its size and style of reference. The entire Accord was encapsulated in just one printed page because it had only three brief clauses. Later, a supplementary agreement with five sub-clauses related to the depositing of weapons was signed on January 5, 1976.[1] The Shillong Accord denied any legitimacy to the Naga National Council. As stated before, the text of the Shillong Accord described the signatories from the Naga side as "Underground Nagas." In fact, the failure to secure the bare minimum of recognition as an organization from the Indian government, after having led the Naga armed struggle for nearly 20 years, was later responsible for the withering away of the NNC, leaving the space to be occupied by the breakaway National Socialist Council of Nagaland (NSCN). This was a major comedown for the NNC, which in 1947 was recognized as the sole representative organization of the Naga people in the Nine-point agreement. The Shillong Accord must be seen in the historical context in which it was signed. It has been strongly argued by this writer that the Indian government effectively intervened in East Pakistan to deny the northeast Indian rebel groups a regrouping zone in what is now known as Bangladesh. Once the Pakistanis were driven out of the east, the northeast Indian rebel groups were, at least for the time being, denied the use of their nearest foreign sanctuary. Foreign support to the Naga rebellion from China and Pakistan also dropped substantially after the creation of Bangladesh, and the defeat of the Pakistan army in 1971.

II

The Indian government followed this up by going ahead with the territorial reorganization of the northeast in 1972, a move widely seen as an appeasement of the indigenous power-holding elites in northeast India. Some would see the creation of the new states and Union Territories as major concessions to win over the moderate elements, and cement the political space they occupied in rebellion-torn northeast. The political engineering went hand in hand with the fierce counterinsurgency operations in Nagaland, Mizoram, Manipur, and Tripura. A disoriented, weakened Naga rebel movement was either unable to stand up to the might of the Indian military machine whose morale had been boosted enormously by its victory in the 1971 Bangladesh war, or with the guile of its political establishment. In the run-up to the Shillong Accord, the NNC failed to extract any commitment about the future shape of the settlement, that the accord said must emerge in a "reasonable time," between India and the Nagas. And so the Shillong Accord reads like an one-way traffic—the "underground Nagas" agreeing to deposit weapons and abide by the Indian Constitution, and the Indian government merely agreeing to provide "reasonable time" to work out a final settlement. Even this may be seen as a time-buying tactic, because 25 years after the Shillong Accord, the Naga problem is no closer to a solution than was the case in 1975.

In an all-India context, the Shillong Accord was the first of the many accords the Indian government was to sign in the northeast and elsewhere in the country with separatist rebel groups, agitating student organizations, and "moderate" political groups (such as the Longowal faction of the Akali Dal) in the second quarter of the Republic. The first quarter (25 years) of the Republic was marked by fierce military responses to any separatist challenge. But in keeping with the Kautilyan traditions of statecraft, that largely determine the way the Indian nation-state functions, Delhi also came up with a whole mix of political initiatives, largely tactical, but some obviously guided by long-term perceptions of strategic interests. The political initiatives mainly aimed at getting the agitator or the insurgent to the table, to win him over by an offer of wide-ranging concessions (but all framed within the constitutional parameters of

the country) of autonomy and statehood, and if the rebel leadership proved too intransigent to appeasement, then to split the
movement and its leadership in an attempt to forge an understanding with the so-called moderates. The craft centred on
creation of political space in which the "moderates" could maneuver and get a share of power, that would, in the long run,
undermine the rebellion and its raison d'etre.

For those who are inclined to see the Naga rebellion as the
first violent challenge to the post-colonial Indian nation-state,
it would be useful to know that the tribesmen in Tripura, under
the leadership of the undivided Communist Party of India, were
the first ethnic group in India's northeast to resort to armed
struggle, immediately after India's Partition. Their rhetoric was
not secessionist like that of the Nagas. It was left to later-day
insurgent groups in Tripura, like the Tribal National Volunteers
(TNV), to echo the secessionist rhetoric they picked up from
the Naga and Mizo separatists. But, by the end of 1950, the
Tripura rebellion was crushed. With the Communist Party's
change of line (from armed struggle to the parliamentary path)
in the early 1950s, and the absorption of the tribal movement
in its fold, the movement returned to the Indian political mainstream. But no accord had to be signed. That sets the historical
record straight. The Naga armed rebellion was not the first of
its kind in the northeast after India became free—that happened
in Tripura. But the intensity of the Naga rebellion easily sur-
passed what the poorly armed Tripura tribesmen of the Communist underground had been able to generate. The Nagas
started off with Second World War vintage rifles, left behind
by the Japanese, and the Allied forces—but they fought bravely
and heroically against vastly superior Indian forces for nearly
seven years before they were properly equipped, first, by the
Pakistanis, and then by the Chinese. Privately, Indian army
officers and jawans recognize the bravery and the commitment
of the Naga guerrillas, and remembered the ferocity of the fighting in the late 1950s and early 1960s. Several of these officers
have told me during interviews that the Nagas "were a tough
adversary to deal with."[2]

I would argue that the Shillong Accord has no reason to be
seen as a political settlement, which is what it was projected
as. While the Naga rebel leaders agreed to cease hostilities,

surrender weapons, and accepted to "discuss other issues for a final settlement," the Indian government agreed to work towards a final settlement within a "reasonable time." And nearly 25 years after the Shillong Accord, those issues have not yet been properly discussed—even during the ongoing talks with the National Socialist Council of Nagaland (NSCN). In the last (few) years, while Delhi has been negotiating with the NSCN, substantive political issues have not been taken up for discussions. It has taken more than three years to agree on the modalities. One could well say, the absence of a strong government at the centre with the mandate to take crucial decisions, may have caused the delays because bureaucrats do not stick their necks out to take decisions during periods of political uncertainty. But one could also argue that the centre has "run out of ideas"[3]; it does not have a clear vision for bringing about a solution to the Naga problem without upsetting other nationalities in the northeast, and is thus bidding for time.

In June 2001, when the Indian government finally acceded to the NSCN's demand for extending the cease-fire "without territorial limits," it appeared (that) the ice had melted. But within a few days, Manipur went up in flames, nearly 20 protestors falling to police bullets. An unnerved Indian government sent Minister of State for Home Mr I.D. Swamy rushing to Manipur. Swamy's team had to reach the Imphal airport from the Governor's house in a helicopter to catch the flight out to Delhi, as their road was blocked by hundreds of protestors determined to face the security forces. On Swamy's recommendations, Prime Minister Mr Atal Behari Vajpayee agreed to "review the cease-fire agreement in its entirety along with all issues arising out of it."[4] This has upset the NSCN and other Naga organizations believed to be close to it. The NSCN has warned of "greater trouble than witnessed in Manipur" if the Indian government reneged on the cease-fire. But a key purpose has been achieved by Delhi. The controversy generated by the cease-fire agreement has split the rebel movement in the Northeast right down the middle. The Assamese and the Manipuri rebel groups said that they would fight the NSCN if the latter "eyed our ancestral lands." Mass organizations in Manipur, Assam, Arunachal Pradesh, and even Tripura have said that they would unite to fight the cease-fire's extension to their areas as a prelude to the possible creation of a "greater Nagaland" as demanded by the NSCN.[5] This now provides the Indian Home Ministry with fresh opportunities. Caught in the cross-fire of conflicting aspirations, it is all the more expected that Delhi will play the game of drift. It has the right excuse for it now. Having brought the NSCN, easily the strongest rebel group, to the table, it may adopt a policy of sporadic negotiations, of buying time, of not trying for a settlement. The idea would be to wear down the NSCN, and finally get them to accept a deal that gives them very little in real terms. The resistance by other ethnic groups to the concept of a greater Naga state by encompassing all Naga-inhabited areas of India, if not of Myanmar, will be used as a strong excuse for any delay in reaching a final settlement with the Naga rebel groups.

In a way, history has come full circle for the Nagas. The NSCN leaders who denounced the Shillong Accord as a sell-out, now find themselves in the same predicament. Having decided to negotiate with India, the NSCN leaders are beginning to discover "it is perhaps easier fighting the Indians in the hills than fighting them on the table."[6] The question that is bound to arise is how could the leaders of South Asia's one of the strongest ethnic rebellions settle for so less, when they signed the Shillong Accord? To find an answer to this, one would have to look back at the course of the Naga insurrection itself. That will make it clear that the Naga rebels did not negotiate the Accord when their movement was at its peak. There was a time in the late 1960s when Prime Minister Indira Gandhi, upset with the growing Chinese and Pakistani support to the Naga rebel movement, and worried about its growing military strength, was prepared to concede any "legitimate political demand" short of giving up Indian sovereignty over Nagaland. In fact, some Naga rebel leaders and Indian officials close to Prime Minister Indira Gandhi say that she was at one stage on the verge of "accepting a Bhutan-style protectorate arrangement with Nagas."[7] But the moment Indira Gandhi found the Naga National Council divided along tribal lines (Sema vs Angami), she shelved the proposal, and covered it up so well, that very few people are aware of it now. As the NNC split and the Sema leaders formed a separate parallel government (the Revolutionary Government of Nagaland or RGN), Mrs Gandhi and her advisers sidelined the NNC, and boosted the RGN, aggravating the divide within the Naga society and its once-powerful underground.

III

Then came the war of 1971, and the Indian forces crushed Pakistan, liberating its eastern wing. Independent Bangladesh was born. In one stroke, Delhi had deprived all northeast Indian rebels of its main regrouping zone. China, though still keen to help train, and arm the rebels, was too far away. Mrs Gandhi not merely unleashed a powerful military offensive to further weaken the Naga rebel movement and the local administration continued to secure large scale surrenders, but also went in for a comprehensive reorganization of the northeast immediately after the Bangladesh War, and that led to the creation of new states and ever-new power-sharing mechanism that would lead to the co-option of the local elites in the national power structure. A brief review of circumstances leading to the Shillong Accord would justify my contention. In the process, I would seek to highlight (a) the political failure of the Naga underground in making the most of its military success at the right time, (b) the emergence of the Nagaland state, and the space it created for political groups that sought a middle road between the Indian political establishment and the underground.

As India waited for its freedom from the British, the Nagas said they must have theirs as well. The argument put forward by the Naga National Council was straight and simple: Down the centuries, the Nagas had lived a free existence, bereft of kings or overlords until the British came and conquered them. So, they said, they should be left alone, free as before, once the British left. But the leaders of independent India would have none of it. Any area deciding to opt out of India was seen as a threat to the infant post-colonial nation-state. So in the confusion that prevailed in the last days of British rule, with millions killed in unprecedented communal riots, a Nine-point Agreement was worked out by Assam's Governor Sir Akbar Hydari in June 1947 with the Naga National Council. This agreement provided the first framework of administration in the Naga Hills, but it said in no uncertain terms in its preamble:

"The right of the Nagas to develop themselves according to their freely expressed wishes is recognized." In fact, the ambiguity in this Nine-point Agreement was believed to be responsible for the future discord between India and the Naga National Council. In its last paragraph, the Agreement said: "The Governor of Assam as the Agent of the Government of the Indian Union will have special responsibility for a period of 10 years to ensure the due observance of the agreement." At the end of this period, the Naga National Council was to be asked whether they require the agreement to be modified.

The NNC interpreted this clause as right to withdraw from the Indian Union if it so desired. The Indian government interpreted it as an option to change the administrative structure in the Naga Hills—but nothing more than that. "The nature of the Naga question is a typical example of the problems arising from the process of decolonization in many parts of the world."[8] The creation of multi-racial post-colonial states has led to the emergence of majoritarian nation-states in the Third World, in which the voice of the smaller ethnic minorities, such as that of the Nagas, has been suppressed. So, in 1955, with the Indians consolidating their grip in the Naga Hills, and rejecting any attempt by the NNC to open a political dialogue on the "the future of the Nagas," the NNC decided to take the path of armed insurrection. Once it started, it spread quite quickly to the Naga Hills and other Naga-inhabited areas of Manipur. Within a year, the Naga Army's ranks had swelled from 500 to 15,000 soldiers.[9] Later, the Burmese Nagas also joined cause with the NNC, forming the Eastern Naga Revolutionary Council. That made the Naga Army the largest rebel force in South Asia at that point of time.

But the intensity of the rebellion varied in different parts of the Naga Hills and from tribe to tribe. The Indian pacification campaign adopted a tribe-by-tribe approach—win over the elders of a particular tribe, use them to open negotiations with the underground in a particular area, and then bring about their surrender by accepting essentially local level demands. Once Nagaland became a state in 1963, the administration reverted back to a district-by-district approach for pacification/ containment. Mr S.C. Dev of the Indian Frontier Administrative Service, who served in several districts of Nagaland, played a key role in the Indian pacification/containment strategy, and his account provides a rare insight into Indian decision-making in Nagaland during its most critical years.[10] It becomes clear from Mr Dev's account that the Indian administration supplemented the ongoing military campaigns with a propaganda drive to isolate guerrilla bands, to be followed by negotiations with their leaders through church leaders, local *dobhasis* (interpreters), or their relatives. It targeted the grassroots organizations of the Naga National Council/Federal Government of Nagaland in specific areas for surrenders, rather than attempting a comprehensive settlement through talks until 1964. Delhi was repeatedly advised by its officials that India should negotiate from a position of strength, not from a position of weakness, and that it should wait "until we gained the upper hand over the rebels and could clearly dictate terms."[11] This answers why India could finally manage to impose something like the Shillong Accord on such a strong rebel movement as that of the Nagas. While India carried on political pacification at the grassroots and managed to create a "democratic alternative" in the Naga Hills through the Naga Peoples' Convention (and later the NNO), it persisted with military action against the rebels until they were weak enough to be played around with, and the external environment had gone against them.

IV

In 1956, as fighting intensified between the Indian security forces and the Naga rebels, the first fissures in the NNC came to surface with the mysterious murder of Thieyieu Sakhrie. The NNC chief A.Z. Phizo was blamed for the assassination, as a note found on Sakhrie's dead body said, "This is the man who betrayed the Nagas." A case is still pending against Phizo for the alleged complicity in Sakhrie's murder, an incident that shocked a lot of Nagas who were beginning to have doubts over the success of the armed rebellion. Sakhrie had played no mean a role in boosting the NNC machinery, as he "wrote everything from memorandums to recruitment appeals." It is perhaps a strange coincidence that Sakhrie's death was followed by Phizo's departure from the Naga Hills. With Pakistani help, Phizo reached London where he spent the rest of his life, trying in vain, to internationalize the Naga issue. But Sakhrie's death also led to the first desertions from the underground—leaders like Phizo's one-time lieutenant John Bosco Jasokie left the NNC in sheer disgust. Later, even leaders like T.N. Angami left. This created the first nucleus of a returnee leadership that the Indian government could use against the NNC.

In 1957, a few Naga leaders convened a meeting under the banner of the Naga Peoples' Convention, saying they wanted to "mediate" between the Indian government and the Naga National Council. The NPC was made up of several former underground sympathisers, many of them fed up with the bloodshed. Its first convention was held in Kohima between August 22–26, 1957. The NNC initially agreed to send representatives but later backed out, "sensing that this was an Indian ploy to get us to the table at any cost."[12] The NPC's resolution maintained that "an early answer to the Naga question was to find a satisfactory political settlement."[13] The NPC said that "in order to create the conditions necessary for a political settlement," it was necessary to merge the Naga Hills District with the Tuensang Frontier Division of the North Eastern Frontier Agency (NEFA) into a single administrative unit, which should then be placed under the External Affairs Ministry. The NPC also appealed to all Nagas to "give up the cult of violence," and it promised to work for a peaceful settlement to end hostilities that would lead to the withdrawal of the army and the de-grouping of the villages.

On September 27, 1957, an NPC delegation led by its president Imkongliba Ao met Prime Minister Jawaharlal Nehru in Delhi, and Nehru accepted all the proposals put forward by the NPC. Delhi's political offensive, to create an alternative centre of power to that of the Naga National Council, had started. On December 1, 1957, the new administrative unit known as the "Naga Hills Tuensang Area" (NHTA) was formed, and placed under the External Affairs Ministry. A general amnesty was granted and the de-grouping of the villages was undertaken. The NNC rejected these moves, dubbed the NPC as "stooges of the Indian government," and remained un-reconciled.

However, the NPC now shifted to a different gear. Its initial stand was to "mediate" between the underground and the Indian government. But in its third convention held at Mokukchung during October 22–26, 1959, it drew up a 16-point memorandum, which ultimately formed the basis for the 16-point Agreement between the Indian government and the NPC in 1960. That led to the creation of a separate state called Nagaland, incorporating the Naga Hills district and the Tuensang frontier area. Phizo, then in London, denounced the NPC–Delhi understanding, but once Nagaland became a full-fledged state, the underground had clearly lost the first round.

The 16-point Agreement was a substantive agreement between two parties. The Indian government took a big step forward by making Nagaland a state. The northeast had been kept out of the process of linguistic reorganization. Except the erstwhile princely states of Tripura and Manipur, the rest of the region was administered from Assam, or as parts of Assam. As the Naga insurrection began to peak, Delhi proceeded to placate the Nagas. The creation of Nagaland as a separate state was intended to take the sting out of the rebellion—it was to put in place a new moderate leadership, which would accept the Indian constitution and its control over Nagaland for substantial concessions, in terms of autonomy. So, in a way, the NPC got much more out of Delhi in the 1960 agreement than the rebel leaders could manage in the Shillong Accord. In fact, the 16-point Agreement constituted the basis of Nagaland's future political status within India—a status that has so far remained unchanged. As Nagaland became a separate state, the rebels unleashed a furious guerrilla campaign. Attacks on security forces mounted, and "moderate" Naga politicians were also killed. The assassination of the NPC president, Dr Imkongliba Ao, as he came out of his clinic in Kohima, further divided Naga society, as those Nagas who were fed up with the killings and the fighting sympathized with Dr Ao. But the NNC continued to send handpicked guerrillas for training to East Pakistan to intensify their separatist campaign against India. Between 1959 and 1963, when the political initiative to make Nagaland a state was taking place, the NNC sent at least four batches of rebels for training to East Pakistan. Though the Naga rebels did not take advantage of a substantial troop pullout from Nagaland during the 1962 border war with China (the reasons for this is not clear), they intensified their armed campaign once the first of the armed batches returned from East Pakistan. Each batch contained anything between 100 and 300 rebels; they were heavily armed by the Pakistanis and equipped with explosives as well. For those who think the Bodos started the explosions in a big way in Northeast, it must be mentioned that the Naga rebels set off major explosions in rail stations and on trains in 1963, 1964, and 1965 (three of them killed nearly 160 people) in areas of Assam bordering Nagaland.

The fierce rebel campaign evoked an equally strong military response. Additional military formations continued to pour into Nagaland and the counterinsurgency operations were intensified. The civilian population continued to suffer, caught between the army and the rebels, between the two governments, one run by India, the other by the NNC. But the essential problem remained, and it only became more and more complicated. After months of bitter fighting, and amidst fresh initiatives by the Baptist Church, the Peace Mission came into existence in February 1964. Assam Chief Minister B. P. Chaliha, Sarvodaya leader Jayprakash Narayan, and British missionary Michael Scott were inducted into the Peace Mission. Within a few weeks, it managed to establish contacts on both sides. Both the army and the rebels needed a breather. Under the stewardship of the Peace Mission, the Suspension of Operations Agreement, popularly known as the Cease-fire Agreement, was signed on August 15, 1964. Under the Agreement, the security forces undertook to suspend—(a) jungle operations, (b) raiding of rebel camps, (c) patrolling beyond 1,000 yards of the security posts, (d) searching of villages, (e) aerial action, (f) arrests, and (g) imposition of forced labor as punishment. The Naga rebels undertook to discontinue—(a) sniping and ambushing, (b) imposition of taxes, (c) kidnapping and sabotage, (d) fresh recruitment, (e) raiding or firing on security outposts, towns and administrative centres, and (f) movement with arms.

Negotiations for a political settlement began, after the ceasefire had come into effect, at Chedema over two phases—the first phase involved talks between Indian officials and the Naga leaders, and they spread over seven rounds of discussions, while the second involved the Indian political leadership and the Naga leaders, and that spread over six rounds. The inclusion of Nagaland's first Chief Minister Shilu Ao was vehemently opposed by the NNC, but finally, he was taken in as "observer." Another interesting thing about the composition of the Indian official delegation was that it was headed by Foreign Secretary Y.D. Gundevia and his deputy secretary N.G. Suntook. No Home Ministry officials were involved. But the wide difference of views found no meeting point in round after round of discussion. The Indian officials insisted that any kind of further autonomy could be conceded to the Nagas, but not sovereignty, while the NNC leaders insisted that "nothing short of independence would be acceptable to the Nagas." Mutual recriminations continued throughout the seven rounds of official-level talks. The NNC, for instance, demanded the "closing down of concentration camps in Nagaland" and "withdrawal of Indian occupation forces in Nagaland." The Indian officials said there were no concentration camps in Nagaland, and the forces could only be withdrawn if the NNC accepted Indian Constitution, and came to a durable settlement by giving up violence. At the second round of talks, the Peace Mission stepped in with the proposal to get both sides to "renounce violence." That seemed to produce an understanding. Both sides agreed to a renunciation of the use of force "as a means of achieving a political settlement."

But several successive meetings could not work out the modalities for implementing the Peace Mission plan, as the NNC insisted on "internal observers" to supervise the withdrawal of security forces, something that the Indian side found unacceptable. On the eve of Christmas, 1964, the Peace Mission came up with an interesting proposal—the NNC, it said, had the right of self-determination but it should exercise that in favor of staying with India, following which, further discussions could be held on the future relationship of Nagaland and India." Many would believe, this was the beginning of the protectorate proposal, though not articulated as such, in an embryonic form. The NNC demanded a plebiscite on the proposal of joining India and upgrading of the talks to "ministerial level." Despite frequent violations of the cease-fire, 1964 ended with a bit of hope. But when the talks were resumed on February 23, 1965, the NNC reiterated the demand for a plebiscite and the Indians rejected it. In the next round of talks in May that year, the NNC demanded the inclusion of the London-based Phizo in the talks and the involvement of Indian ministers. Delhi agreed but Phizo did not turn up for the future rounds of talks, which were upgraded to "ministerial level." The ministerial level talks spread over nearly 18 months (from February 1966 to October 1967), and it involved the Indian prime minister and the "Ato Kilonser" (prime minister) of the federal government of Nagaland.

By holding these talks in Delhi, the Indian government, by default, gave scope for massive publicity to the Naga cause. Suddenly, the global media was interested in the Nagas as well. But two significant developments had happened by the time the ministerial level talks started. India faced another war with Pakistan, and even as its relations sharply deteriorated with China, Beijing made its first decisive move in the Northeast. It agreed to train and "educate" the Naga rebels. By the time the NNC leaders sat down with Mrs Gandhi, the decision to send a guerrilla batch to China for training and arming had been taken. Interestingly, on the very night the NNC leaders arrived in Delhi for talks in February 17, 1966, a powerful bomb allegedly planted by the Naga undergrounds ripped through the Assam Mail at Tinsukia, killing 37 persons and injuring 52. Few minutes later, another explosion in a station killed 23 people. The explosions were seen as an attempt to sabotage the talks between the NNC and the Indian ministers by the armed wing (or a "hard-line section of the underground"). With the bombings looming large over the talks, the first round did not yield much. But at the second round of the ministerial level talks on April 11–12, 1966 the two prime ministers (Kughato Sukhai, "Ato Kilonser" of the FGN and Mrs Indira Gandhi) met without aides. This created tremendous mistrust within the NNC/FGN set-up, and though Kughato stuck to the Naga demand for sovereignty, some of his colleagues openly denounced Kughato and even accused him of taking bribes from the Indian government. And as the talks ended, more bomb attacks on trains and railway stations (Lumbding and Diphu) left 110 killed and more than 200 injured. Mrs Indira Gandhi, though hard-pressed by her own party-men to cancel the talks, insisted that "it was the need of the hour to exercise utmost restraint, without which the long standing Naga problem cannot be solved."[14] Many close observers of Naga politics argue that this was the stage when the Naga rebels could have got anything out of India short of sovereignty. In fact, the Indian External Affairs Minister Dinesh Singh said during these talks that Mrs Gandhi was "willing to meet any legitimate demand that would meet the aspirations of all sections of Nagas."[15]

V

I am not inclined to get involved in the debate here on whether it was moral for India to force the Nagas to accept Indian overlordship. But can we say any nation-state, in the First, or the Third World would have behaved differently? The hypocrisy of the whole exercise becomes evident when India, while steadfastly refusing to deny Nagas the right of self-determination, would, within a few years, back the Bengali nationalist struggle in East Pakistan to the point of a decisive military intervention. On the other hand, Pakistan, which backed the Nagas and now backs the "freedom struggle" in Kashmir, would deny the Bengalis the autonomy proposed under the Six-point programme of Awami League. Delhi could well say the Naga and the East Pakistan situations were different. But in the initial stages (during the 1950s), the desire for full independence was as strong among the Nagas as amongst the Bengalis in East Pakistan in 1970–71, if not more. The state response may have made much of a difference. While Pakistan reacted bluntly to enforce a military solution by perpetrating genocide and triggering a massive refugee crisis, the Indians used in the Naga Hills a clever mix of military operations and political initiatives. In the process, it successfully divided the Naga society and politics, and created a section that would depend on India for its existence. The carrot-and-stick (or the Kautilyan *sham-dam-danda-bhed* (the four options of amity, monetary inducement, force, and split to tackle the enemy) policy of India brought to the surface the inner contradictions within the Naga underground—the schism on tribal lines, the crisis over leadership, and the differences over tactics to be adopted. A society, where the tribe and the clan were still very strong institutions and where "nationalism" essentially exists in reaction to the Indian state, could not long keep under wraps the fissures that had existed. They surfaced soon after the ministerial level talks had started. While Kughato

Sukhai negotiated with Indira Gandhi, not only was the NNC's military wing, so long content with classic hill guerrilla warfare tactics, turning to modern urban terrorism with the bomb explosions, they were also hobnobbing with one of India's major rivals, China, for weapons and training. In June 1966, led by Thinoselie and Muviah, the first batch of Naga rebels left for China for training. A year later, another group led by "General" Mowu Angami and "Foreign Minister" Issac Chisi Swu followed their footsteps. The discovery of the China connection upset Mrs Gandhi considerably. By mid-1966, the Indian government was upset with the role Michael Scott was playing in the Peace Mission, and he was asked to leave the country. With Scott's departure, ended the Nagaland Peace Mission; Jayprakash Narayan left over a furore caused by one of his statements which drew considerable flak from the underground; Chaliha resigned after he had faced serious criticism over the Naga rebel bombings of Assam's railway stations.

Immediately after the ministerial talks broke down, the Naga federal parliament (Tatar Hoho) passed a resolution condemning Kughato Sukhai for the failure of talks with India. A no-confidence motion was passed against him and Sukhai resigned on October 24, 1967. His brother Kaito Sema, the dashing underground general, was also removed from the position of defence minister—in fact, he was ousted from the Tatar Hoho itself. Scato Swu was removed from the position of president, replaced by Mehiasiu Angami, who "assumed all executive powers." Scato was Kughato's and Kaito's brother-in-law. On the other hand, the new chief of Naga army, Mowu Angami and the new president Mehiasiu Angami were from Phizo's village, Khonoma. The changes in the NNC leadership brought the Sema–Angami rivalry to the fore. The appointment of Zimik Ramyo to the post of Home Minister also upset the Semas still further. But as if this was not enough, an *ahza* (decree of death) from the *Oking* (rebel headquarters) was issued for "General" Kaito. On August 3, 1968, Kaito was assassinated, presumably on orders from the Federal Government of Nagaland. The Sema rebels immediately responded by kidnapping Zimik Ramyo, perhaps because he was suspected of passing the orders for Kaito's liquidation.

These incidents drove a clear wedge in the rebel government, much to Delhi's glee. And that was the beginning of the decimation of the NNC/FGN and the Naga Federal Army. They never again regained the initiative, until they succumbed to India's military–political offensive, and signed the Shillong Accord. The Semas formed "Council of Naga People," and declared unilaterally, the dissolution of the Federal Government of Nagaland. Later, on November 2, 1968, they formed the "Revolutionary Government of Nagaland." Scato Swu was elected the "Prime Minister" of the RGN, which committed itself to a "peaceful solution" of the Naga problem. The formation of the RGN was, predictably, denounced by the NNC. The Nagaland State Government headed by Chief Minister Hokishe Sema however tried to win over the RGN. On paper, the RGN was an underground group, but their fighters could move around freely in the state. The army backed them and used them against the NNC/FGN/Naga Army. In a way, the RGN was the precursor to the SULFA (Surrendered United Liberation Front of Assam), and such other state-sponsored guerrilla outfits and militant groups. While Hokishe Sema was seen as close to the RGN (mostly from his own Sema tribe), S.C. Jamir was seen as close to the FGN. Jamir had already been a minister in the Indian government, and was Sema's archrival in the Naga Nationalist Organization (NNO), which was ruling the state. Hokishe wanted a settlement with the RGN, excluding the FGN totally, while Jamir insisted that without a settlement with the FGN, there would be no durable peace in Nagaland. By then, the United Democratic Front (UDF) had emerged as a party, ready to challenge NNO that finally joined the Congress. The UDF was strongly supported by the NNC/FGN, and they demanded that talks should only be held with the FGN. The formation of these over-ground parties and the underground developing strong links with them, served to further dilute the underground, which was already riven with dissensions.

The 1971 Bangladesh war further deprived the Naga rebels of a foreign base, a regrouping area, which could be used for training, and expansion of the rebel army. The government of Bangladesh was not inclined to shelter any anti-Indian guerrilla army, as the Pakistanis had done. The frustration in rebel ranks was evident when they tried to assassinate Chief Minister Hokishe Sema in August 8, 1972. Sema miraculously escaped but his driver and bodyguards were killed. The car had taken 57 bullets. Sema may have been attacked because he was about to attend an UN conference as a member of the Indian delegation, because he was wooing the RGN, which later surrendered in 1973, and because he was not seen as obstructing a settlement between Delhi and the RGN. The assassination attempt on Hokishe Sema reflected the FGN's frustration rather than its strength. The attack on Sema was followed by the imposition of a government ban on the federal government of Nagaland, Naga National Council, and its armed wing, the Naga Federal Army. B.K. Nehru, who was then governor for northeastern states including Nagaland, said in an All India Radio broadcast immediately after the attack on Sema:

> The continuous breaches of peace in Nagaland by the underground culminating in the recent attempt on the life of the Chief Minister has caused deep anguish. The government of India has reviewed its policies and has taken certain decisions with a view to further strengthening amity and the establishment of permanent peace.[16]

This was followed by relentless counterinsurgency operations, the surrender of many FGN commanders and the fresh attempts to bring peace. But those attempts failed. With the advent of President's Rule, the Nagaland government and the army coordinated the military-political offensive with more gusto. S.C. Dev says that the "President's Rule provided the ideal situation in which we could operate, free from interference of politicians." He argues that the "softening off the FGN" was directly related to the "free hand" the army and the administration got during the President's Rule in Nagaland. Hundreds of Naga rebels and their over-ground supporters were arrested and the rebel organization was pushed into a corner. Mr Dev says that "a series of successive surrenders within a short span of time demoralized the Federal remnants and more surrenders in the Angami and Chakesang region would have completely smashed the rebel movement."[17] It is in that context that the Nagaland Peace Council was formed with several church leaders in it, along with

Kevi Yalley, Phizo's brother. According to Mr Dev: "Both the Liaison Committee and the underground leaders had fully realized that the game is over." He also points out that the administration was promised by some Peace Council members that "they (the underground) are willing to sign anything that the Governor might like them to."[18] The meeting between the Peace Council members, the underground representatives, and the Governor and his advisers continued in Shillong for a while before it culminated in a one-page accord on November 11, 1975. The Accord was a victory for India. The underground leaders agreed to accept the Indian constitution of their own volition, deposit their arms at appointed places, and "formulate other issues for discussion for final settlement." A supplementary agreement detailed the process of depositing weapons and other modalities for housing the underground members in peace camps. The Naga rebel leaders got nothing out of the accord—absolutely nothing. The detractors of the Shillong Accord—men like Muivah, denounced it as "sell-out" and as a "complete betrayal." Twenty years of bloodshed were (rendered) unnecessary if this is what the rebel leaders were finally willing to settle for. Interestingly, the Shillong Accord was signed with "representatives of the Naga Underground" rather than with an organization like the NNC, or the FGN. Phizo never publicly endorsed the Shillong Accord but did not denounce it either. In a way, it might be his way of recognizing the ground realities—the underground had very little fight left in it. In the process, the FGN/NNC was completely sidelined before it withered away from the Naga scene.

So though a small minority in the Naga rebel movement in 1975, the breakaway faction that formed the National Socialist Council of Nagaland, or the NSCN could establish its organization without much difficulty. Nagas who were still not reconciled to be a part of India (and their number even today are not inconsiderable) were to rally behind the NSCN, as it grew, in Muivah's words, "on the ruins of the Shillong Accord." The Shillong Accord marked the end of the most volatile phase of the Naga rebellion, an era when the movement was broad-based, militarily strong, and relatively free from the virus of tribalism. The NSCN emerged as a strong rebel organization, it managed to completely overshadow its parent organization, and it became a rallying point for other guerrilla groups in the region. But it never enjoyed the kind of popular support that the NNC enjoyed at its peak.

But the Shillong Accord left behind many problems in the sense that subsequent administrative effort veered round organizing surrenders, and recovering arms; Delhi completely overlooked the need to discuss for a final settlement. It is now discussing with the NSCN (Issac–Muivah faction), but progress has been slow. The discussions have so far been held outside India. And after the June 2001 agreement between the Indian government and the NSCN to extend the cease-fire "without territorial limits," furious protests have rocked Manipur and threatened to spread to the rest of the region. The Prime Minister A.B. Vajpayee promptly agreed to review the June agreement signed between Indian mediator K. Padmanabiah and NSCN General Secretary Thuingaleng Muivah. The NSCN has threatened to go back to the jungles and "fight for another 50 years" if Delhi went back on the June agreement. Forty-five years after the first Naga guerrilla bands attacked Indian security forces and 25 years after the Shillong Accord, the Naga problem remains a festering wound in India's body politic.

NOTES AND REFERENCES

1. See text of the Shillong Accord and the supplement agreement.
2. Interview with Major General K.K. Ganguly, June 23, 2001.
3. Thuingaleng Muivah, Interview with BBC World Service on July 5, 1996.
4. I.D. Swamy, in a press conference in Delhi, telecast on Star TV, July 3, 2001.
5. Since June 16, 2001, fierce protests against the extension of the Naga cease-fire have rocked Manipur. Most Meiteis believe this is a prelude to a partition of their state, and creation of Greater Nagaland by merging Naga areas of their state in Nagaland. Initially the protests were led by All-Manipur Students Union and All-Manipur United Clubs Organization, but now an apex body, United Committee for Manipur has taken over the leadership of the movement. Nearly 20 protestors have died in the police firings during the agitation. The United Committee of Manipur says they will continue the agitation unless the cease-fire's extension to Manipur is revoked.
6. Muivah's interview on BBC World Service, July 5, 1996.
7. Muivah's version was corroborated by B.K. Nehru in an interview to the author on January 20, 1984.

8. Ulrich Schweinfurter, "Problems of Nagaland" in Charles Fisher (ed.), *Essays on Political Geography*. USA, 1968.
9. M. Horam, *Naga Insurgency: The Last Thirty Years*. Delhi, 1988.
10. S.C. Dev, *Nagaland: The Untold Story*. Kolkata, 1988.
11. Y.D. Gundevia, *War and Peace in Nagaland*. Delhi, 1975.
12. Zashie Huire, former NNC President, interview with author, June 13, 1984.
13. Nirmal Nibedon, *Nagaland: The Night of the Guerrillas*. Delhi, 1983.
14. Y.D. Gundevia, *War and Peace in Nagaland*. Delhi, 1975.
15. Nirmal Nibedon, *Nagaland: The Night of the Gurrilla*. Delhi, 1983.
16. Broadcast over All India Radio (AIR), Kohima, September 1, 1972.
17. S.C. Dev, *Nagaland: The Untold Story*, Kolkata, 1988.
18. Ibid.

9

GENDERED NATION, GENDERED PEACE: A STUDY OF BANGLADESH*

Amena Mohsin

This chapter reflects upon the construction of a gendered and hegemonic state, and its impact upon the minorities. In this context, the cases of Bengali women and the Hill people of Chittagong Hill Tracts (CHT) of Bangladesh would be taken up. The chapter also attempts to show how the ideology of nationalism has been used to marginalize women, as well as the Hill people within the state of Bangladesh. The chapter first of all seeks to show how the state assuming the role of a patriarch had silenced the voices of women in post-1971 Bangladesh. This indeed was the beginning of the construction of a gendered state. The patriarchy and gender bias are built in the idea of nation. The second section takes into account the connection between the idea of nation and the construction of politicized minorities within the state. These minorities however have failed in evolving any alternative vision for them or, their emancipation, and remain trapped within the nationalist construction. A consequence of the above is the gendered nature of the CHT Peace Accord signed between the government of Bangladesh and the Parbattya Chattagram Jonoshonghoti Samity (PCJSS), the body that was at the centre-stage of the autonomy movement for the Hill Tracts (HT) on December 2, 1997, the day the Accord was signed. The Accord establishes, on the one hand, Bengali hegemony over the Hill people, and on the other hand, Chakma dominance over other Hill communities living in CHT.

* Originally published in the *Indian Journal of Gender Studies*, vol. 11, no. 1, February 2004.

Most importantly, the women's question is totally absent in the Accord. An analysis of the above issues along with the Peace Accord is the main thrust of the third section of this chapter.

THE PATRIARCH STATE AND WOMEN

The 1971 liberation war of Bangladesh is regarded as one of the bloodiest wars in the history of humankind. The Bangladesh government alleges that 3 million people were killed by the Pakistan army; while the *New York Times* (August 20, 1971) and the *Washington Post* (August 23, 1971) estimated that between 200,000 to 300,000 Bengalis were killed after March 25. The subsequent history of the liberation war has glorified the sacrifices made by its people for the attainment of independence. I however would submit here that this glorification has a distinct gender bias.

The accounts of the war while contain the number of deaths do not have a corresponding list of the women who had died, or were killed during the nine-month-long war with Pakistan. In the category of *Shaheeds* (martyrs who sacrifice their lives for the cause of their country, or are killed in the genocide), the names of only two women, that too belonging to the intellectual segment, have been included.[1]

Susan Brownmiller[2] has pointed out that about 200,000 Bengali women had been raped by Pakistani soldiers in 1971. Yet the 14 volumes of officially documented history of the war of independence carry only a few testimonies of rape. The government had set up a rehabilitation centre in each district for the affected women. The centres however did not keep any records of the affected women. The idea at that time was to rehabilitate these women in the society as quickly as possible. Therefore, at present, no proper record of the rape victims is available, nor were they ever properly compensated. According to Maleka Khan, who was in charge of a rehabilitation centre in Dhaka, a doctor at the centre had told her that during the first three months of 1972, 170,000 rape victims were aborted, and more than 30,000 war babies were born. This list however is not an exhaustive one and excludes the most marginalized women.[3] Most of the war babies were given up for adoption despite protests and pleadings from their mothers. In this context, Neelima Ibrahim points out that she had called upon Sheikh Mujib-ur-Rahman, the Father of the nation to decide about the fate of these children. His response was: "Send the children, who have no identity of their father abroad. Let the children of human beings grow up like proper humans. Besides I do not want to keep that polluted blood in this country."[4]

The attitude of the Father of nation epitomized the hegemonic and gendered attitude of the state and society. It reified the privileged position of men in society, and more importantly, over women. At this point one may however ponder over several critical questions, like where was the voice of the women who had lost and suffered most during those nine months? Who gave the state the right to snatch away the child from her? The state never made any attempt, or created any space for these women to rehabilitate themselves psychologically. Values of society meant values of men, where in order to grow up like proper human beings one needed the identity of one's father; why do we then glorify the mother figure in our nationalist construction; are we then talking of a mother sanctified and legitimized by a male?

Susan Brownmiller has pointed out that the Bengali men were totally unprepared to accept these women; even some of them were rejected by their own family members. In an attempt to elevate them and make them acceptable to the society, they were given the title of *Birangona* (war heroines) by the Father of nation. Such coinage however was resented by the women activists at that time. It was resented because the title did not offer them anything else, in other words, there was nothing beyond the title. Moreover the expectation that the title *Birangona* would make them acceptable to the society did not really work out. Instead the women became marked. Such exaltations, therefore, held little meaning for the affected women.

In this context Meghna Guhathakurta mentions:

Despite the official attempt to recognize the sufferings of these women by calling them *Birangonas*, the program for reintegrating these women into society turned into a "marry them off" campaign which misfired tragically; tragically that is for the women. Few prospective bridegrooms stepped forward, and those who did made it plain that they expected the government, as father figure, to present them with handsome dowries.[5]

Neelima Ibrahim has detailed in her two volumes of *Ami Birangona Bolchi* the frustrations and agonies of the *Birangonas* at the state and the society. In the seven cases narrated in the two volumes they express their dismay at the state's role in silencing them. They point out that the sacrifices of the freedom fighters (mostly men) have been properly recognized and acknowledged by the state. Roads have been named after them. Martyrs' domes and cenotaphs have been built. They and their children still continue to enjoy many state benefits. They are honoured in many state functions. But the *Birangonas* are nowhere. There is no memorial or road to remind the people of their sacrifices. They cannot even come out and state with pride that they are the *Birangonas*. The Bangladeshi state as well as the society even after 30 years has not prepared itself to accept them. A *Birangona* has aptly summarized the contradictions and hypocrisy within the state and society by posing the following question: "Why is it so? Is it only because we are women that we are unholy; whereas the *Razakars* and *Al-Badars* (Bengali collaborators of the Pakistan army), despite their sins have been accepted and today constitute the elites of the society."[6]

I would like to submit here that through bestowing the title of *Birangona* upon the rape victims, the state had assumed the role of a patriarch. It only strengthened the idea of patriarchy inherent to the modern state.

STATE HEGEMONY AND THE CONSTRUCTION OF THE JUMMAS

The nationalist state went ahead with its agenda of creating a homogenous Bengali state. Bangladesh however is home to 45 different ethnic communities. However no reflection of the same could be found in the political, institutional, and cultural arenas of the state. The hegemonic idea of power guided the modern state. The constitution, as well as the state institutions, epitomized the hegemony and control of the Bengali "nation" over the non-Bengali population of the state. The Hill people, however, in the light of their past experiences of exploitation in the state of Pakistan felt it necessary to have constitutional safeguards for their protection as a separate community. On February 15, 1972, a Hill people's delegation led by Manobendra Narayan Larma (the lone elected member to Bangladesh Parliament from CHT) called on Sheikh Mujib, and demanded political and economic autonomy for the Hill people with a constitutional guarantee for a continuation of their traditional system.

The above demands were unacceptable to Sheikh Mujib. He insisted that there could be only one "nation" in Bangladesh. He therefore asked the Hill people to forget about their separate identity, and to become Bengalis. He further threatened to turn them into minorities by sending Bengalis to the CHT.[7] Mujib's refusal can be explained in terms of his conception of a modern state, which for him implied a culturally homogeneous state. This was unacceptable to Larma who by then had emerged as the champion of the Hill people's cause. He, accordingly, formed a regional political platform, the PCJSS, (The United People's Party of CHT) on March 7, 1972. Subsequently, an armed wing, the Shanti Bahini (SB, Peace Force) was added to it. The seeds of *Jumma* nationalism—an identity that the PCJSS claimed for the Hill people, were sown by Mujib's refusal to accept the Hill people as a separate community distinct from the Bengalis within the state of Bangladesh. The formation of the PCJSS signalled the formal break of the CHT from the state-sponsored model of nationhood. Henceforth, the PCJSS emerged as the main mouthpiece for the Hill people.

The constitution of Bangladesh adopted by the Bangladeshi Parliament on November 4, 1972 legally consolidated the hegemony of Bengalis over the ethnic minorities of Bangladesh. It was a reflection of the ideals of Bengali nationalism. The constitution of Bangladesh in its preamble (paragraph 2) accepted "nationalism," "socialism," "democracy," and "secularism" as state principles. Article Eight Clause One reiterated these. Article Nine defined Bengali nationalism as:

> The unity and solidarity of the Bengali nation, which deriving its identity from its language and culture, attained sovereign and independent Bangladesh through a united and determined struggle in the war of independence, shall be the basis of Bengali nationalism.[8]

Language and culture thus became the basis of Bengali nationalism, in other words, the state acquired a Bengali identity. This identification with the dominant cultural group had put the other groups in a marginalized and disadvantaged position. Apart from language and culture, secularism too was a plank of Bengali nationalism. In the construction of nationhood in Pakistan, religion had been used as the main tool of domination of the Bengalis by the Pakistani regime. Again in 1971, the Pakistani regime had employed the rhetoric of religion in carrying out one of the worst genocides of the century. Secularism was therefore a logical outcome of the spirit of the liberation war of Bangladesh. It also accommodated the religious minorities in Bangladesh. But while religious communalism was prohibited, the Bengali elite failed to take note of the communalism that its own assimilationist nationalism could breed.

Article 1 Part 1 declared Bangladesh to be a unitary state. Through Article 3 Part 1, Bengali was adopted as the state language, and Article 6 Part 1 stated that the citizens of Bangladesh were to be known as Bengalis. The unitary system ruled out the possibility of having a separate legislature or autonomy for the CHT, as was demanded by the CHT delegation. Throughout its political career in united Pakistan, the Awami League had fought for regional autonomy for East Bengal through its demand for a federal structure between East and West Pakistan. Yet it itself opted for a unitary system thus denying the Hill people a separate legislature, as was demanded by them. Linguistic autonomy was a major political demand of the Awami League, but here again through the imposition of Bengali as the state language and the medium of academic instruction, the Awami League, or for that matter the Bengali elite, adopted the very position that it had fought against. The imposition of Bengali nationality over all the citizens of Bangladesh gave the final touch to the phenomenon of Bengali hegemony upon the Hill people. Instead of religion, culture and language had now become the instruments of domination. Manobendra N. Larma refused to endorse this constitution.

The 1972 constitution of Bangladesh indeed made no provision for a special status of the CHT. Article 28 of the constitution whereby all disadvantaged citizens of Bangladesh are given preferential treatment could hardly satisfy the Hill people.

Larma rejected outright the imposition of Bengali nationality upon the Hill people. The quest to turn the Hill people into Bengalis did not end there. In an electoral speech at Rangamati in 1973 Mujib declared: "From this day onward the tribals are being promoted into Bengalis."[9]

This was the first (and last) visit of Sheikh Mujib to Rangamati. The Hill people had come to hear him with great expectations, but this statement created many misgivings among them. It implied that Bengalis were at a higher echelon of civilization. This attitude helped crystallize the sense of nationhood among the Hill people. On January 23, 1974, Parliament passed a Bill declaring Bangladesh a uni-cultural and uni-lingual nation-state. The stage was thereby set for carving out a homogenous nation-state patterned around the dominant Bengali culture.

Following changes in the political scene in 1975, Islamic ideals were incorporated into the constitution. By the proclamation of Order No. 1 of 1977, "Bismillah-ar-Rahman-ar-Rahim" (in the name of Allah, the Beneficent, the Merciful) was inserted at the beginning of the constitution, before the preamble. Through the same proclamation the principle of secularism, previously set forth in Article Eight as one of the state principles, was dropped from the constitution, and was replaced by "the principles of absolute trust and faith in the Almighty Allah, nationalism, democracy and socialism, meaning economic and social justice, together with the principles derived from them" shall constitute the fundamental principles of state policy.[10]

Article 12, through which communal political parties were banned in Bangladesh, was also dropped. Article 9 which stressed the lingual and cultural unity of Bengali nationalism was likewise omitted. In place of "Bengalis," the citizens of Bangladesh through Article 6 Clause 2 were now to be known as "Bangladeshis." These changes were given effect through the Fifth Amendment to the constitution on April 5, 1977. Bangladeshi nationalism was based on the elements of race, the war of independence, Bengali language, culture, religion (in this instance Islam, the religion of the dominant community), land (geographical area), and economy. There was thus no space for accommodating the minorities within this new discourse of the state. Through the Eighth Amendment to the constitution of Bangladesh on June 7, 1988, Islam was declared as the state religion of

Bangladesh (Article 2 Clause A). The ethnic minorities of Bangladesh thus found themselves to be minorities both in the ethnic and religious senses. The Islamization of the Bangladesh polity at the direct behest of the state has seriously eroded the confidence of the minority communities in the state.

Thus at the political level, the state acquired a hegemonic form. It is therefore no wonder that Bangladesh under the regime of Bangladesh Nationalist Party (BNP) did not observe 1994 as the year of the Indigenous Peoples as was declared by the UN. It categorically maintained that there were no indigenous people in Bangladesh. Granting the recognition would have implied that the latter gets all the protections offered by the UN Declaration. The subsequent regime of Awami League under Sheikh Hasina was also very ambivalent on the issue. She did not recognize the existence of any indigenous people in Bangladesh. According to her, at best, there were some *Nritattik jongoshti* in Bangladesh. The implications of the term are quite vague. Its nearest English equivalent is ethnographic people. A remarkable consensus exists among the Bengali political elite on the question of Bengali hegemony, no matter whether the rubric is Bengali or Bangladeshi nationhood, for nation in essence is a hegemonic construction.

The states' development policies have also benefitted the dominant Bengali community at the cost of the Hill people. The latter have been alienated from their land and forest resources, which constitute the basis of their economic, cultural, and social lives. The following exposition will make this clear:

Land

In a resource poor and agrarian country ownership of land is associated with the power structure of the community. In the CHT the indigenous people have been alienated from their land through a state-sponsored project of settlement of Bengalis in the Hills. Presently, there are two groups of Bengalis in the HT. The Hill people call them "*adivashis*" (indigenes) and "settlers." The *adivashis* are the people who had migrated to the Hills in a natural way in search of jobs, or as farmers and traders. This migration initiated from the pre-colonial period continued after the Partition of India in 1947. There is no record of ethnic

violence between the *adivashis* and the Hill people. This suggests that the Hill people did not oppose the natural migration
of Bengalis for they had not come as land grabbers, or posed
any threat to their survival.

The pattern of migration changed from "natural" to "political"
in the Bangladesh period. In 1979, the government through
an amendment to Rule 34 of the CHT Manual did away with
the restrictions against settlements of CHT lands by non-
residents. It decided to settle 30,000 landless Bengali families
on government-owned "Khas" land, in CHT the following year,
and Taka 60 million was allocated for the project. According to
one estimate around 400,000 Bengalis were settled in the CHT
by 1984.[11]

The settlements proved popular with Bengalis for obvious
reasons. In Bangladesh, the per capita land today is 0.29 acres.
In such a "land-hungry" situation the settlements were bound
to be popular with the Bengalis. But here one has to be mindful
of the fact, as our following analysis will show, that land is also
scarce in CHT. It is posited here that the real motive of the
government in making this move is to "colonize" the HT by bringing about a demographic shift in the region. The exposition that
follows will make it clear.

In making this move the government had argued that Bangladesh is an overpopulated land. The population density in the
plains in 1980 was 1400 persons per sq mile. On the other hand
vast tracts of land in the CHT were lying empty. Moreover,
Bengalis have been settled on "Khas" land, i.e., government owned
land, so there has been no encroachment on privately owned
land.

The much-publicized notion of "emptiness" in the Hills is a
myth. The fact of the matter is that, the area of cultivable land
in the Hills is very small. A research carried out by a group of
Soil Scientists on CHT land in the 1960s revealed that only
3.2 percent or 104,304.64 acres of CHT land was suitable for
all-purpose agriculture (A–category land), about 15 percent or
505,225.60 acres were suitable for fruit gardens and forestry
(B–category land), and 77 percent of the land in the region, i.e.,
about 2,509,830.40 acres was suitable solely for afforestation
(C–category land).[12]

In consideration of the life-supporting capacity of CHT land, even as early as 1918, when the CHT population was about 200,000, it was found necessary to restrict the migration of plains people into the HT to protect the economy of the region. Even before the construction of the Kaptai dam (completed in 1960), it was found that the available cultivable land was insufficient for the CHT population.... The situation was aggravated by the construction of the reservoir. Apart from uprooting about 100,000 people, the reservoir inundated more than 54,000 acres of the prime plough land in the CHT. In exchange the government could only compensate for one-third of the lost land. Until today, a large number of displaced people have not been properly rehabilitated mainly due to scarcity of land. In view of the land situation, the government imposed a ceiling of five acres of land on private ownership (of land) in case of the Hill people in the CHT. Interestingly enough, this ceiling is not applicable in case of the Bengalis residing in CHT, nor is there any such rigid limit in other parts of Bangladesh. The land ceiling on private ownership in the plains is 33.3 acres. By the early 1970s most of the land in CHT was under occupation. The population of CHT in 1974 stood at 508,199, i.e., 80,000 to 100,000 families. Thus theoretically, each CHT family could have between 3.7 to 4.63 acres of land; this was less than the government-assessed minimum of 5 acres. Even within this, a large area was not available, for most of it was Unclassed State Forest (USF).[13]

In this context, the question that comes to mind is: from where would the land be made available for settling 400,000 Bengalis? A few thousand acres of forest reserve containing both mixed and hilly lands were released for settlement, but these lands hardly amounted to one-tenth of that required. The problem was solved by the government by ejecting the Hill people from their traditional lands. The settlement policy rendered around 100,000 Hill people homeless. About half of them crossed over to the nearby states of Tripura and Mizoram in India as refugees. The rest are scattered around the CHT. The Hill people thus had been turned into "international," as well as "internal" refugees. The internal refugees live either as dependents upon their relatives, or they have moved into the forests and practise *jhum* (shifting, slash and burn cultivation) on basically fragile land. According to experts a society that practises shifting cultivation with a fallow period of two to five years can support 25–50 persons per sq mile. The population density of CHT in 1988 was 140 persons per sq mile and the fallow period had been reduced to two–three years. It is thus evident that the notion of "emptiness" in the Hills is a myth. Its propagation however has enabled the state to settle around 400,000 Bengalis in the Hills, albeit through the displacement of about 100,000 Hill people from their land. The Bengali settlement program had far-reaching consequences. It deepened the alienation of the Hill people from the Bengali regime(s), and from the Bengali population of the state.

The government claims that Bengalis have been settled on "Khas" lands, i.e., government owned lands. This is also subject to interpretation. Differences exist in the conception of "Khas" land between the Hill people and the Bengali elite. What the government regards as "Khas" land is essentially the Hill peoples' traditional *jhum* land and forestland. For the Hill people this land is common property, belonging to the community, kinship groups, and even members of the spiritual world. The roots of the conflict between these contradictory notions lie in the British colonial period. The colonial state had declared all land in the CHT as government property; the indigenous people were given tenancy rights. This however did not create any conflict, as according to the Hill peoples' notion of land owner-ship, individuals and individual families cannot own land, they only have the right to use it. The government ignores this indi-genous view of "Khas" land, which is regarded by the Hill people as a gross violation of their inalienable rights.

This suggests that the government position on the settlement of Bengalis is deliberately deceptive. Its real motive, as sug-gested earlier, is to "colonize" the HT, by bringing about a demo-graphic shift in the region. A demographic shift indeed has taken place in the HT. In 1947, the Hill people constituted more than 98 percent of the CHT population. The Bengali population in the region rose to 9 percent in 1956, 12 percent in 1961, 40 percent in 1981, and 50 percent by 1991.[14] In Banderban and Khagrachari districts, Bengalis are in a majority where they account for 53 percent and 52 percent of the total population, respectively.[15] This change in demographic composition of the region is viewed with alarm by the Hill people. They regard the government policy of Bengali settlement as "ethnocide." The local leaders constantly refer to the fate of Indians in America, and fear that a similar fate awaits them.[16] This perception deepens their alienation from the Bengali regime(s).

Forest Resources

In the 1970s, the government of Bangladesh assigned to the Swedish International Development Agency (SIDA) a US $6 million forest development project. This was part of a much larger afforestation program, which involved, during a period of 20 years, the planting of about 1,000 sq miles of seedlings involving an area of about 20 percent of Unclassed State Forests. The completion of the project would have meant that the *jhumias* (the *jhum* cultivators) would eventually be deprived of more than half of their traditional land.[17] In view of this, there were large-scale protests by Hill people against the project, and reports of human rights violations, i.e., the forced ejection of *jhumias* from their traditional lands also appeared in the Swedish press. Finally, in 1981, SIDA withdrew from the project. In a statement it observed:

> Due to the political situation in the CHT and the policies pursued by the Bangladesh government ... the Swedish government decided in 1976 not to continue to support the programme after its termination in June 1981. Such extensions of project agreements are usually quite common. The main reason for the decision was the inability to give the programme such a direction as to benefit the ethnic minorities in the area.[18]

In 1980, the government undertook a scheme of rubber plantation in the HT to make the Hills commercially profitable. Accordingly, it allotted more than 550 plots of 25 acres each on a trial basis to Bengali entrepreneurs, on the understanding that further land of up to 100 acres or more, would be granted on the successful performance on the first 25 acres. In this way more than 14,000 acres of forest hilly land were allotted to Bengalis in the district of Banderban. Thereafter, a few hundred plots of 25 acres each were allotted to Bengali entrepreneurs in the three districts. The allotment policy clearly favored the Bengalis—for instance, between 1980 and 1986, a total of 64 plots were allotted in four mouzas[19] of Banderban. Out of these 64, only one belonged to a Hill man. The government blames the lack of interest and capability of the Hill people for this situation. On their part, the Hill people do not deny these allegations, but point out that the government has not taken any measure to encourage them, or to protect the interests of willing local entrepreneurs vis-à-vis the Bengalis, for it is a matter of fact that at this stage they cannot compete on an equal footing with the Bengalis. The scheme, therefore, meant the enrichment of Bengali entrepreneurs, and more land alienation for the Hill people. Besides the project also has detrimental effects on the environment. At a seminar held in Dhaka on "Forest, Forest Dwellers and Forest Culture" on April 20–21, 1994, experts identified rubber planting to be a prime cause of soil degradation. It was argued that rubber is a monoculture crop, which leads to cutting off of coppices that regenerate natural forests. Consequently, forests are destroyed. It was further pointed out that the rate of deforestation in Bangladesh has reached an alarming rate of 3.36 percent per year; while in South Asia in general, it is 0.6 percent. Commercial logging for furnishers by Bengali entrepreneurs, and the clearance of forestland for agricultural purposes are also causing deforestation.

The Chittagong Hill Tracts Development Board (CHTB) was formed in 1979 for the economic development of the region. Since the inception of the Board a number of construction works have been undertaken at the Board initiative. This construction also entails the use of wood as fuel for brick industries. The government has enacted a law prohibiting this, but it has not been possible to implement this ordinance effectively and fuel wood is still extensively used as fuel in brickfields.

It is ironical that the government blames the *jhumias* and *jhum* cultivation for soil degradation and deforestation. But the fact of the matter is that *jhum* has been banned in half of the total area of CHT for more than a century now in order to create Reserve Forests (RF), and the land in which Hill people normally *jhum* now, is not virgin forest land, but common mouza lands which have been cultivated by *jhumias* for centuries.

Nonetheless, in 1992, the government decided to declare 76,000 acres of land in Rangamati, 37,387.5 acres in Khagrachari, and 7,389.2 acres Banderban as RF.[20] The decision caused widespread resentment among the local population, for it would displace about 50,000 local families, and turn them into refugees either within, or outside CHT. These people do not have any titles to the land they had been occupying so there is no way for them to acquire any compensation from the government. The signing of the Peace Accord has not brought any substantial change in the state position, and government continues to acquire forestland in the name of development.

THE JUMMAS AND THE CHT PEACE ACCORD

The persecution in the CHT had led the PCJSS to demand for a separate nationhood for the Hill people. This party had since the mid-1980s been referring to the Hill people as the "*Jumma* nation." The demand for a separate nationhood was not equated by the PCJSS with statehood. The party, as well as the Hill people, insist that for them "nation" is a cultural category. The party's nationalistic agenda had been explicitly spelt out in its manifesto, where it stated that its main objective was to achieve the right to self-determination of the various small nationalities in the CHT, with a separate entity status of CHT, with a constitutional guarantee. It recognized CHT as the homeland of various multi-lingual nationalities, who together had been referred to as the *Jumma* people.[21]

The PCJSS maintained that this "construction" of *Jumma* nationhood could satisfy the aspirations of self-identity and autonomy of the Hill people within the state of Bangladesh. *Jumma* nationalism bases itself on the traditional mode of cultivation of the Hill people, i.e., *jhum*; on the special relationship of the Hill people with their land,[22] and the cultural and economic separateness of the Hill people from the Bengalis. The Hill people have also constructed martyrs' domes at different places in the CHT to commemorate the killings of the Hill people by the Bengalis.[23] These constructions draw the lines between the Bengalis and the Hill people in which the Bengalis emerge as the oppressors and exploiters, and the Hill people are the victims.

Jumma nationalism is however a negative and problematic construction. To begin with, the idea of nationalism itself is a hegemonic construction. *Jumma* nationalism also sought to impose an artificial homogeneity upon the Hill people. The smaller communities saw it as hegemonism of the Chakmas— the dominant community in the CHT.[24] Second, it is understandable that within the framework of a nation-state the demand was unrealizable. The failure of the PCJSS to come out of this category was indeed indicative of their intellectual dependence upon borrowed concepts, for the idea of nation as invoked by the PCJSS is alien to the Hill people. Members of the smaller communities preferred to be identified in their own generic names. The category of *"Jumma* nation" as used by the PCJSS thereby lacked the vision and spirit of creating a truly non-homogenous and non-hegemonic society.

Nonetheless the CHT Peace Accord as pointed out earlier is a gendered and hegemonic accord. On the one hand, it has established the hegemony of the Bengali "nation" over the Hill people. On the other hand, it has consolidated Chakma hegemony over the smaller communities of the HT. Also significantly enough, the women's question is totally absent. The peace negotiations were initiated during the reign of President Ershad in the 1980s, and continued through the Khaleda regime, and ultimately, the accord was signed during the Awami League regime of Sheikh Hasina. In other words, two women headed the Bangladesh government during the course of negotiations, yet throughout the negotiating process one does not find a single woman representative either from the government side, or from the Hill people. An analysis of the accord would also reveal its hegemonic and gendered nature. This indeed can be explained by the masculinized paradigm through which politics is conducted within a modern state.

The main provisions of the accord can be classified under the following heads and each of them as we will see, is hegemonic and gendered:

(a) *Cultural:* The PCJSS had constructed the idea of a *Jumma* nation to counter the hegemony of Bengali nation. It was assumed that this construction would put them at par with the Bengalis.

But the peace accord has recognized the CHT as a tribal-inhabited region. It is indeed ironic that the PCJSS had to accede to the pressure of the government on this count.[25] It denied them the equality that they had been fighting for. The state thereby has retained the hegemony of the Bengali nation. The constructions of categories like "tribal" and "nation" within a modern state, indeed, sets the parameters for state policies, where "nation" appears as dominant and "tribal" as subordinate.

(b) *Political:* Self-government or political autonomy had been a major demand of the PCJSS. In order to realize this, PCJSS had demanded that the constitution should recognize the CHT as a special administrative unit with regional autonomy. The three districts of CHT—Rangamati, Khagrachari, and Banderban —should be merged into one unit, and the region should be renamed Jummaland. An autonomous Regional Council (RC) should administer *Jumma*land. This Council would be elected directly by the people on the basis of adult franchise.... The RC would be called *Jumma*land Regional Council (JRC), to be headed by a Chairman and consisting of 48 members of whom 35, 7, 3 and 3 will be drawn respectively from the general *Jumma* people, the *Jumma* minorities (excluding the Chakmas, Marmas, and Tripuras since they constitute the numerical majority), the Bengalis, and the women who would be elected by other members of the Council.

The JRC should have an Executive Council (EC). The Chairman of the JRC would decide the membership number of this body. The majority party would form it for a term of five years. The above arrangements would have to be constitutionally guaranteed with the provision that no change could be brought about in the administrative structure of the HT without the prior holding of a referendum on the issue within the region itself.

This demand was rejected by the previous regimes. In this context, subsequent governments pointed to the creation of three District Councils for the three Hill Districts by the Ershad regime. The latter through the passage of a Parliament Act on February 28, 1989, had established three District Local Government Councils for the districts of Rangamati, Khagrachari, and Banderban. Each of these councils is headed by a chairman, who has to be an indigenous person. It is composed of 30 members of whom two-third will be indigenous and one-third Bengali. The indigenous seats are proportionally divided on the basis of population among the different groups of the districts. The Council is elected directly on the basis of adult franchise...

The District Councils were rejected by the PCJSS on the ground that the District Council Act had no constitutional basis. But the subsequent governments maintained that through the creation of the above institutions, the government has conferred autonomy, as well as special administrative status on the region. It also maintained that there was no historical basis for converting the name of the region. The PCJSS also subsequently moved away from its demand of *Jumma*land, but stuck to its demand for regional autonomy.

Under the present accord a three-tier administrative system has been evolved. These are the Hill District Councils (HDC), the Regional Council (RC), and the Ministry of CHT Affairs.

The three Hill Districts Local Government Councils have been renamed Hill District Councils. The composition and electoral process of the HDC remain as before. But their powers and functions have been increased in the following areas through an amendment:

- increase in the number of subjects that are to be transferred to HDC;
- increase of administrative powers over the functions of the subjects of the HDC;
- increase of powers of taxation;
- power to receive a part of the income/royalties from extraction and exploration of forest and mineral resources;
- all development projects in the CHT are to be implemented and funded through the HDC including those initiated at the national level;
- the HDC can independently formulate and adopt administrative regulations, and the GOB is to consult the HDC prior to the adoption of any rules under the HDC Act;
- no land in the CHT, including khas land, can be transferred, purchased, sold, or leased without the permission of HDC. The RF, Kaptai Hydro electric project, and other state owned lands and properties are excluded from this.

As per the demand of the PCJSS, a RC has been formed though its composition, powers, and functions are much different. The following is the composition of the RC:

- Chairman (tribal)–1;
- Members (tribal)–12 male;
- Members (tribal)–2 female;
- Members (non-tribal)–6 male;
- Member (non-tribal)–1 female.

Among the total male tribal members, five will be elected from the Chakmas, three from the Marmas, two from the Tripuras, and one each from the Murongs and the Tanchongyas. In case of female members one from the Chakmas and one from another tribe would be elected. Two persons would be elected from each district in case of the non-tribal members.

The members of the Council will be elected indirectly by the elected members of the three Hill District Councils. Chairmen of the three HDCs will be the ex-officio members of the council and they will have the right to vote. The elected members of the RC will indirectly elect chairman of the RC. The Council will be elected for five years. The Council will co-ordinate and supervize the general administration; law and order, and development activities of the three HDCs. Tribal laws and dispensation of social justice will also come under the council. It will co-ordinate disaster management and relief activities with non-governmental organizations (NGOs), and give license for heavy industries. The government will enact laws relating to CHT in consultation with the Council.

The accord also provides for the setting up of a ministry to be headed by a tribal person. The ministry is to function as an apex body with supervisory and executive authority over the CHT self-government system. The ministry will also co-ordinate the activities of CHT affairs at the central level. Its major powers include the residual jurisdiction of the government to legislate on matters relating to CHT; revisional authority over the functions of the HDC, the district administration headed by the Deputy Commissioners, and the RC; allocation of funds for the HDC and RC.

The PCJSS had also demanded that three seats be reserved in the national parliament for the Hill people from the CHT constituency. This demand was rejected on the ground that three seats are already reserved for the CHT region. It however needs to be mentioned here that those seats are for the geographical constituency of the HT—not for the Hill people alone. Any Bengali person from the HT may also be elected from there. Given the present demographic composition of CHT where the Bengalis now constitute 50 percent of the population, this is not an impossible scenario. However, it is submitted here that even if three seats were reserved for the Hill people, there is very little that they can do in a majoritarian democracy in a House of 300.

(c) *Economic* (Land, control over natural resources, and Bengali settlement): The PCJSS had demanded that all lands in the CHT, except the Kaptai power station, Betbunia satellite station, state owned industrial areas, and state acquired land be placed under the jurisdiction of the Council. A constitutional ban ought to be put on the purchase of land in the CHT by outsiders. Deeds made to lease out land to Bengalis for rubber plantation and forestry be cancelled and the lands be placed under the Council's jurisdiction.

Under the present accord, as pointed out earlier, the HDCs have been given significant powers over land issue. The government also cannot acquire or transfer any lands, hills, and forests under the jurisdiction of the HDC without prior discussion and approval of the RC. The accord also provides for the formation of Land Commission to settle disputes pertaining to land. The Commission is to be headed by a retired judge of Bangladesh High Court. Its members include the chairpersons of the HDC, a representative of the RC chairperson, the three traditional chiefs, and the commissioner of Chittagong Division. The Commission is to make its judgments on the basis of ownership of deeds to lands, customary rights, usages, and practices of the Hill people. Its decisions cannot be challenged in a court of law. The accord also stipulates that a land survey would be undertaken in the CHT to ascertain ownership rights.

Since the state-sponsored Bengali settlement is considered by the Hill people as the most important factor behind their land alienation, the PCJSS demanded that the constitution must put a ban on Bengali settlements in the region. It further demanded that all outsiders, who have settled in the area after August 17, 1947 should be withdrawn from the region.

Subsequent governments had remained uncompromising on the issue of withdrawal of Bengalis from the HT. The present accord makes no reference to the question of Bengali withdrawal, though the PCJSS insists that there was a verbal commitment to this effect by the government.[26] Regarding accusations of land alienation due to Bengali settlements, the Land Commission is supposed to decide on the validity of the accusations.

The PCJSS had also demanded the natural resources of the Hills and their exploitation be placed under the jurisdiction of the RC. As mentioned earlier, the HDCs are to get a certain percentage of royalty from the exploitation of the natural resources, though the state retains control over the exploitation of the resources.

(d) *Refugees:* The PCJSS had demanded that all international and internal *Jumma* refugees should be properly rehabilitated. The previous regime of BNP had promised that a grant of Tk.10,000 would be given to each returning family. The government promised that land belonging to the returnees would be restored to them; a general amnesty had been declared, besides the returnees were promised educational and employment facilities and opportunities. The present package signed separately between the GOB and the *Jumma* Refugees Welfare Association (JRWA) on March 9, 1997 is not much different from the earlier agreement, though the amount of money has increased from Tk.10,000 to Tk.15,000. Each JSS returnee has also been given Tk.50,000.

(e) *Security:* The PCJSS had demanded that an autonomous indigenous Police Force consisting solely of the Hill people should be formed. Quotas should be reserved in the defence services for the Hill people. The region should be demilitarized, and for the purposes of guarding the borders, only the Bangladesh Rifles (BDR, a paramilitary force for border patrolling) could be deployed along the borders. The demand for demilitarization was made in view of the military excesses, human rights violations, and full-scale militarization of the region during the insurgency period.

The state has remained uncompromising on the issue of demilitarization. Its position is that Bangladesh is not a demilitarized state, and CHT constitutes an integral part of Bangladesh; more importantly, the region is economically and strategically important. The three hill districts are bounded on the north by the Indian state of Tripura, on the south by Myanmar, and on the east by the Arakan Hill Tracts and the Lushai Hills. The insurgency in India's northeast and in Myanmar, according to Bangladesh military planners, makes it imperative that a military presence remains visible in the region.

Under the present accord the military will remain in the CHT, though it will be withdrawn to the permanent cantonments. The temporary camps of army—Ansar (a paramilitary force), and the village defence forces, excepting the BDR, will be gradually withdrawn. The members of the armed forces can be deployed under the state rules, and procedures in case of deterioration of law and order situation, and in times of natural calamities, or like other parts of the country, under the control of civil administration. The RC may request the appropriate authorities for such help and assistance, if required.

AN APPRAISAL OF THE ACCORD

The accord has put an end to more than two decades of armed insurgency in the Hills, but it has failed in establishing peace, for absence of war does not constitute peace. Instead, as suggested earlier, it contains seeds of future conflicts and polarizations within the Hills. This is because the accord is flawed on several counts and levels.

HEGEMONIC PEACE

The accord lacks the principles, and vision of creating a non-hegemonic society that can only be the basis of sustainable peace in the region. Hegemony is evident at various levels and forms....
Through recognizing the HT as a tribal-inhabited area the state has only reaffirmed the hegemony of the Bengali "nation" within the state of Bangladesh. These constructions have important policy implications in a nation-state as these categories are

based on power equations. In the context of a modern state, the "nation" is the core or dominant group. The PCJSS's demand for recognition as a nation was a demand for, and assertion of, equality of the Hill people vis-à-vis the Bengalis. This recognition has implications for the other minorities of Bangladesh, who are struggling for the recognition of their customary rights over land, and as indigenous people. The latter are indigenous people living in the plains alongside the Bengalis. The accord has recognized the CHT as a tribal-inhabited area; hence certain rights have been given to them. None of the other groups can claim such an area for itself. Hence, they remain deprived of any special rights as well. The accord thus has negative implications for the Hill people, and the other indigenous people of Bangladesh as well.

The accord established the hegemony of the Chakmas who constitute the numerical majority, as well as the dominant community over other minority communities of the region. This hegemony was latent in the construction of *Jumma* nationalism as well.... (T)his conception was a negative and problematic one.

The hegemony is most evident in the composition of the RC. Here one needs to ask, how representative the RC is of the different communities of the CHT. This would determine the degree of participation of the Hill people in the political body. A look at the composition of the RC reveals the predominance of the majority Chakma community. Thirteen ethnic groups inhabit the CHT, and in actuality, only four will have their representation in this body, as the Mrung and the Tangchongya together will have one representative. The other nine communities will have to be content with one representative. This is a very imbalanced situation. The smaller communities feel deprived, and point out, that the RC is representative of different communities in the HT, not of numbers. A Bengali cannot represent a Chakma, likewise, the latter cannot represent a Kheyang, or a Tangchongya. They feel this ought not to have been the case in the RC for it is a selective body, not a directly elected one. In other words, the RC is replicating and reproducing the hegemony that it had been purporting to fight.[27]

At a national conference held between December 18–20, 1997 on *adivashis* (indigenous people), the smaller communities of

CHT expressed their resentment against the proposed composition of the RC. Members of other ethnic communities (Garos, Manipuris, Saontal, and others), also expressed their resentment, and demanded representative bodies for themselves. They further demanded that instead of a ministry for CHT Affairs, there ought to be a ministry of Adivashi Affairs.

The autonomy demand of the Hill people is indeed a justifiable one, but equally justified is the claim of the other ethnic minorities. Because of the majoritarian democracy, it is impossible for members of any ethnic group to get elected in national parliament. Even when they do so, it is invariably on the ticket of the mainstream political parties. This particular provision has created an imbalance in the CHT, between the Bengalis and the Hill people, and also amongst the Hill people. It has also created a schism between the ethnic communities of Bangladesh, and particularly, between the Bengalis and the Hill people. In order to overcome this, it is important that strong local government bodies be set up for each division.

The accord is a highly gendered one. Based on majority/minority equations it only strengthens the masculine values of politics.[28] The composition of the RC with only three seats for women, in a House of 22, is reflective of this gender imbalance and male hegemony. It also needs to be pointed out here that women had played an active role in the Hill people's struggle for autonomy. They had not only cooked for and nursed the SB men, but also acted as their informers under tremendous pressures and risks. The women's wing of the PCJSS had its organizational set-up even in the remote villages, where they organized the village Hill women, and made them aware of the objectives of the organization, and garnered support for the movement. It goes without saying that women were the worst victims of the conflict, but many of them overcame this victimhood and acted as agencies of change. The Hill Women's Federation (HWF) formed in 1990, through its democratic movement within and outside, the CHT had succeeded in creating a general awareness of the human rights violations, more specifically against the women, committed in the HT, by the military. It became active on the issue of rape as an instrument of counterinsurgency.[29] It is regrettable

that no woman from the HT was ever made part of the negotiation process that sprawled over two decades. The accord also
does not have any provision that deals with women's question.

It is perhaps pertinent to point out here that among the Hill
communities excepting the Marmas, the Hill women do not
inherit their parental property. The PCJSS agenda has remained
silent on the issue of women's right to succession of land, despite
waging their struggle for land rights of the Hill people. A common argument in this context is that land rights to women might
result in land alienation in case of a woman marrying outside
the community, especially a Bengali.[30] The women's question
thereby is subsumed under the "national" question.

PEACE WITHOUT JUSTICE

During the period of insurgency the CHT had undergone total
militarization. The entire administration was under the military
control, and the entire region was turned into a military camp.
The military had divided the entire area of CHT into three zones:
white, green, and red. The white zones covered an area of two
miles adjacent to the Army headquarters, and were jointly populated by Bengali settlers and Hill people. These were considered
as neutral zones. Bengali settlement areas were identified as
green zones. Areas in the interiors of forests, and those populated by the Hill people alone constituted the red zone, and
there the military carried out its counterinsurgency operations.

In the name of counterinsurgency, massive violations of human
rights had been committed by the military. These included cases
of forced religious conversion and religious persecution, forced
eviction, arrests, tortures, and kidnappings. There were also as
many as 11 massacres of Hill people. Women were the worst
victims of violence, yet they had played an active role in the
autonomy struggle of the CHT. The physical, as well as, economic security of women was threatened by the state especially
due to military activities. Women were the most marginalized
as the state took over the forest resources. Nearly two decades
of insurgency had turned many houses in the CHT into woman-
headed households. While men crossed over and fought with

guns, the women had kept the fabric of family and society alive. They had to go around and do their daily chores amidst a hostile environment. Women who crossed over to India also suffered as refugees. Within HT itself they became the victims of military oppression, including rape. In the construction of a nationalist cause, rape has played a central role, for women as child-bearers are considered important for the reproduction, that is to say, the biological continuation of a nation. Rape, therefore, is used systematically as a deliberate tactic to destroy or damage the enemy. Women are victimized by the military in two ways—as a member of the "enemy," and as female individual. It has been reported that between 1991 and 1993 over 94 percent of the rape cases of Hill women were by the security personnel. Over 40 percent of the victims were women under 18 years of age.[31] The Hill women had protested against military atrocities through the Hill Women's Federation. These protests took place at the regional, national, as well as, the international levels. Members of the HWF also had to suffer for their activities. Kalpana Chakma, the Organizing Secretary of the HWF, was abducted in 1996 allegedly by a military officer, but till date, her whereabouts remain unknown.

The accord makes no reference at all to the human rights violations committed in the Hills. There is no provision for the compensation of the victims of violence, nor any mention of rehabilitation or counselling of the rape victims. It needs to be pointed out here that Bangladesh is a signatory to the International Criminal Court (ICC) Convention that declares rape as a crime against humanity. Bangladesh has also officially demanded apology from Pakistan for the human rights violations, and more specifically, for the rapes committed by the Pakistani military on the Bengali women during the liberation war of 1971. In this backdrop the total absence of any justice clause for the Hill people is reflective of a number of things. First, it speaks of the hegemonic position of the Bengali nation over the Hill people; second and more significant, of the weakness of democracy. The accord was signed by a democratically elected regime; yet it failed in doing justice to a segment of its population for excesses committed by its military. It also showed the preponderance of the military in Bangladesh politics.

REFUGEES AND REHABILITATION

Since the signing of the accord in 1997 the refugees have returned from their camps in India. But they have come back to a very polarized and tense situation. It is important to point out here that India had played the critical role in getting this accord signed. It also gave a one month ultimatum to the refugees, and gradually, their ration was stopped. Under the circumstances, it is difficult to say that they have come back willingly. A survey carried out by this author among 100 returnees in the Khagrachari district between September 3–10, 1999 found that about 92 percent among them felt that the situation was still uncertain and unstable, and 8 percent felt that it was bad. Important point to bear in mind here is that none of them felt that the situation has settled down for them. The accord also does not provide for any rehabilitation or counselling centres for the victims, more specifically, for the women victims, many of whom had been raped as well.

Hence, it appears that in its nationalist construction, the state of Bangladesh has marginalized and silenced the voices of minorities—women, as well as ethnic communities. This chapter has argued that the idea of a nation-state has a homogenizing and hegemonizing thrust built in it. Bengali, as well as Bangladeshi nationalism, both variants of state-sponsored models of nationalism gave birth to *Jumma* nationalism. This nationalism too has its problems. It is exclusionary and is identified mainly with the Chakmas, whereas there are 13 ethnic groups in the CHTs. It is also silent on the women's question. Nonetheless, within the context of a modern state, the hegemony of the dominant Bengali nation has prevailed, and it is evident that many of the contentious issues that had led to the autonomy movement in the Hills have remained unresolved. At each instance, the state of Bangladesh had sought to impose its hegemony upon the subordinate communities in the HT. The CHT peace accord is only an extension of the above. The accord has not only consolidated Bengali hegemony over the Hill people, but has also sowed the seeds of polarization in the region. The Hill people are now divided into pro-accord and anti-accord groups. On the part of the Hill people as well, they have failed in thinking innovatively on ways of emancipation. Instead, by adopting the nationalist path, they have taken recourse to an equally hegemonic and gendered notion of polity. Consequently, the peace accord is beset with hegemonism, and a gendered notion of political and economic emancipation in which women remain a marginalized category. It is perhaps time that the Bengalis, as well as the Hill people, realize that the way to emancipation, a viable peace, and counterhegemony does not lie in the signing of peace accords or such constructions, that draw lines between human populations; rather in their struggle for emancipation, the dominated Hill people should take the dominated *adivashis* and Bengalis as well, and endeavor towards the creation of a non-hegemonic un-gendered society comprising citizens, and not nations.

NOTES AND REFERENCES

1. These two women are Saleena Parveen, a journalist; and Meherunessa, a poet.
2. Susan Brownmiller, *Against Our Will: Men, Women and Rape.* Harmondsworth, 1975, p. 79.
3. Shahriar Kabir, "Ekatture Birangona: Bhindeshi Nayanikar Obhiggota" (in Bengali) (The war heroines of 1971: The experience of foreigner Nayanika), *Janokantho,* October 7, 1998.
4. Neelima Ibrahim, *Ami Birangona Bolchi*, (in Bengali) (I am a war heroine speaking), vol. 1, Dhaka, 1994, p. 19.
5. Meghna Guhathakurta, "The Bangladesh Liberation War: A Summon to Memory," in Abul Kalam (ed.), *Internal Dynamics and External Linkages.* Dhaka, 1996, p. 26.
6. Neelima Ibrahim, *Ami Birangona Bolchi*, vol. 2, Dhaka, 1994, p. 42.
7. This was stated to the author by Ananta Bihari Khisha, a member of the delegation in a personal interview on October 19, 1993.
8. *The Constitution of the People's Republic of Bangladesh.* Dhaka, 1972, p. 5.
9. Siddharta Chakma, *Proshongo Parbattya Chattagram.* Calcutta, 1986, p. 49.
10. *The Constitution of the People's Republic of Bangladesh.* Dhaka, 1994, p. 10.
11. *The Guardian,* March 6, 1984.
12. Raja Devasish Roy, "The Erosion of Legal and Constitutional Safeguards of the Hill peoples of the CHT in Bangladesh: An Historical Account," paper presented at a seminar on *The CHT Problem in Bangladesh,* organized by the Manoghar Shishu Sadan, Rangamati, April 20–22, 1992, p. 10.

13. Raja Devasish Roy, "Key Features of the Land Crisis in the CHT," Unpublished Paper, 1992, pp. 2–6.
14. M. Nurul Amin, "Bangladesher Jatishottar Shomossha O Shangbidhanik Shomadhaner Onushandhan," (in Bengali) (The Nationality Crisis in Bangladesh and Investigation into a Constitutional Solution) in Emajuddin Ahamed (ed.) *Bangladeshe Shongshodiya Ganatantra: Prashangik Chinta Bhabna.* Dhaka, 1992, p. 118.
15. *Life is not Ours': Land and Human Rights in the CHT Bangladesh.* The CHT Commission. Denmark, 1994, p. 8.
16. This was stated to the author during her visits to the CHT in 1992, and again in 1997.
17. "The Genocide Charge. Human Rights in the CHT of Bangladesh." Paper for the Conference on the CHT, Amsterdam: Research Institute of Oppressed Peoples, 1986, p. 139.
18. Anti-Slavery Society, *The CHT: Militarization, Oppression and the Tribes.* Series 2, London, 1984, p. 34.
19. A revenue unit constitutive of several villages.
20. *Sangbad,* August 13, 1992.
21. "The Genocide Charge. Human Rights in the CHT of Bangladesh." Paper for the Conference on the CHT, Amsterdam: Research Institute of Oppressed Peoples, 1986, pp. 129–30.
22. Willem V. Schendel, "The Invention of the 'Jummas': State Formation and Ethnicity in Southeastern Bangladesh," *Modern Asian Studies*, vol. 26, no. 1, Cambridge, 1992, pp. 122–23.
23. *Keokradang,* September 9, 1993, p. 8.
24. This was revealed to the author by members of the Tripura, Mong, and Mru communities during personal interviews. The interviews were taken in November 1993 and again in September 1994.
25. This was stated by Rupayan Dewan, member PCJSS in a workshop on "The CHT: Problems and Prospects," organized by RDC in Dhaka on May 22–23, 1999.
26. The RC Chairman and President of PCJSS stated this to the author in a personal interview on April 4, 2001.
27. Stated to the author by members of smaller communities during her visit to the CHT in May 2001.
28. For an exposition of this see, Rebecca Grant and Kathleen Newland (eds), *Gender and International Relations.* Open University Press, 1991.
29. Meghna Guhathakurta, "Women's Narratives from the Chittagong Hill Tracts," in Rita Manchanda (ed.), *Women, War and Peace in South Asia: Beyond Victimhood to Agency.* New Delhi, 2001, pp. 252–93.
30. This was stated to the author by male as well as female members of the Hill people.
31. The CHT Commission, *Life is Not Ours',* Denmark, 1997, p. 9.

10

IMPROVING INDIA–PAKISTAN RELATIONS*

Mubashir Hasan

Last May I spent some time in Bombay working on my books.
The Birds of the Indus, at the best library and museum on the
subject in the world. In its reading room, one day, a young
Maharashtrian woman, researching in Marine Biology, asked
me if I was from Pakistan. "Do you hate us?" was her next question in a friendly but confident tone. "No we don't hate you but
we are scared of you." She did not let me complete the sentence
and almost shouted. "But we are scared of you." It was my turn
to ask: "India is a much bigger country than Pakistan. You have
a very large army, air force and navy. Why are you scared of
us? "We are scared of Muslims. They live in our country, and
when there is a match between Pakistan and India, they take
out Pakistani flags and back Pakistan, and not India. They
should not be doing that." She related how tense she had felt a
few days ago while riding bus through a Muslim area. She raised
her hands, placed the finger-tips of one against the other and
said, "I was all the time like this, not sure of what might happen
to me the next moment." In answer to my questions she said
neither she nor anyone she knew had a bad experience, nor
had she read of any such account in newspapers. She said she
was scared of Muslims because "my parents have told me so."
On learning that her fears of Pakistan were unfounded, that
Indians are received in Pakistan in a friendly way, her next question, with wide open flashing eyes, was "How is Imran Khan?"

* Originally published in *Strategic Perspectives*, vol. 1, no. 1, 1999. Published
with the permission of Pakistan–India People's Forum for Peace and
Democracy.

and the next was "How is Miandad?" On hearing the answers she was all smiles and thanked me for what I explained to her.

We must recognize that perceptions about Muslims among non-Muslims are hugely distorted. And this is true not merely among non-Muslim Indians in general, but non-Muslims in Palestine, Serbia, Croatia, Armenia, Azerbaijan, Philippines, indeed America and Europe and so many places in the world. Edward Said has traced the history of these misperceptions and bigoted notions in several of his works. Muslims, weak, poor uneducated, and unorganized are under pressure all over the world. While the responsibility of removing misperceptions in the Indian minds lies primarily with the Indian government, the government of Pakistan should also do what it can.

In modern India, the first big setback to the efforts of Muslims to continue with a united political platform with others occurred in 1920 at Nagpur. At the annual sessions of the All-India Muslim League and the Indian National Congress, the hitherto recognized apostle of Hindu–Muslim unity, the author of the Lucknow Pact, Mohammad Ali Jinnah, was totally isolated. The Congress and the Muslim League could never come together afterwards. After Independence the relation between Pakistan and India, partly based on hostile perceptions deeply rooted in the psyche of the two peoples, and partly as a result of the objective situation on the ground, started on the wrong foot and have continued on suspicious, and at times hostile, and all along on unfavorable terms.

Today, on the one hand, the danger of yet another war lurks over the heads of the two peoples like the sword of Damocles. On the other hand, the perennially dismal situation has begun to develop a faint silver lining which requires to be taken note of with due prudence.

The number of senior and experienced Indians who are favourably disposed towards improving relations with Pakistan is fast growing. Among them are retired judges, governors, editors, secretaries to government, generals, air-marshalls, ambassadors; some serving professors, vice-chancellor, businessmen, and even some former ministers. And this development is not without its counterparts in Pakistan. In our Punjab, also, where live the tens of millions who had to bear the brunt of the ravages of the migrations at the time of Partition and of three wars, the opinions held for two generations have begun to change. For anyone trying to collect signatures on an appeal for peace and cooperation between India and Pakistan, the going is surprisingly easy.

The contentious issues between the two countries are formidable. Among them, the high priority questions for Pakistan are of Kashmir, of military imbalance, of peaceful uses of nuclear power, of Indian sabotage networks in Pakistan, and of the safety of Muslims in India. In its turn, India links the problems of Kashmir under its rule and in Punjab to the covert aid and propaganda from Pakistan. History has its own ways of resolving stubborn problems, or of letting them continue unresolved. We often shudder to think what may be in store for India and Pakistan should the present tendencies continue.

In the long run, however, what will greatly help in the resolution of problems between the two countries, is the removal from the minds of many Indians the emotionally based and immensely exaggerated view (that) ... Muslims are not some kind of monsters who cannot be trusted, must be suspected, if not feared, or despised. False perception, inherited by generations of non-Muslims must be combated in a practical manner. Why not let as many Indians, as can afford, come to Pakistan, and see for themselves that Pakistanis are experts in not solving their own internal problems, and that they are in no position to harm any of their neighbors.

Why not let people of both the countries read each other's newspapers and begin the process of countering false propaganda and encouraging dissemination of the reality? Why should there not be a meeting between editors and owners of daily newspapers of India and Pakistan to come to some understanding to stop hostile propaganda against each other's countries? Such a meeting has the potential of being extremely beneficial to the cause of peace and co-operation.

Why should not the anomalies in our communication systems be sorted out? Why should Indians pay Rs 11 to send a letter to Pakistan, while Pakistanis send a letter to India in Rs 4? While Indians pay Rs 45 for a three-minute telephone call to Pakistan, which is as much as they pay for a call from Bombay to Delhi, why should Pakistanis pay Rs 168 for a three-minute call to

India, while they pay for the same duration call, Rs 64 for Bangladesh, Rs 78 for Thailand, Rs 118 for Holland, Rs 121 for Japan, and Rs 132 for Ecuador? Why should India stop Pakistanis crossing the border at Wagah by road while Pakistan allows Indians to do so? Why should not Pakistanis be able to read several recently published books and articles in India which reveal the personality of the Quaid-I-Azam in much better light than he was painted in India during the last half a century?

In their present state of social, economic, and political disarray both India and Pakistan should consider these small measures as giant steps forward towards improving their ties.

11

THE MAHAKALI IMPASSE AND INDO-NEPAL WATER CONFLICT[*]

Dipak Gyawali
Ajaya Dixit

On January 29, 1996 in Kathmandu, after about three days of deliberations, India's External Affairs Minister Pranab Mukherjee and Nepal's Foreign Minister Prakash Chandra Lohani initialled the Mahakali Treaty—known formally as the *Treaty between his Majesty's Government of Nepal and the Government of India concerning the integrated Development of the Mahakali River including Sarda Barrage, Tanakpur Barrage and Pancheshwar Project.* Immediately, there was an unseemly scramble among Nepali politicians to take credit for the Treaty. From the former speaker of parliament to the general secretary of the Nepal Communist Party (United Marxist–Leninists), then in opposition, from hard-line panchayati politicos of yesteryears to hardboiled bureaucrats, all claimed a share in the glory, or sang hosannas.[1] Today, except for those whose names have been directly enmeshed with the Treaty, one is hard-pressed to find a champion who would risk defending Mahakali heart and soul.

There is a need to analyze this predicament because it holds deep lessons for future efforts in collaborative water management in the Ganga basin, as well as development in general. The Mahakali impasse has roots deep in Nepal's history, and ramifications beyond water resources into political economy,

[*] Published with the permission of Nepal Water Conservation Foundation, Kathmandu, Nepal and the *Economic and Political Weekly*, February 27, 1999.

diplomatic relations between India and Nepal, as well as governance in south Asia. While the complex events surrounding it do need much deeper socio-political analyses than is possible here and in so close a time period after the events, a beginning needs to be made that can serve as a prelude to future studies from a variety of other viewpoints. The purpose of this essay is to put into perspective the complex set of events that led to the signing of the Mahakali Treaty, and the impasse it has since been enmeshed in. It first presents the chronology of events leading up to the Mahakali impasse. With this overview, it then asks some open-ended questions that may uncover a rich agenda for further research. Several undercurrents emerge with this historical overview that need not only further insightful analyses but also some redeeming statesmanship, both in Nepal and India.

I CHRONOLOGY OF EVENTS

Early Years

The Sugauli Treaty of AD 1816 defined the national frontiers of present day Nepal. It forced the Gorkhali Empire, which had extended up to the Satluj in the west, to give up the conquered lands west of Mahakali (called Sarda in India), and fixed this river as the western boundary between Nepal and British India.[2] Given the remoteness of the headwater reaches where the arms of the Nepali state had only a feeble presence, not much is heard of conflicts in this area. In the southern reaches, however, where the land was gifted back by the British to Nepal in recognition of the services provided by Shogun Jung Bahadur Rana in suppressing the Sepoy Mutiny of AD 1857, the braided nature of the river as it debouches onto the plains presented problems. Neither the thalweg nor centreline principle could be satisfactorily used to define the boundary, and it was taken as the midstream of the river with reference pillars on either side. Because of the shifting nature of the river course, a realignment of the boundary was ordered by the British India government in AD 1909. After much correspondence and many meetings, the demarcations were completed in February 1912 during the Shogunate of Rana Chandra Sumshere.[3]

Soon thereafter, the British India government contemplated building the Sarda barrage to provide irrigation to western United Provinces. After a series of negotiations, it managed to realize a Sarda Treaty in 1920, which transferred 4,000 acres of the eastern banks of the Mahakali to India to build the Sarda barrage in exchange for 4,000 acres of forested land in areas to the east, as well as Rs 50,000 to Nepal. Furthermore, the Treaty allowed Nepal to withdraw 4.25 cumecs of water in the dry season and 13 cumecs in the wet season, which could be increased to 28.34 cumecs if water were available. What India could withdraw out of the approximately 650 cumecs average annual flow of the Mahakali was, however, not specified. In effect, it was limited only by the scale of the technology it was free to employ.[4] This left room for critics of the 1920 Agreement to call it an "unequal treaty" and, with perfect economic and technological hindsight of today, to fault Chandra Sumshere for undervaluing the left bank of Sarda barrage. There were also questions raised about where the 4,000 acres of land received in exchange from the British were located.

After a major flood in the Mahakali "circa" 1953, India extended the left afflux bund of the Sarda barrage about a 100 m into Nepali territory beyond the border pillar BP 6A between 1954 and 1958. This extension of the Sarda afflux bund is physically similar to the case in Tanakpur in 1991. However, it is not known publicly if Nepal government provided permission for this in any form. If it was an incursion, there is no record of any protest over this by any Nepali government then, or afterwards—neither during the panchayat years, nor even while the Tanakpur debate raged on after the restoration of democracy during the first half of the 1990s.[5]

During the 1950s, there were no major initiatives on the Mahakali, but major flood control embankment building and irrigation projects were undertaken in north Bihar and Uttar Pradesh plains by the Indian government. To further these initiatives for the north Ganga plains, India entered into two major river treaties with Nepal in this period: the Kosi agreement on April 25, 1954 (revised subsequently on December 19, 1966) and the Gandak agreement on December 4, 1959 (amended on April 30, 1964). These treaties, and the projects they gave birth to, have had their own, less than salubrious, impact on Nepali polity, and popular perceptions of Indo-Nepal water relations, the details of which are beyond the scope of this essay.

Panchayat Raj (1961–April 1990)

Nepal, with a loan from the World Bank, began the Mahakali Irrigation Project in 1971 to utilize its share of the waters of the Mahakali as allowed under the Sarda agreement of 1920. By the second decade of Panchayat rule, Nepal's water resources development activities had begun to acquire a donor-led, statist bias, precluding other (private or community-based) institutional possibilities. Private initiatives in power generation were discouraged by HMG's (His Majesty's Government) new industrial policy of 1972 that nationalized electricity production to make bilateral and multilateral donor involvement easier.[6] There was extensive World Bank, UN, ADB, USAID, etc., involvement in irrigation, power, and water supply projects. The ministry of water resources, with irrigation, flood control, electric power, and water supply within its brief, became the largest infrastructure ministry in the country overtaking the ministry of works and transport. With the exception of the 21 MW Trisuli and 14 MW Devighat hydroelectric projects, there was not much inclination for furthering water resources projects that would be mutually beneficial to both India and Nepal.

Heavy investments were made in irrigation and power projects during this period—66,000 ha Sunsari–Morang on the Kosi (1965–ongoing), 34,000 ha Narayani (1967–ongoing), 7,000 ha Kankai (1970–90), 25,000 ha Kamala (1975–85), 10,400 ha Chitwan Lift (1973–88), 36,000 ha Bagmati (1980–ongoing), 60 MW Kulekhani I (1974–80), 32 MW Kulekhani II (1977–87), and 69 MW Marsyangdi (1982–89), etc. From 1985 onwards, the ministry of water resources was preoccupied with the 402 MW Arun 3 (later scaled down to 201 MW, and finally abandoned in August 1995 after the World Bank pulled out of it because of criticism for its excessive cost that was four to five times more than that of private sector projects in the Himalayan region).[7] The significance of Arun 3 to Tanakpur and Mahakali episodes is that this project, which had overtaken the entire

water and power establishment in Nepal, saw every other alternative to Arun 3 such as Sapta Gandaki, Burhi Gandaki, West
Seti, etc., as rivals to be suppressed or sidelined, rather than
examined with an open mind. As a result, during the Panchayat
rule, Nepal's water establishment was never able to approach
India openly, question its plans, and propose a co-operative
alternative that was better suited to Nepal's interests.

In 1983, India completed the technical study of a 120 MW
hydroelectric project on the border River Mahakali near the
town of Tanakpur in Nainital district. Nepal raised its concerns
with India regarding possible damage to Nepali land and territory, including the Mahakali Irrigation Project. The 120 MW
Tanakpur power plant, which uses all the waters of the Mahakali
during the dry season, would have emptied its tailwater into
the Sarda canal feeding the UP system and not into the river
upstream of the intake of the Sarda barrage from which Nepal's
Mahakali Irrigation Project receives its water. India agreed to
redesign its project and release the Mahakali water back into
the river so that Nepal's existing irrigation project would not
be left high and dry. It also agreed to, and constructed, some
river abutments to ameliorate bank cutting on the Nepali side.[8]

By 1988, India had completed the construction of the Tanakpur
barrage and the powerhouse with the exception of the left afflux
bund that was needed to tie the barrage to the high ground on
the left bank in Nepal. Despite its earlier insistence that this
was a wholly Indian project in fully Indian territory, and thus
of no concern to Nepal, it became necessary for India to request
for 577 m of Nepali land for this purpose. However, around this
period, relations between Nepal and India deteriorated with
Nepal importing Chinese light arms, and India imposing a
peacetime economic blockade of Nepal in March 1989. The
matter of extending the left afflux bund was not pursued further
in view of other pressing concerns, but the essential strategic
thrust of Indian government vis-à-vis Nepal's water resources
made itself felt in its diplomatic proposals.

In November 1989, with the main architect of the blockade
Rajiv Gandhi not faring well in the Indian parliamentary elections, the foreign ministers of the two countries were able to
meet in New Delhi in January 1990. Even as the anti-Panchayat
agitation led by the Nepali Congress and the United Left Front

continued in the country, the royal regime toned down both its promotion of "Nepal as a Zone of Peace" concept and its opposition to the 1950 Treaty of Peace and Friendship with India, and agreed to India preparing a new draft agreement on mutual co-operation. In a bid to extract maximum benefit out of the political turmoil in Nepal, India put forth a draft proposal on March 31, 1990 that included more stringent demands on Nepal vis-à-vis Indian security concerns than the 1950 Treaty. It was reminiscent of what one scholar has described as the "Krishna Menon syndrome."[9] It included Article Three of Part Four Economic, Industrial and Water Resources Co-operation that stated:

> The two Contracting Parties being equally desirous of attending complete and satisfactory utilization of the waters of the commonly shared rivers, undertake to (i) plan new uses or projects subject to the protection of the existing uses on the rivers and (ii) co-operate with each other to formulate and modify the planned new uses or project taking into consideration the water requirement of the parties.

The phrase "commonly shared rivers" was to make a comeback later during K.P. Bhattarai's interim government, and the prior rights issue expressed as "existing uses on the rivers" was to be resurrected in the "package deal" on the Mahakali with the UML government.

On April 9, 1990, King Birendra lifted the ban on agitating political parties and multi-party democracy was restored in Nepal. The post-panchayat interim government was under pressure from the Indian government to allow the construction of the left afflux bund of Tanakpur barrage especially after the economic blockade was relaxed following the restoration of democracy in April 1990. Soon after becoming prime minister of the interim government consisting of Nepali Congress and the communist United Left Front, Krishna Prasad Bhattarai visited New Delhi on the invitation of Indian Prime Minister V.P. Singh with an entourage that included Sahana Pradhan, then chairperson of the United Left Front and a minister in the interim government. On June 10, 1990, a joint communique was issued at the conclusion of his visit that included the phrase "common rivers" and the expediting of their development. It was to become an election issue in May 1991 as an alleged example of Nepali Congress's "sell-out" to India.

With the restoration of status quo ante of the pre-blockade days following Prime Minister Bhattarai's successful visit to India, the diplomatic initiatives from Delhi for Nepal's acquiescence to building Tanakpur's left afflux bund inside Nepali territory began to gather momentum. Meanwhile, the issue of Tanakpur, which had been wrapped within bureaucratic secrecy, began to unfold slowly in the public arena. Because the interim government's primary agenda was to frame the new constitution and hold elections, the matter of Tanakpur's left afflux bund was not pursued with any alacrity, but it continued to have its effect on Nepal's body politic. The new constitution of Nepal, which was being drafted in the meanwhile, was promulgated on November 9, 1990. It included a constitutional provision in Article 126 that required any resource-sharing agreement to be ratified by a two-thirds majority in parliament if it was of "pervasive, serious and long-term nature."

The interim government subsequently did try to find a way out of the difficulty brought about by India's unilateral decision to construct a barrage on a common border river. Because of the geometry of the land swapped in 1920, if India tied the afflux bund to the high ground in its territory, significant portion of Brahmadeo Mandi in Nepal would be submerged. There was a need to look for a variant which would cause the least submergence in Nepal, and water resources minister of the interim government Mahendra Narayan Nidhi asked his technical team, on December 28, 1990, to make a review of the Tanakpur problem. This team recommended, on February 22, 1991 the best variant that Nepal could agree to was to meet Indian requests. The team also mentioned Nepal's needs for additional irrigation in Kanchanpur district, as well as highway connection to the Mahakali barrage that functions as the only AA class bridge over the river in this area.

On April 15, 1991, the cabinet of the interim government— which included members of the communist United Left Front— authorized HMG's negotiating team to conduct discussions with India within certain parameters, including the least harmful afflux bund variant, provision of 1,000 cusecs of irrigation water, and "some electricity" in return for agreeing to provide India 577 m of Nepali land for building the left afflux bund of the Tanakpur barrage.[10] On May 17, 1991, Indian Prime Minister Chandra Shekhar wrote to his Nepali counterpart Krishna Prasad Bhattarai, asking for Nepal's permission to build the afflux bund, especially since the monsoon would be soon approaching. (If a record flood occurred, it could—unless prevented by an afflux bund—outflank the barrage with devastating consequences.) Because general elections were going on in Nepal, the matter remained unattended.

Centrist Majority Government and after

Nepali Congress won a majority in the general election even though its interim Prime Minister Bhattarai lost to the general secretary of the UML, partly due to the "common rivers" issue. The new Congress Government was headed by Girija Prasad Koirala as prime minister. He replied to Indian Prime Minister Chandra Shekhar, on June 10, 1991, that the permission requested from the Bhattarai government regarding Tanakpur's left afflux bund could only be given after detailed study, and an agreement between the two governments.

Prime Minister Koirala visited India between December 5–10, 1991 at the invitation of India's Prime Minister Narasimha Rao. Possibly because inadequate homework was done as regards Tanakpur, a decision seems to have been made not to discuss the matter with India in Delhi. This is highlighted by the fact that neither the water resources minister, nor the secretary of water resources, nor any other water resources experts were included in the 72-member strong official delegation that accompanied the prime minister to New Delhi. However, despite a possibility of breakdown of talks, a last-minute set of agreements was entered into with the government of India, which included trade and transit, and development issues, as well as plans to develop major high dams in the Nepal Himalaya.[11] Among other things, this December 1991, agreement explained as a mere "understanding" and not a treaty that would have to be presented before parliament, allowed India the use of 577 m of

Nepali territory to complete the construction of the left afflux bund of the Tanakpur barrage. Nepal was to receive "free of cost" 10 million units of electricity as well as 150 cusecs of water for irrigation.

On December 15, 1991 Prime Minister Koirala gave a public speech about his India visit at Kathmandu City Hall. In the interest of transparency, and to counter allegations of any "secret treaty," he promised to make public the agreements via the official *Nepal Gazette,* which was subsequently done on December 24, 1991. The details of the "understanding" that began to emerge after Koirala's return to Kathmandu raised a lot of suspicion and hackles. It allowed India to hastily start the construction of the left afflux bund by December 15, which was before details of the "understanding" had been made public in Nepal. Construction of flood protection works was slated to start in November 1991 even before the "understanding" was initialled in Delhi. The newspaper reports and gazetted notices continued to confuse 10 million units (KWh) of electricity with 10 MW of power, prompting a debate of what Nepal had actually received for allowing its left bank to be used for the project.

On December 17, 1991 advocate Bal Krishna Neupane filed a writ at Supreme Court challenging this "understanding," and appealing to the court to have it declared a treaty requiring parliamentary ratification by a two-thirds majority as per Article 126(2) of the Constitution of Nepal. On February 28, 1991, during the winter session of the parliament, the communist opposition gheraoed the rostrum of the lower house for eight hours, and prevented parliamentary proceedings in a bid to force the government to table before the house all documents relating to the Tanakpur "treaty." The treasury bench, on the other hand, maintained that it was only an "understanding" and everything relating to it had already been published in the *Nepal Gazette* of December 24, 1991. A 19-member all-party special committee of the parliament was formed to try and find a consensus. On March 11, 1991, Prime Minister Girija Prasad Koirala presented written reply to the Supreme Court defending his government's position. Street agitation against the treaty dominated national politics and newspapers for months. In end July–beginning August, Prime Minister Koirala attended the non-aligned summit meeting in Jakarta, where he is understood to have met India's Prime Minister Narasimha Rao, and discussed the Tanakpur imbroglio.[12]

The all-party special committee of the parliament held extensive meetings and invited external specialists, as well as government experts to the hearings. It was, however, unable to reach a consensus as sharp divisions remained regarding the actions of the government, and the interpretations of the constitutional provision. Instead of a single document, there were three different reports presented by the committee to the Lower House of parliament on September 7, 1992. In a memorandum submitted to the chairman of the Upper House dated September 9, 1992, eight communist factions (including the UML, Unity Centre, United, and Masal) state that the Tanakpur "understanding" signed by Prime Minister Koirala was a treaty which could only be implemented after ratification by a two-thirds majority in parliament. They demanded to know from the government where the 4,000 acres of land swapped with British India, in 1920, is located. The communists stated very clearly that it was wrong to link the Pancheshwar Project with Tanakpur. Pancheshwar high dam, they wrote, is a separate project requiring a separate treaty with parliamentary ratification, and there is no need for Nepal to compromise her future bargaining position at this stage.

In October 1992, India's Prime Minister Narasimha Rao visited Nepal during which the Tanakpur "understanding" was negotiated. The quantum of electricity that Nepal was to receive from the project "free of cost" was raised from 10 to 20 million units. Future upstream water developments such as Pancheshwar Multipurpose Projects were delinked from the agreement on Tanakpur with the provision that both countries were free to negotiate on upstream projects independent of whatsoever is agreed to at Tanakpur.

On December 15, 1992, the Supreme Court of Nepal decided that the Tanakpur agreement was indeed a treaty and not just an "understanding," and that it would have to be presented to the parliament for ratification as per Article 126 of the Constitution of Nepal. The Court, however, failed to provide a ruling on the second point of the petitioner, which was to require parliamentary ratification by a two-thirds majority as per

Clause Two of Article 126. It left it upon the Parliament to decide whether the ratification should be by a simple majority or, if the matter was deemed to be "pervasive, serious and long-term," to be ratified by a two-thirds majority.

A month after the Supreme Court decision, the government constituted a committee (Baral Commission) to evaluate the impact of the agreement. The committee fixed six criteria to define whether this river development initiative, and the agreement associated with it, constituted "all encompassing, serious and long-term" issues. They were:

(a) if a single treaty was done regarding use of several different river basins of Nepal, the treaty should be considered "all encompassing, serious and long-term";

(b) if a treaty is made for an entire river basin, then the treaty should be considered "all encompassing, serious and long-term";

(c) run-of-river hydroelectric projects (with no water storage) will be excluded from this definition;

(d) this definition would apply to storage projects of capacity greater than 1000 MW and capacity factor less than 0.3;

(e) this definition would also apply to projects whose costs would be large compared to economic indicators, such as annual GDP, and where sovereign loans are involved which would have to be paid back not just by the current generation making the decision, but by future generations, or which would be difficult to pay given the state of the economy; and

(f) the definition would apply to projects with large reservoirs, where resettlement is difficult to handle within Nepal's finance, land availability, etc.

Based on these criteria, the compensation that Nepal received for allowing India to use 577 m of Nepali land to complete the 120 MW run-of-river, the renegotiations that occurred during the visit to Kathmandu by the Indian Prime Minister Narasimha Rao that delinked Tanakpur from future developments upstream at Pancheshwar, as well as other benefits that would accrue to Nepal from the barrage such as transport, irrigation, as well as diplomatic goodwill, the Baral Commission concluded that the Tanakpur Agreement was of a simple nature and not an "all encompassing, serious, and long-term" one.

Subsequent to this report and other consultative works, the government made a move to present the Tanakpur Treaty to the parliament. It is suspected that the government intended to present it as a treaty of a simple nature that needed ratification only by a simple majority. It is also not clear if the government had set forth any criteria, new or otherwise, for defining the nature of the treaty as such. A meeting of the parliamentary committee of the Nepali Congress had been called. The Nepali Congress supreme leader Ganesh Man Singh refused to attend the meeting, and fired, what is popularly known as, a "letter bomb" to the chairman of the Nepali Congress. In his epistle of March 8, 1992, the Congress supremo declared: "Passing the Tanakpur Treaty by a simple majority of the lower house of parliament would be the equivalent of signing a death warrant. My conscience prevents me from putting my signature to it. Please do not compel me to go against my conscience."[13]

His letter, just as the Supreme Court's decision, skirted the difficult but germane issue of defining the criteria for calling Tanakpur Treaty an "all encompassing, serious and long-term" matter. The Ganesh Man faction of the Nepali Congress had been clamouring for Koirala's resignation on moral grounds after the Supreme Court decision. The speaker of the Parliament (who came from the Bhattarai faction of the Congress) had compromised his nonpartisanship by declaring that the House belonged to the opposition, and by not co-operating with the Koirala government in this matter.[14] Ganesh Man Singh's letter effectively derailed any political chance of the issue being resolved politically in parliament by any initiative from the Koirala camp. It was thus left hanging in limbo. Even the very first meeting of the newly formed high level National Water Resources Development Council—held on the eve of V.C. Shukla's visit to Nepal, chaired by the prime minister, and including in its composition all important politicians and bureaucrats—did not discuss at all projects of controversy such as Tanakpur and Arun 3.[15]

In December 1993 the Indian Water Resources Minister V.C. Shukla visited Nepal and managed to extract from the

Nepali government an "action plan" on how to proceed with the implementation of the Tanakpur agreement even when the main treaty had not been approved by the Parliament as was required by the Supreme Court verdict of December 1992.[16]

Soon thereafter, the Nepali government—which was embroiled in the Arun 3 controversy—granted a private Australian company a "hunting licence" to build the approximately 750 MW west Seti hydroelectric storage project upstream of the Karnali Chisapani Dam site and to sell the electric power to India. The matter was not presented to parliament, no questions were asked about the benefits of regulated flow that would accrue to India, and no political party or figure showed any interest or need to raise the matter, even though this issue had implications regarding Article 126(2) of the Nepali constitution. Another attractive scheme, the Sapta Gandaki run-of-river hydroelectric project, found the site of its powerhouse and desilting basin given away to a private medical college for setting up its campus. It was speculated that this was done to remove these projects from the list of contenders to Arun 3.

Meanwhile, the special all-party committee of the parliament failed to make any headway. Because of strong personal animosities among political leaders of different parties, this special committee was also unable to define what constitutes "all encompassing, serious and long-term" water sharing issue as per Clause 126(2) of the Nepali constitution. During the agitation against the Tanakpur "understanding" by the Koirala government, his opponents from the Opposition, as well as from within his own party, had hyped up the rhetoric to such an extent that an acceptable resolution of this impasse was well-neigh impossible. Committee discussions became a lacklustre buying of time, and parties began to exhibit early signs of "Tanakpur fatigue."

In July 1994, the Koirala government fell when MPs of his own party boycotted the house, and a bill elaborating his government's policy was voted down. The row over Tanakpur and the Supreme Court's verdict were considered among the significant factors that contributed to the brewing of this situation. Midterm general elections were held in November 1994, which resulted in the Nepali Congress losing the majority it commanded in the outgoing house.

The communist UML, which had vociferously opposed the Tanakpur Agreement, emerged as the single largest party in a hung parliament and formed, on December 9, a minority government. In the heat of the debate, both the communist UML and the RPP had called for renegotiating the Tanakpur Agreement. India saw no reason why it should live up to the hype of Nepali opposition leaders. To resolve the impasse, the UML government, ostensibly after receiving signals from India's CPM, put forth in April 1995 a "package deal." This plan proposed increasing the quantum of electricity and water to be made available to Nepal, but requires Nepal agreeing to the construction of a massive (315 m high, 6,480 MW) storage high dam at Pancheshwar in the mountains upstream of the Tanakpur site on the border of Mahakali River. It was this very linkage of Tanakpur with Pancheshwar that the UML had opposed previously.

Pancheshwar was a dam that India had wanted all along for over two decades but for which Nepalis had not shown much interest because of their smaller requirements for water and power. There was also a lack of clarity from the Indian side regarding power purchase price, as well as valuation of irrigation benefits and India's security concerns over control of the dam that would have compromised Nepal's sovereignty. Former Prime Minister Kirti Nidhi Bista had warned the powerful general secretary of the UML and Deputy Prime Minister Madhav Kumar Nepal before the latter left for talks with New Delhi, that he did not agree to the Indian demand on Mahakali. He said that he had turned down Indira Gandhi's request for a pact on the Mahakali in 1972.[17] The minority UML government, however, was not able to push it ahead because of differences within its ranks about the implications of the "package deal." Also, it soon got embroiled over the controversial Arun 3 hydroelectric project from which the World Bank withdrew support in August 1995 during its tenure, allowing the Nepali Congress to blame it for "setback to development."

The minority UML government fell in September 1995, and a three-party coalition of the Nepali Congress, the RPP, and the Sadbhawana Party formed a new government headed by Sher Bahadur Deuba. Because of the need to accommodate as many MPs as possible in a shaky coalition, Deuba formed the largest cabinet in the history of Nepal, and also created a new ministry of science and technology. By now, "Tanakpur fatigue" had overtaken all parties in small or great measure, and Nepali politicians were too embroiled in infighting among parties and groups for perks and privileges to worry about long-term interests.

During November–December 1995, in what has subsequently come to be known as the Pajero scandal, the Deuba government allowed initially MPs, and later senior bureaucrats and judges, the favor of importing luxury vehicles duty-free without disclosing their sources of income. It was seen as a violation of Article 67 of the Constitution, as well as Facilities for Members and Officials of the Parliament Act 2052, that specifies what members are entitled to as perks and privileges. The said Act does not allow MPs the facility to import luxury vehicles duty-free. Only a handful of MPs did not avail of this facility, and an even smaller number openly criticized the government's move, which was seen as institutionalizing corruption and buying off parliamentary votes.

On January 26, 1996, just before the arrival of Indian Foreign Minister Pranab Mukherjee to Kathmandu, a meeting was called amongst the representatives, two from each of the three major parties—the Nepali Congress, the UML, and the RPP—who put their signatures on what is called a "National Consensus on the Use of the Waters of the Mahakali River."[18] This so-called "consensus agreement" was done outside the Parliament and its committees, including the All-Party Committee on Tanakpur; the smaller parties, as well as opposing factions within parties, were not represented; and it basically furthered the earlier UML proposed "package deal" on the Mahakali.

On January 29, 1996 the foreign ministers of Nepal and India (Prakash Chandra Lohani and Pranab Mukherjee, respectively) signed the "Treaty concerning the integrated development of the Mahakali River, including Sarda barrage, Tanakpur barrage, and Pancheshwar project." The treaty provides 50 million units of electricity to Nepal from the Tanakpur powerhouse and barrage, over and above the 20 million agreed between Girija Koirala and Narasimha Rao. It also provides more water for irrigation as well as environmental needs below Sarda barrage, but wrests from Nepal the consent to build the Pancheshwar high dam—which would generate nine billion units of electricity that would be consumed mostly by India. It also had some water and cost sharing provisions, which subsequently became controversial as their implications began to unfold. The agreement was clear, and without doubt of an "all encompassing, serious and long-term" nature, and needed two-thirds ratification by Parliament. However, it became clear that Nepal's rights to 50 percent share of the waters of a border river had again been compromised by Article Three of the treaty, as well as Clause Three of the accompanying Lohani–Mukherjee exchange of letters.[19]

The prime ministers of Nepal and India re-initialled the treaty during the visit to India of Nepali Prime Minister Sher Bahadur Deuba on February 12, 1996. A day later, on February 13, 1996, the Communist Party of Nepal (Maoist) led by Puspa Kamal Dahal (Comrade Prachanda) and the United Peoples' Front led by Baburarm Bhattarai declared the Maoist "peoples' war," an insurgency which has taken more lives than most past revolutions in Nepal. Among their many demands was, and is, the abrogation of the unequal treaty on the Mahakali.

On February 17, 1996 in Bombay, during a continuation of the Nepali prime minister's India visit, the Nepali secretary of the ministry of water resources and the Indian secretary of the ministry of power signed an umbrella "agreement between His Majesty's government of Nepal and the government of India concerning the electric power trade." This agreement allows any governmental, semi-governmental, or private enterprise in Nepal or India to buy and sell power to each other determining, in the process, their terms and conditions. Meanwhile, public debate began to heat up prior to the parliamentary ratification of this treaty. This debate was very strong within the left and right parties. There was, however, practically no debate or discussions within the centrist Nepali Congress that had, since coming to power in 1991, jettisoned the principles of "democratic socialism" in favor of economic liberalism.

Two weeks after the treaty was initialled on April 10, 1996, because of public pressure, the 26th Central Committee Meeting of the UML formed a working group to study the treaty and its implications, even though its Janakpur meeting welcomed the signing of the treaty. Meanwhile, on August 20, 1996, Water Resources Minister Pashupati Sumsher Jung Bahadur Rana tabled the Mahakali Treaty for parliamentary discussion and ratification.

In what is widely seen as an effort to pressurize the UML into ratifying the Mahakali Treaty, the British Minister of State for Parliamentary Affairs Liam Fox and the US Assistant Secretary of State for South Asia Robin Raphael hinted during their visits to Nepal around August 26, 1996 that non-ratification of the Mahakali Treaty would send a wrong signal driving away private international investments in Nepal.[20]

On 2 September UML's study committee on the Mahakali Treaty (Oli Commission) presented its report to the general secretary, which highlighted 26 flaws with the Treaty. Among the flaws reported (for the first time) was the presence of Indian troops at Kalapani in Nepal near the headwaters of the Mahakali.[21] In terms of seriousness regarding matters pertaining to Nepal–India relations, it subsequently overshadowed the Pancheshwar high dam issue. This report virtually split this main Opposition party (without whose votes the Treaty would not muster the required two-thirds majority in parliament) into two—the majority Bolsheviks who felt that the Treaty should be ratified first and the negative points taken care of during the preparation of the engineering report (DPR) of the high dam project, and the minority Mensheviks who thought the Treaty should not be ratified until all the flaws had been cleared up with India (and who later split off as the ML faction).

The working committee and central committees met in almost continuous sessions to iron out the differences between the Bolsheviks and the Mensheviks. The 28th meeting of the central committee of the UML was held from September 4–9, 1996. This meeting decided that the Treaty can be ratified only after HMG and the Government of India gives written commitments to rectify the following items:

- demarcate Nepal's western border with India within a fixed time-frame;
- remove Indian military checkpost from Darchula;

- give Nepal 36.67 acres of land that should have been given when the Sarda barrage was constructed;
- declare Mahakali River as basically a border river;
- have written commitment from India that it will buy Nepal's share of the electricity from Pancheshwar dam on the principle of avoided costs;
- assure that Nepal will have half the rights to the water produced from Pancheshwar dam, that Nepal will have unhindered right to use her share of the water, and that India will not raise any objections to Nepali irrigation projects in the Tarai;
- review 1950 Treaty;
- assure alternative transit point for Nepal through Bangladesh;
- assure that the transit treaty between Nepal and India will be for long term;
- manage scientifically Nepal's border with India;
- regulate Nepal–India border;
- assure Indian help in solving the problem of the Bhutanese refugees;
- assure that India will provide Nepal navigational access to the sea.

The UML wrote a letter to HMG asking for its, and Indian government's, written commitments on these points before it would consent to ratifying the Mahakali Treaty. On 2 September Prime Minister Deuba replied to the UML that all these issues are either covered in the Treaty, or will be done, by technical teams to be constituted between two governments. The Indian ambassador, in letters of 10 and 19 September declined to comment on these issues as diplomatically inappropriate to him; but he assured "that the government of India would be happy to discuss these and other relevant matters and reach mutually satisfactory understandings on them after ratification of the Treaty, at the time of finalizing the detailed project report." The Bolsheviks are satisfied that this letter is enough of a written commitment on the above issues, whereas the Mensheviks call it a worthless receipt.[22]

At the penultimate moment before the parliamentary vote for ratification, an equally split 29-member central committee of the UML approved with 17 vote's majority against 16 votes to ratify the treaty. The chairman of the party, former Prime Minister Man Mohan Adhikari—who had spoken out against the Treaty—claimed indisposition, and he was replaced temporarily by an alternate member of the general secretary's choice who voted in favor of ratifying the Treaty. The party's Mensheviks called this a "counterfeit majority." Students ransacked the UML parliamentary party office and locked up leaders, who had to be rescued by the police. There was an attempt by small parties opposed to the Treaty to encircle the parliament, but police action, including arrest of some Opposition politicians, including former Prime Minister Kirti Nidhi Bista, prevented this from happening.[23]

The Mahakali Treaty was ratified close to midnight by a more than two-thirds majority of the joint Upper and Lower Houses of the Nepali Parliament, as per the constitutional requirement and Article 126.[24] However, before the Treaty was ratified, the parliament unanimously passed a stricture on the Treaty ("sankalpa prastav"), which is binding on the Nepali government. The stricture, inter alia, redefines water rights, especially as stated in Article Three in the main Treaty text, as well as in Clause Three in the letter exchanged with the Treaty. The four elements of the stricture are:

(a) Nepal's electricity to be bought by India will be sold as per the "avoided cost" principle.
(b) When the Mahakali Commission is constituted, it will be done only upon agreement with the main Opposition party in parliament as well as parties recognized as national parties.
(c) "Equal entitlement in the utilization of the waters of the Mahakali River without prejudice to their respective existing consumptive uses of the Mahakali River" means equal rights to all the waters of the Mahakali; and
(d) Saying that "Mahakali is a boundary river on major stretches between the two countries" is the same as saying it is "basically a border river."[25]

In the debate leading to the voting on the Treaty, UML parliamentarian Khadga Oli said that the Mahakali Treaty was done to correct the treason ("rastraghaat") committed in Tanakpur by the government of Girija Prasad Koirala. This allegation was not countered or challenged by the Nepali Congress, which en masse votes in favor of the Treaty, even though senior leaders such as Sailaja Acharya had voiced misgivings. The unanimous passage of this stricture essentially means that the Treaty has been given conditional ratification. The argument was put forward by those in favor of the ratification, that the defects in the Treaty, as well as the provisions of the parliamentary strictures, would be taken care of during the preparation of the detailed project report (DPR) of the Pancheshwar high dam project. As per Article Three (a) of the Lohani–Mukherjee exchange of letters with this Treaty (re-initialled again by Narasimha Rao and Sher Bahadur Deuba on February 12, 1996 in New Delhi) this DPR had to be prepared within six months of the entry into force of the Treaty, i.e., March 19, 1997.[26]

Because of the controversy surrounding the Treaty, and the fact that it had been passed with an unanimous parliamentary stricture, the parliament constituted a joint parliamentary committee to monitor the Mahakali Treaty on October 10, 1996. Its objective was to guide the implementation of the Treaty, and assure the inclusion of those points that have been missed in the Treaty, such as the "sankalpa prastav." There were 10 members from different parties in the committee, which was chaired by the speaker of the House of Representatives Ram Chandra Paudel.[27] Like the previous all-party parliamentary committee on Tanakpur, this committee too was unable to provide any guidance. The members visited the site and came back as confused as before. To add to their worries, India's joint secretary of water resources, responding to questions from Nepali journalists regarding the "sankalpa prastav," said that India is not concerned with what such "prastavs" say. Rather, India is only concerned with the wordings in the Treaty itself.[28] The much heralded statements by political leaders, that all defects in the Treaty would be taken care of during the preparation of the DPR and that India has agreed to do so, is thus proved wrong.

Even as the two governments remained unable to prepare the DPR of the Pancheshwar project under the Mahakali Treaty, the Deuba government signed a memorandum of understanding with India to study the mammoth Kosi high dam project on January 7–9, 1997. This agreement, signed by Anand Bahadur Thapa, executive director of HMG/N Water and Energy Commission and Ramesh Chandra, chairman of the India's Central Water Commission, allowed the establishment of liaison offices in Nepal by India for the purpose of preparing these projects, committed Nepal to providing data to India on its water projects within this area from Birganj to Biratnagar within a month, without India reciprocating along the same lines, and agreed to India paying for the perks and privileges of Nepal government employees on this exercise.[29]

Politicians of Nepal seem to have been guided by the view that large water resources projects are synonymous with Nepal's development. Nepali party functionaries fear political allegations that a project, any project, is not moving forward due to their action or inaction, regardless of technical, economic, or developmental demerits of such projects. Hence, they prefer to be seen "for" projects rather than questioning them. With the collapse of Arun 3, Nepali politicians have gone overboard blaming the opposition for its cancellation by the World Bank. To be seen as promoting water resources development, the Deuba government continued its "distress sale" type of approach to large-scale water resources development.

It proposed giving a "hunting licence" to Enron Renewable Energy Corporation of Texas for the Karnali project. Enron highlighted in its proposal that it was willing to build the Arun 3 as part of the Karnali–Arun 3 package, with Arun 3 costing only 700 million US dollars as opposed to the aborted World Bank/HMG plan which required 1.1 billion US dollars, of which approximately 42 percent was to be borne by the Nepali consumer through stiff tariff hikes. His cabinet minister for water resources Pashupati Rana opposed Deuba in this attempt because the matter involved downstream irrigation and flood control benefits that would accrue to India, and upstream costs, such as submergence to Nepal.[30]

In end February 1997, again because of party indiscipline, the centre–right Deuba government collapsed, and an incongruous right–left coalition formed the government.

After the Treaty

Lokendra Bahadur Chand of the RPP became prime minister on March 3, 1997 after Sher Bahadur Deuba's government collapsed when some Nepali Congress MPs refused to show up during a crucial vote. Chand led a right–left coalition government of ex-panchas and the communist UML with Bam Dev Gautam as the deputy prime minister. This government exchanged the instruments of ratification of Mahakali Treaty with the Indian government on June 4, 1997 without including the provisions of the "sankalpa prastav" of the parliament. It also went ahead with an agreement with the private Australian Snowy Mountain Engineering Company regarding the export-oriented multipurpose west Seti storage project, without discussing downstream water rights issues. The powerful deputy prime minister claimed in parliament that this was done because it is only a hydroelectric project and that "claiming downstream benefits from India may lead to India claiming damages from flooding from the waters released from the reservoir."[31]

The state of affairs of the body politic is highlighted by the following statement in *Kathmandu Post*:

Ex- and soon-to-be prime minister Surya Bahadur Thapa's interview given to *Kathmandu Post's* Akhilesh Upadhyay:
TKP: What could be the interests of "unseen forces" trying to destabilize democracy?
SBT: The biggest destabilizing force is the politics of commission. (Agents of) Arun 3, Karnali, Enron, etc., have come to play a crucial role in the frequent changes in government and the distribution of portfolios within a given government. For this class, its petty economic interests prevail over the national interests. This force has no scruples.[32]

The joint parliamentary monitoring committee came to an impasse. It directed the government to do a thorough homework regarding the source of the Mahakali and the status of the western border of Nepal.[33] After a long silence since the People's Movement in 1990 that overthrew the panchayat system, its last Prime Minister Marich Man Singh Shrestha broke his silence and gave an interview. He accused the government of caving in before India, and claimed that his government had rejected the Mahakali project proposed by India because of the border problem at the headwaters. He further claimed that because of his government's nationalistic stance regarding Tinkar (Kalapani) and Mahakali, India imposed the economic blockade of 1989.[34]

Pashupati Sumsher J.B. Rana, erstwhile water resources minister in several governments but not in this right–left one, in an interview given to Binod Dhungel, executive editor of *Janata Saptahik,* on June 17, 1997, expressed amazement that the very forces which opposed the Mahakali Treaty are now moving forward to exchange the instruments of ratification without incorporating the provisions of the "sankalpa prastav."

In what has come to be known as the "Good Bye, Monika!" episode, two otherwise warring newspapers, *Dristi* of the UML and *Punarjagaran* of the Ganesh Man-Bhattarai (or alternatively, anti-Girija) faction of the Nepali Congress jointly hosted a farewell reception for a press officer of the Indian embassy at the pricey Shangrila hotel. The press officer had been responsible for assuring favorable coverage during the passage of the Mahakali Treaty. What was even more incongruous diplomatically was the presence of senior UML and NC leadership of ministerial rank at this reception.[35] An all parties' meeting of August 3, 1997 wanted the government to write a letter to Enron of Texas for investment in the 10,800 MW Karnali–Chisapani hydro-project. Enron publicized its intention to sell electricity to China some 3,500 km across the Himalayas to the north to the delight of left-wing comrades and to build the Arun 3 project.[36]

By September 17, 1997, the much talked about and publicized completion of the preparation of DPR of Pancheshwar multipurpose project ran into deep waters after a proposal of water sharing was put forth by an Indian technical team. Highly placed government sources who participated in the meeting of joint group of experts are reported as telling *Kantipur Daily* that India came forward with an altogether new and unheard of proposal during the talks which stunned the Nepali technicians. Their proposal was that the sharing of Mahakali waters should be done only after ensuring that the flow of water to the lower Sarda project situated about 160 km downstream from the Sarda barrage at the Nepal–India border is assured prior use. In fact,

India made prior rights claims based on the size of its canals (built without Nepal's co-operation or permission) which amounts to more water than there is in the river itself. India thus used Article Three of the Mahakali Treaty to its advantage as suspected by many when the Treaty was initialled.[37]

Lokendra Bahadur Chand's government collapsed between October 4–6, 1997 when differences arose in the RPP about the wisdom of unprincipled coalition with the communists. A government led by Surya Bahadur Thapa of the RPP was formed with the largest parliamentary party, the Nepali Congress, as junior coalition partner. On December 4, 1997, the six-month period for the preparation of the DPR stipulated in the letters exchanged with the Mahakali Treaty, and counted from the date of exchange of instruments of ratification, lapsed with no progress. Those who opposed the Treaty as unequal and flawed in 1996 argued that the Treaty has lost its legitimacy and can be considered as having lapsed. There was talk that this is a "procedural" matter, which can be sorted out bureaucratically, but the counter argument made is that only the body, which ratified the Treaty (two-thirds of the parliament), has the right to change it.[38] On January 9, 1998 the RPP split into the Thapa faction which is seen as pro-Mahakali Treaty and the Chand faction which is seen as opposed to it. On March 5, 1998, the Menshevik faction of the communists, most of whom abstained from voting for the Mahakali Treaty broke away from the UML to form the Nepal Communist Party (Marxist–Leninists) or ML, for short, as opposed to the UML, who were responsible for ramroding the Treaty through parliament.

Between April 10–12, 1998 the Nepali Congress forced Surya Bahadur Thapa to resign, and formed a minority government headed by Nepali Congress president Girija Prasad Koirala with support by the Mensheviks from the outside. In the new cabinet, Sailaja Acharya became deputy prime minister and minister of water resources. She openly advocated the "Small is Beautiful" philosophy, and mentioned flaws with the Mahakali Treaty for which she was attacked by the pro-Mahakali Thapa faction of the RPP and the UML.

In May 19, 1998 the Chinese deputy minister for water use and vice-president of Chinese Federation of Commerce and

Industry Yan Kikung visited Nepal. In reply to questions of China buying electricity from Nepal from the Karnali and Arun 3 projects, the minister said categorically that China had no intention of doing so, that for Tibet, she was going to develop solar energy because of the dispersed nature of the settlements.[39] This came as a jolt to those Nepali politicians and policymakers, who have been sold on the dream of exporting electricity to China as well as India. The presence of Indian troops at Kalapani on the Mahakali was protested by students of the ML faction, Former Foreign Minister Rishikesh Shah said that the Indian troops moved in when he was in the ministry during the reign of King Mahendra who did not wish to irritate India any more than he already had.[40]

There was a campaign to discredit Deputy Prime Minister Sailaja Acharya because of the letter she has had her ministry write to Enron on July 24 effectively, not giving it the Karnali project survey licence it had asked for. She and her ministry argued that Karnali was a multipurpose project, and the issues involved were not just of electricity exports, but also significant downstream flood control and irrigation benefit issues in India. This matter needed further discussions with the lower riparian, and was related to how much progress was made in the difficulties regarding the Pancheshwar project and the Mahakali Treaty.

Against her were aligned not just the Thapa faction of the RPP, but also her rival in the Nepali Congress led by ex-Prime Minister Sher Bahadur Deuba, the latter accusing Acharya of "murdering" Karnali. In perhaps, what could be the only event of its kind worldwide of a communist leader, openly advocating for a multinational company, the leader of the opposition UML and former Prime Minister Man Mohan Adhikary accused the government of cold-shouldering Enron and threatened to make this an issue.[41] The deputy prime minister was made to stand at the rostrum of the lower house and heckled for two hours. In her reply, she quoted the joint parliamentary committee members monitoring the Mahakali Treaty as saying that the Treaty was as good as dead, which infuriated the pro-Mahakali lobby. She, however, claimed that without adequate progress on the Mahakali Treaty, a new project such as Karnali Chisapani cannot be initiated since the issues in both were linked in terms of downstream water rights.[42] While she stuck to her ground, her party's central committee decided that Pancheshwar and Karnali Chisapani projects were not linked, and that Enron should be invited for talks to give it the survey licence.

On August 26, 1998, the breakaway Menshevik communist faction of the ML formally joined the Koirala government and took up cabinet assignments. In an article in a local weekly, former foreign minister and Nepal's permanent representative to the United Nations Shailendra Kumar Upadhyay mentioned that the commission agents against Sailaja Acharya were the very forces which ousted minister D.P. Adhikari from the water resources ministry, during the panchayat days in 1979, when he initiated the small hydro-development projects.[43] Deputy Prime Minister Acharya mentioned in an interview in the official daily that the "water mafia" which has benefitted from kickbacks in foreign aid projects would like to see her removed.[44] In a continuing bout of national amnesia, despite the Chinese deputy minister's statement six months earlier, Prime Minister Girija Prasad Koirala said to Japanese businessmen during his visit to Japan on November 5, 1998 that they should invest in hydropower development in Nepal, and sell electricity to Indian and Chinese markets.[45]

The ML, which was ideologically closer to other communist factions, came under pressure from the other eight left groups ("aath baam samuha") to either force its Congress coalition partner to curb police activities against the Maoists and agree to other left demands, or to quit the government. On December 10, 1998, all its ministers in the cabinet resigned en masse. On December 24, 1998, Girija Prasad Koirala again formed another government, this time with the UML as coalition partners on the condition that he recommends dissolution of the house and holds fresh elections.

The leaders of the UML had met Indian Prime Minister Atal Behari Vajpayee in New Delhi on September 19, 1998, and assured him that they would co-operate in furthering the Mahakali Treaty, as they had done during its ratification. They assured him that they were doing this not for petty interests or a few billion rupees, but for furthering friendship and bilateral relations with India.[46] The UML, in its Bhairawa meeting, had passed a

resolution demanding the DPR of Pancheshwar Project be prepared forthwith. Immediately, upon assuming the portfolio of
water resources minister in the new coalition, UML politburo
member Pradip Nepal called for a meeting of senior officers of
the water resources ministry, as well as finance and foreign affairs
secretaries of HMG, and authorized the transfer of Rs 15 million
from various projects to the Pancheshwar Project office for the
preparation of the DPR.[47] This action was criticized by other
left parties as unbecoming of a government which was effectively
an interim government that was only mandated to hold fresh
elections.[48]

II Larger Questions

The three-year saga of the Mahakali Treaty presents itself as a
forensic resource to study and understand Nepali polity and its
relationship with its big southern neighbor. The Treaty is a
classic case of "marry in haste and repent at leisure," as the
current impasse over its implementation amply demonstrates.
It is standing proof that for the major political forces in Nepal
and their leaders, international treaties have value more for
their outward form than for their internal substance, more to
look "nice" as "development-oriented" politicians in the short
term than to have the nation benefit from their substance in
the long term. Given the unseemly haste with which the Treaty
was rammed through parliament and the barrage of pejoratives
that was fired at those raising caution regarding the highest
rockfill dam in the world in seismic Himalaya, it may be safely
predicted that conflict and paralysis will probably mark the
way forward unless redeemed by farsighted statesmanship.
However, selective amnesia that filters out difficult questions
of resource management seems to be pandemic among Nepal's
political set, which does not leave much room for sanguinity.

The fact is that Nepalis are prisoners of their own hype. There
is the pervasive and naive belief that global capital and/or
the foreign aid machine would do the needful for harnessing
the Himalayan waters and selling the electricity generated to
India, after which they could be rich as the sheikhs of Arabia.

Without adequate homework on the details of costs and benefits, as well as on the intense and complex bargaining required to realize these dreams, they will find themselves ill-prepared to face the forces of the market. As in the past, it will lead them to a perpetual post facto feeling of having always received a raw deal. More fundamentally, the idea of generating electricity by harnessing Himalayan water, exporting it, and developing the country from the revenue generated is simplistic on several counts, from hydrogeology to macro-economic finances. There has never been any serious articulation of what the multiple risks are, how much the actual revenue will be, or what linkage there is between water resources development and the eradication of pervasive poverty in the Himalaya-Ganga. Indeed, without such upstream–downstream linkages with the economy's overall capacity and development, the experiences of other countries from Ghana to Laos to Paraguay point to the possibility of such high-risk projects leading straight to impoverishment instead.[49]

A fundamental flaw of those "marrying in haste" is their inability to distinguish between the purpose of a Treaty and that of a DPR under the Treaty. The former is a political document that defines rights and the boundaries of those rights on the entire Mahakali basin. It is the job of politicians to secure those rights, and their success or failure is judged by how well they do this job. By demonstrating casualness and carelessness regarding the implications of Article three of the Treaty, as well as Clause three of the Lohani–Mukherjee exchange of letters that form an integral part of the Treaty (re-initialled subsequently by two prime ministers), the current crop of leaders have not fared well with their task of protecting Nepali rights and interests.

By contrast, the Pancheshwar DPR on which all aspirations are now pegged (or to put it more bluntly, behind which skirts major political leaders), is a technical engineering document regarding the construction of a very high dam—one of the highest in the world—within the framework of the Treaty. It cannot change or challenge that framework. It cannot negotiate rights on water, nor can it negotiate the modality for fixing the price of electricity ("cost plus" or "avoided costs"). Political leaders alone can do that, but being prisoners of their past, they show little will in being able to do so. The all-party parliamentary committees formed to find a consensus and guide the DPR preparation is "as good as dead," and along with it, the Treaty it ratified three-years ago with such fanfare.

Even on professional matters, government expertise and organizations that are supposed to do the expert homework on the technical issues have eroded their own credibility with their past unprofessional performance on Arun 3 and other water resource-related issues. This sad state of affairs has come about because of political interference, failure of senior bureaucrats to stand up for professionalism, as well as the rampant growth of a culture of "zamindari" research, an attitude wherein in-house homework is substituted with a total reliance on expatriate consultants. This has not only sapped their intellectual vigour, but has also made them incapable of providing sound professional advice to the medley of political masters of the day. There has also been a less than satisfactory performance by other constitutional organs of the state. The crux of the matter from Tanakpur to Mahakali lay in defining the three adjectives of Clause 126 of the constitution of Nepal—what constitutes "pervasive, serious and long-term" issues in a resource sharing Treaty—and the Supreme Court was asked to do so in a writ petition. While the court ruled that the "understanding" reached by Prime Minister Koirala in December 1991 was a Treaty that needed parliamentary ratification, it failed the petitioner on his second point, i.e., whether the matter constituted an "all encompassing, serious and long-term" issue, and thus required ratification by two-thirds majority. The court sent the matter back to the parliament for it to decide, and the parliament has, to this day, with all their all-party committees, failed to do. Once the court has been asked to provide judgment on this issue, it should have done so (taking the help of appropriate amicus curae of experts, if necessary), without saying, let the parliament decide and then we will judge whether the parliament's decision is correct or not. This is a major reason why the matter hangs in political and judicial limbo.

The Mahakali impasse has also forced upon us questions regarding the role of the "durbar." While it is fashionable not to see any wrong with the durbar since monarchy went constitutional in 1991, several things are worth noting. First, the current constitution gives joint executive powers to the durbar and the executive, and the durbar's role does include warning the executive of what it would see as improper in the larger national interests. Given that both the Tanakpur and Kalapani issues originated during the "active and dynamic leadership" of the durbar pre-1990, and the fact that it functioned as the de facto secretariat of the country where much of the relevant documents resided (as opposed to the de jure secretariat, especially since the 1975 second, and the 1980 post-referendum third amendment of the constitution), its role in providing timely warning to the new executive system was essential. This was not done.

In recent interviews, former Foreign Minister Rishikesh Shah has opined that Mahakali Treaty is not a Treaty but only a *note verbale* since it has not been approved by the durbar.[50] The point is moot since the Treaty laws in force do not have such a provision; but the legal right as well as moral responsibility to provide timely warning does rest with it under the present arrangements. This provision has not been used to benefit the nation in a timely fashion as far as the Tanakpur–Mahakali issue is concerned.

Second, the issue of Mahakali is now inextricably linked with that of the presence of Indian troops at Kalapani. How this relates to the durbar is in the following. Foreign troops were stationed on Nepali soil during the period of active and absolute monarchy, and the army—one of whose elementary functions is to guard the country's frontier from encroachment—is still under the durbar, and not fully under the elected government under the present democratic dispensation. For such institutions, not to have done anything about foreign troops on its soil, raises many disturbing questions, and the durbar's attempted aloofness on this matter, can leave it open to interpretation of reluctant cooperation with the new dispensation.

In resolving the Mahakali impasse, national exercises are needed which rise above partisan interests not only of political groupings, but also of the durbar and the rent-seeking bureaucracy in singha durbar. But how can that be achieved? While one can debate various ways of achieving it, one can at least begin by outlining those activities that must not be done if a way out is to be found:

- Nepalis should stop reflexively blaming the Indians. They are only taking advantage of an attractive bargain, at throwaway price, offered by Nepalis with their lack of effective homework. Such a favorable situation would be something any party on the other side of the bargaining table would avail of.
- Those who wish to see the Pancheshwar high dam built should not continue to deny the obvious. A good beginning could be made by admitting that the Mahakali Treaty done in haste has serious flaws in it. A Treaty ratified with strictures is no ratification, especially since the Indian side has not accepted those strictures, and the Nepali side cannot move away from those strictures. Very pertinent in this regard is the near absolute lack of any debate within the Nepali Congress on this issue. While both the RPP and the UML/ML have seen debates on Mahakali, this silence on the part of the oldest and major centrist party of Nepal does not bode well for an open and democratic polity.
- Certain statesmen-like norms need to be established that do not misuse provisions of the constitution for partisan ends. If the court and the constitution demand that a criterion for defining "all encompassing, serious and long-term" is required, parties in parliament should not shirk from that responsibility, but get that task done before moving forward with other resource sharing agreements, whether bilaterally, multilaterally, or through the private sector. Otherwise, one merely exports Tanakpur–Mahakali type imbroglios into the future for other projects.
- There is no need to continue being prisoners of hot political rhetoric and hype. It has only divided the nation and put national leaders up for ridicule. The homework that should have been done before the Treaty was formalized has not been done even into this third year after it was signed (even though it was rather thoughtlessly promised in ratified writing to be done in six months); and given the complexity of the issues involved, both technical and socio-economic, there is little chance of its being completed well into the life of the next parliament. All indications point to the possibility that the hyped-up benefits projected for this Treaty are just not there.

- The bureaucracy and their political masters should not shut off their ears to civil society voices. The Mahakali Treaty has been characterized, among other things, by the refusal of those in power to listen to any alternative arguments. Those arguments have now come to haunt all the three fractured parties in Nepal.
- If development is to be real and sustainable, there must no longer be any shirking from an honest assessment of the real capacity of national institutions and the need to build up these capacities. The project that the Mahakali Treaty aims to execute—Pancheshwar high dam—is at 315 m, the second, if not the highest rockfill dam in the world. The implementation of an engineering project of such a magnitude is replete with challenges and uncertainties, meeting which, the managerial and technical capacities of Nepali, and possibly, Indian water related institutions in their current stage of evolution are questionable.

There are also major lessons for India's water bureaucracy as well. Water resource management in the semi-arid tropics that is the Himalaya-Ganga, albeit punctuated by short monsoon cloudbursts, is a slow proposition which not only needs to assure fairness with the societies it is dealing with, but must be perceived and accepted as being fair as well. Agreements through political pressure, diplomatic maneuvering and legal point scoring from a strong and large neighbor may bring forth agreements in the short term but, as Mahakali has shown, nothing will move forward in the long term. Even if it did, the social and political costs may make the victory too expensive. Since India is to be the major beneficiary of reservoirs in Nepal, it will have to go the extra length in providing creative leadership, that is not just legally, but morally unassailable. The need of the region and the times is for sagacious water management at the micro- and meso-levels so that agricultural, health, and sanitation securities are assured, and its impact can be translated into quick and tangible economic benefits. However, given the continuing preoccupation of the Indian water establishment with new constructions, and a failure to conduct a credible review of past mistakes, there is little hope that South Asia's

largest water bureaucracy can provide the required statesmanship. This job is made all the more difficult because of the colossal
vested interests built into the political economy of embankment
and canal construction industry in India.

The answer, therefore, probably lies in growing activism, not
only of the environmentalists, but also of the judiciary, journalism, and the sections of the bureaucracy that are concerned
with issues of equity, such as social and rural development
wings; therefore, reassess, reconsider and renegotiate in good
faith. Indian water and energy requirements on the ground are
quite different from that which is projected by its construction-
oriented water bureaucracy. Those requirements cannot be met
at reasonable costs from the type of technology and programmes
offered by the high dam option, at least, in the short to medium
term of the next 20 years. The same is true of Nepal's own needs.

Proper water management in the Himalaya-Ganga is a pressing need of today which has to be done based on principles of
low cost options, short gestation projects, contractual reliability,
especially for industrial and agricultural consumers, national
capacity building for effective maintenance and technology
transfer, and a balance of equity in regional and urban–rural
contexts. Given what has happened around the world, both in
developing and industrialized countries in this regard, it is quite
easy to see how the Mahakali option fails on these criteria compared to other paths and options.

The delegitimization of mainstream political actors in Nepal,
despite democratic polity, has its genesis in their inability to
conceptualize modalities of ushering security to the Nepali
people by addressing the eco-structural contradictions that the
country is enmeshed within. The process is further aggravated
by their inability to define the path of harnessing the country's resource, particularly water, to the advantage of the country's disadvantaged sections. The response by all political parties
across the board to harness water resource vis-à-vis India has
so far in the last halfcentury been one-track and rooted in the
notion of sharing of the largesse from a mega "project." The
end result has been many words, but little or no deeds to show
for the hype, leading to erosion of the state as an institutional
resource and the crises in governance that the country currently
faces.

The alternative approach of national capacity building, local government participation, use of cheap and reliable electricity to give national industries a competitive edge, etc., would obviate much of the current ills in Nepali body politic. This approach (as opposed to that of only inviting external contractors and consultants) will enhance local resilience that will contribute to demonstrable societal well-being. The difficulty, however, is in transcending the clogged filters within the water establishment, as well as the current set-up of political leadership in the country.

POSTSCRIPT

This article in EPW was subsequently revised and expanded by the authors, and published in AD 2000 as "Mahakali Impasse: A Futile Paradigm's Bequested Travails" in Dhruba Kumar (ed.), *Domestic Conflicts and Crisis of Governability in Nepal*, Centre for Nepal and Asian Studies (CNAS), Tribhuban University, Kathmandu. The impasse, which is coeval with the Maoist insurgency in the Kingdom, continues into its eighth year despite ratification by the Nepali parliament with an over two-thirds majority. The "detailed project report" or DPR on the 315 m high Pancheshwar High Dam that was to have been completed within six months of the signing of the treaty is still mired in disagreement. Whenever it is prepared, its provisions would have to be approved anew by the parliament.

This is made difficult by the failure of past House sessions (since the Tanakpur imbroglio in 1991) to define the three qualifiers in Article 126 of the Nepali Constitution: if a treaty is of a "pervasive, serious and long-term" nature it should be ratified by a two-thirds majority of the parliament, otherwise any government with a simple majority should be able to implement it. There have been recent attempts to clarify that definition, which is discussed in A. Dixit, P. Adhikari and S. Bisanghke (eds), *Constructive Dialogue on Dams and Development*, Nepal Water Conservation Foundation, Kathmandu, 2004.

The contentious issues in the preparation of the DPR centre on interpreting water rights that accrue to the two countries as well as on the location of the re-regulating dam. Nepal wants it at Rupaligad close to the main dam itself, whereas India wants it further downstream at Poornagiri, which would submerge much of the fertile Jogbuda Valley and which is actually the site for a second high dam in the Mahakali cascade. These divergent positions are further complicated by India's river linking proposal, the implications of which for Nepal have been discussed by A. Dixit in the article "Rivers of Collective Belonging," in the October 2003 vol. 16, no. 10 issue of *Himal South Asia*.

NOTES AND REFERENCES

1. General secretary of CPN (UML) Madhav Kumar Nepal (who said on Nepal TV that the mango tree had really been planted by the UML but when time came for plucking the ripe mango, the Nepali Congress happened to be in power); former speaker of parliament Daman Nath Dhungana (who wanted credit for not allowing Tanakpur Treaty to be passed by the Girija Koirala government); and former Royal Palace bureaucrat responsible for the water resource portfolio during the panchayat years Govinda Das Shrestha (who wrote in *The Kathmandu Post* of February 1, 1996 that ["the new Treaty] is indeed a happy occasion for all Nepalis....But it is an undertaking and obligation no political party or government can or should possibly balk at or withdraw from.")

2. M.C. Regtni, *Kings and Political Leaders of the Gorkhali Empire 1765–1814.* Hyderabad, 1995.

3. D. Gyawali, "Tanakpur on the Thames," *Himal,* vol. 6, no. 4, Kathmandu, 1993.

4. D. Gyawali and O. Schwank, 1994: "Interstate Sharing of Water Rights— An Alps Himalaya Comparison," *Water Nepal*, vol. 4, no 1, Kathmandu.

5. Ibid.

6. See case study of Butwal Power Company in D. Gyawali, A. Dixit, S. Sharma, and N. Dahal. "Fractured Institutions and Physical Interdependence— The Challenges to Local Water Management in the Tinau River Basin in Nepal." Study by Nepal Water Conservation Foundation, Kathmandu with support from IDRC/Canada, 1999.

7. D. Gyawali, "Foreign Aid and the Erosion of Local Institutions—An Autopsy of Arun 3 from Inception to Abortion" in C Thomas and P Wilkin (eds.), *Globalisation and the South. International Political Economy Series*, London, 1997.

8. The statist bias in all of this, both in Nepal and India, is obvious when one considers that amelioration measures were only limited to civil engineering structures: during the construction of the barrage, the bank cutting in Nepal from diversion works affected about 80 families, but they were not compensated. See Report of the Commission formed to assess the impact of the Tanakpur barrage agreement, also known as the *Baral Commission Report* (in Nepali: *Tanakpur Bandit Pariyojana Sombandhi Samjhautako Asar Mulyankan Sujhav Samity Dwora Prastut Nepal Ra Bharat Beech*

Tanakpur Bandh Pariyojona Sumbandhi Samjhauta Ko Asar Mulvankan Pratibedon, Falgun 3, 2049) February 14, 1993, His Majesty's Government, Kathmandu.

9. See Dhruba Kutnar, "Asymmetric Neighbours" in D. Kumar (ed.), *Nepal's India Policy.* Kathmandu, 1992. This publication also contains the draft of Indian proposal of March 31, 1990 entitled "Agreement between the Government of India and His Majesty's Government of Nepal on Mutual Co-operation."

10. See *Baral Commission Report.*

11. Information from delegation members who were told to come down for breakfast packed for departure while the two prime ministers had a one-on-one meeting. It is said that upon assurances from his bureaucrats that such an "understanding" would not need to be presented to parliament that prime minister Koirala decided to initiate such an "understanding" on Tanakpur.

12. Report in "Tanakpur Now To Be Resolved in Jakarta?," *Nepal Post,* August 2, 1992.

13. See Ganesh Man Singh's historic letter—"There is No Alternative to National Consensus," in *Punarjagaran,* March 9, 1993.

14. See "Allegations that Speaker is the Opposition," *Hindu Dainik,* September 3, 1992.

15. See editorial "Need for Understanding in Water Resources Development" in *Suruchi Saptahik,* December 26, 1993.

16. See "Nepal–India Relations—Signing of the Water Resources Development Action Plan," in *Gorkhapatra,* December 29, 1993.

17. See interview "I Turned Down Mrs Gandhi's Request" in *Crosslines,* February 2–8, 1998.

18. The members who put their signature on the so-called "national consensus" were: Madhav Kumar Nepal and Khadga Prasad Oli of the UML (who are with the Bolshevik UML and not the Menshevik ML); Prakash Chandra Lohani (then foreign minister), and Pashupati Sumsher Rana (then water resources minister) of the RPP (both of whom subsequently became part of the Thapa faction of the RPP as opposed to the Chand faction); and Chiranjivi Wagle and Bimalendra Nidhi of the Nepali Congress (both known to be of the anti-Koirala Chhattise camp—"Group of 36," which abstained from voting and led to the fall of the Koirala ministry).

19. The wordings of Article 3 of the Treaty:

> ... and hence both the parties agree that they have equal entitlement in the utilization of the waters of the Mahakali rivers without prejudice to their respective existing consumptive uses of the waters of the Mahakali river.

Paragraph 3 of Article 3 of the Treaty:

> The cost of the project shall be borne by the Parties in proportion to the benefits accruing to them ....

Clause 3 of the exchanged letters:

It is understood that Paragraph 3 of Article 3 of the Treaty precludes the claim, in any form, by either party on the unutilized portion of the shares of the waters of the Mahakali River of that Party without affecting the provision of the withdrawal of the respective shares of the waters of the Mahakali River by each party under this Treaty.

This wording basically prevents Nepal from claiming financial benefits from its equal entitlement of the waters of the border river if it does not use it within Nepal and allows it to flow downstream.

20. *Samakalin,* August 29, 1996 and *Jansatta*, August 31, 1996.
21. This was the issue that led to the item in the parliamentary stricture, during the Treaty's ratification, about the status of the Mahakali (of where and, how it is a border river).
22. *Jana Aastha,* September 4, 1996; *Bimarsha,* September 6, 1996; *Drishti*, September 10, 1996, and September 17, 1996. See also Keshav Lal Shrestha, *Mahakali Sandhi Ra Rashtriya Heet Ko Sawal.* Kathmandu, 1996.
23. *Himalaya Times, Prakash Weekly,* etc, September 21–30, 1996.
24. As per voting records in the joint session of both the Houses (total strength of 206 + 60 members). UML chairman was absent, eight MPs voted against the Treaty (3 from UML, 3 from Workers and Peasants' Party, and 2 from Masal). 31 MPs abstained (26 from UML, 1 from RPP and 4 nominated members of the King), and 220 MPs voted in favor of the Treaty.
25. See *Water Nepal,* vol. 6, no 1, July 1998.
26. What exactly is the DPR or when and how should it be completed are points of intense debate. Water Resources Minister (at the time of the Treaty) Pashupati Rana mentioned in an interview to *The Kathmandu Post,* January 21, 1997 stated: "The DPR on the Pancheshwar was all ready at the time the Treaty was signed." He also said in the same interview that the Nepali version of the DPR had been sent to India but that India had not responded, and that the formal instruments of ratification of the Treaty had not been exchanged between the two governments and was expected to be done during the forthcoming Nepal visit of Indian Prime Minister H.D. Deve Gowda. On the other hand, in a separate interview to *The Kathmandu Post* April 25, 1997, Foreign Minister Prakash Chandra Lohani stated that HMG had formally informed India of the passage of the Treaty together with the "sankalpa prastav" already in November 1996.
27. *Himalaya Times*, October 11, 1996.
28. *Gorkhaputra,* November 19, 1996. Also *Himalaya Times*, November 24, 1996.
29. See "Minutes of the Second Meeting of the Joint Team of Experts of Nepal and India on the Sapta Kosi High Dam Multipurpose Project (Nepal)" held in Kathmandu, Nepal, January 7–9, 1997.
30. R. Dahal, "As Enron Came. It Went," in *Himal South Asia.* Kathmandu, 1998.
31. Kedar Subedi, "Maha Adhiveshan Ma Emale Le Ke Payo. Ke Gumayo" in *Saptahik Bimarsha,* February 6, 1998. Subedi claims to be quoting

Gautam's reply in parliament on West Seti.

32. *The Kathmandu Post*, March 28, 1997.

33. *Kantipur*, April 21, 1997.

34. *Tarun Rashtriya Saptahik,* June 16, 1997.

35. News and photo published in *Punarjagaran,* July 29, 1997.

36. The representatives at this meeting are Ram Sharan Mahat, Govinda Raj Joshi and Binayak Bhadra from the Nepali Congress, Khadga Prasad Oli, Jhalanath Khanal and Bim Rawa from UML, and Kamal Thapa, Sarbendra Nath Shukla and Rajiv Parajuli from the RPP (*Kantipur*, August 4, 1997).

37. *Kantipur*, September 18, 1997. See also A. Dixit, "Mahakali Sajha Ho Pani Adha Ko Adha Ho," in *Mulyankan,* 1997 and D. Gyawali *"Mahakali Sandhi—Aba Ke Garne?"* in *Nepali Himal*, May/June, 1997.

38. *The Kathmandu Post*, December 15, 1997.

39. *Kantipur,* May 20, 1998.

40. See interview with Rishikesh Shah "Kalapani Ma Bharatiya Fauj Rakhna Diekai Raja Mahendra Le Ho," *Budhabur Weekly*, July 29, 1998.

41. *The Kathmandu Post*, August 3, 1998. It is surprising that this issue was raised because Pashupati Sumsher Rana, in an interview with *Himalaya Times* when asked if Enron had gone back because of his intransigence replied that he was willing to give the survey licence to Enron provided the issue of downstream benefits ("which would extend all the way to Bangladesh") could be resolved before the production license would be given (*Himalaya Times,* May 10, 1998).

42. *The Kathmandu Post*, August 8, 1998.

43. *Samakalin*, September 17, 1998.

44. See "I am having a difficult time because of the 'water mafia'", *Gorkhaputra,* November 29, 1998.

45. *Kantipur*, November 6, 1998.

46. See Jalanath Khanal, "One Visit Many Benefits" in UML party monthly *Navayug.* Mangsir, November/December, 1998. The UML was heavily criticised for this action by both the eight left as well as right parties.

47. See "Decision to Speedily Prepare the DPR of Pancheshwar," *Kantipur* January 2, 1999.

48. See "Why Does An Election Government Want to Implement the Mahakali Treaty?" in *Mulyankan*, Poush (December/January), 1999.

49. For discussion of pitfalls in water-led development strategy for Nepal see P.J. Thapa, "Water-led Development in Nepal—Myths, Limitations and Rational Concerns," *Water Nepal*, vol. 5, no. 1, July 1997. Also Dhungel's examination of the Dutch Disease impact on Paraguay's economy with ltaipu and Yacyreta mega-hydroelectric projects are instructive in this regard. See H. Dhungel, "Macro-economic Adjustments to Large Energy Investments in a Small Controlled Open Economy—A Policy Analysis of Hydropower Development in Paraguay," unpublished Ph.D. dissertation, University of Pennsylvania, 1996.

50. See interview with Rishikesh Shah, "Kalapani Ma Bharatiya Fauj Rakhna Diekai Raja Mahendra Le Ho," in *Budhabur Weekly*, July 29, 1998.

FURTHER READINGS[*]

Abbi, B.L. (ed.), *Northeast Region: Problems and Prospects of Development.* Chandigarh, 1984.

Acharya, Jagat Moni, *Media and Displacement III: Bhutanese Refugees in Nepal: A Sourcebook.* Kolkata, 2004.

Adhikari, Gautam, *Conflict and Civilization.* New Delhi, 1981.

Adiyaraj, Arvind, *In the Shadow of Gunfire: The Dynamics of Ideology and Power Politics in Indo-Pakistan Relations (1982–1991).* Patna, 2001.

Agarwal, H.O., *Kashmir Problem—Its Legal Aspects.* Allahabad, 1979.

Ahmad, Mushtaq, *Politics with Social Change.* Karachi, 1971.

Ahmed, Aijajuddin, Daniel Noin, and H.N. Sharma (eds), *Demographic Transition: The Third World Scenario.* Jaipur, 1997.

Ahmed, A.F. Salahuddin, *India, Pakistan, Bangladesh: Perspectives on History, Society and Politics.* Kolkata, 2001.

Ahmed, Akbar S., *Pakistan Society: Islam, Ethnicity and Leadership in South Asia.* Delhi, 2001.

Ahmed, Feroz, *Ethnicity and Politics in Pakistan.* Karachi, 1998.

Ahmed, Istiaq, *The Concept of Islamic State: Analysis of the Ideological Controversy in Pakistan.* London, 1987.

Akbar, M.J., *Kashmir: Behind the Vale.* New Delhi, 1991.

———, *India: The Siege Within: Challenges to a Nation's Unity.* New Delhi, 1996.

Alexander, K.C., *Culture and Development: Cultural Patterns in Areas of Uneven Development.* New Delhi, 1991.

[*] This bibliography on peace process and peace accords excludes as per the design of this series the sources cited in the essays in the volume. While utmost care has been taken to accommodate the burgeoning peace historiography developed on these themes in the South Asian context during the last 10 years, it is beyond any doubt that there has hardly been any attempt at including them in a volume of this kind and making them part of a critique of the conventionally understood peace studies. Although the rudiments of this critique have always been present in the literature cited below, their bearing on such broader issues as rights, justice including gender justice, civility and democracy has never been brought to the fore by their own right. This bibliography especially focuses on the particular cases of conflict in South Asia that set off organized peace processes and culminated at least on some occasions in the signing of accords and treaties. In some cases, references to writings on other regions and to wider conceptual and theoretical underpinnings have been unavoidable.

Ali, Ansaf, *Broader Dimensions of the Ideology of Pakistan.* Karachi, 1988.

Allen, Douglas (ed.), *Religion and Political Conflict in South Asia.* London, 1993.

Anand, V.K., *Conflict in Nagaland: A Study of Insurgency and Counter Insurgency.* New Delhi, 1980.

Anderson, Benedict, "The War World Disorder," *New Left Review,* vol. 193, 1983.

Anderson, Michael and Sumit Guha, *Changing Conceptions of Rights and Justice in South Asia.* Delhi, 1998.

Avruch, Kevin, Peter W. Black and Joseph Seimecca (eds), *Conflict Resolution: Cross-Cultural Perspectives.* New York, 1991.

Azam, Ikram, *Pakistan's Security and National Integration: A Study of Public Opinion and Popular Points of View.* Islamabad, 1986.

Bachelard, Gaston, *The Poetics of Space,* Maria Jolas trans. New York, 1964.

Bahadur, Kalim and M.C. Paul (eds), *Contemporary India.* Delhi, 2000.

Bailey, F.G., *The Civility of Indifference: On Domesticating Ethnicity.* Delhi, 1996.

Bajpai, Kanti P., and Harish C. Shukul (eds), *Interpreting World Politics.* New Delhi, 1995.

Balakrishnan, Gopal (ed.), *Mapping the Nation.* London, 1996.

Balibar, Etienne and Immanuel Wallerstein (eds), *Race, Nation, Class: Ambiguous Identities.* London, 1991.

Ball, Nicole, *Regional Conflicts and the International System.* Sussex, 1984.

Banerjee, Paula, *Second Civil Society Dialogue on Peace: A Report.* Kolkata, 2002.

Banerji, Arun Kumar (ed.), *Security Issues in South Asia: Domestic and External Sources of Threats to Security.* Calcutta, 1998.

Baral, Lok Raj, *Oppositional Politics in Nepal.* New Delhi, 1977.

———, *Nepal in Regional Cooperation: Quest for a More Equitable Relationship.* Kathmandu, 1984.

Barpujari, H.K., *North-East India: Problems, Policies and Prospects.* Guwahati, 1998.

Baruah, Apurba Kumar, *Social Tensions in Assam: Middleclass Politics.* Guwahati, 1991.

Baruah, Sanjib, "Immigration, Ethnic Conflict and Political Turmoil: Assam 1979–1985," *Asian Survey,* vol. 26, November 11, 1986.

———, "Ethnic Conflict as State Society the Poetics and Politics of Assam Micro Nationalism," *Modern Asian Studies,* vol. 28, July 3, 1994.

Bayley, C.A., *Origins of Nation-Building in South Asia: Patriotism and Ethical Government in the Making of Modern India.* Delhi, 1996.

Bazaz, Prem Nath, *Democracy Through Intimidation and Terror: The Untold Story of Kashmir Politics.* New Delhi, 1978.

Begum, Khurshida, *Tension over the Farakka Barrage: A Techno-Political Tangle in South Asia.* Dhaka, 1987.

Benko, Georges and Ulf Strohmayer (eds), *Space and Social Theory: Interpreting Modernity and Postmodernity.* Oxford, 1997.

Bhargava, Rajeev, Amiya Kumar Bagchi, and R. Sudrashan (eds), *Multiculturalism, Liberalism and Democracy.* New Delhi, 1999.

Bhatt, Sudhir, *The Challenge of the Northeast*. Bombay, 1975.

Bhattacharya, Krishna, *Possible Ethnic Revolution in a Predatory Unitary Hindu State*. Kathmandu, 1998.

Bhaumik, Subir, *Insurgent Crossfire: North-East India*. New Delhi, 1996.

Bhaumik, Subir, Meghna Guhathakurta, Sabyasachi Basu Ray Chaudhury (eds), *Living on the Edge: Essays on the Chittagong Hill Tracts*. Calcutta, 1997.

Bhava, Homi, *The Location of Culture*. London, 1994.

Bindra, S.S., *Determinants of Pak Foreign Policy*. New Delhi, 1988.

Bidwai, Praful, "Ulfa: Assam's Irrational Syndrome," *Sunday Times of India*, December 23, 1990.

Bilder, Richard B., *Managing the Risk of International Agreement*. Madison, 1981.

Blaikie, Piers, et al., *Nepal in Crises: Growth and Stagnation of the Periphery*. Delhi, 1983.

Borbora, Sanjoy, *Experiences of Autonomy in the East and the Northeast: A Report on Third Civil Society Dialogue on Human Rights and Peace*. Kolkata, 2003.

Bordoloi, B.N., *The Dimasa Kacharis of Assam*. Guwahati, 1984.

————, *Transfer and Alienation of Tribal Land in Assam*. Guwahati, 1991.

Borre, Ole, Sushil R. Randey and Chitra K. Tiwari, *Nepalese Political Behaviour*. New Delhi, 1984.

Bose, Arun, Bimal C. Ray and Somesh Dasgupta (eds), *India's Challenge and Response*. Kolkata, 2000.

Bose, Nirmal Kumar, *Selections from Gandhi*. Ahmedabad, 1948.

Bose, Sumantra, *States Nations Sovereignty: Sri Lanka, India and the Tamil Elam Movement*. New Delhi, 1994.

————, *The Challenge in Kashmir: Democracy, Self Determination and Just Peace*. New Delhi, 1997.

Boyd, Govin (ed.), *Regionalism and Global Security*. Toronto, 1994.

Brar, Lt. Gen. K. S., "India's Turbulent Northeast: Over Five Decades of Isolation, Neglect and Alienation," in Sekhar Basu Ray (ed.), *New Approach 2002: Our East and North East*, vol. 11, nos. 1 and 2, 2002.

Brass, Paul, *Ethnicity and Nationalism: Theory and Comparison*. New Delhi, 1991.

Breton, Albert, Gianluigi Galeotti, Pierre Salmon and Ronald Wintrobe (eds), *Political Extremism and Rationality*. Cambridge, 2002.

Brown, T. Louise, *The Challenge of Democracy in Nepal: A Political History*. London, 1997.

Budania, Rajpal, *India's National Security Dilemma: The Pakistan Factor and India's Policy Response*. New Delhi, 2001.

Butalia, Urvashi, *Speaking Peace: Women's Voices from Kashmir*. Delhi, 2002.

Cairns, Allan C., "Constitutional Government and Two Faces of Ethnicity: Federalism is not Enough," in Current Knopf (ed.), *Re-thinking Federalism: Citizens, Markets and Governments in a Changing World*. Vancouver, 1995.

Caplan, Lionel, *Land and Social Change in East Nepal: A Study of Hindu–Tribal Relations*. London, 1970.

Chadda, Maya, *Building Democracy in South Asia: India, Pakistan and Nepal*. Boulder, Col., 2000.

Chakraborty, Saroj, *The Upheaval Years of Northeast India, 1960–1983*. Calcutta, 1984.

Chakravarti, Chittaranjan, *Cultural History of Bhutan*. New Delhi, 1996.

Chambers, Lain and Lidia Curti (eds), *The Post-Colonial Question: Common Skies, Divided Horizons*. London, 1996.

Charney, Evan, "Political Liberalism, Deliberative Democracy, and the Public Sphere," *American Political Science Review*, vol. 92, no. 1, 1998.

Chatterjee, Shibashis, "State, Terrorism and Violence: A Theoretical Engagement" in A. Subramanyam Raju (ed.), *Terrorism in South Asia: Views from India*. New Delhi, 2004.

Chattopadhyay, H.P., *Ethnic Unrest in Modern Sri Lanka: An Account of Tamil Sinhalese Race Relation*. New Delhi, 1994.

Chaube, Sibani Kinkar, *Hill Politics in Northeast India*. Bombay, 1973.

Chaudhury, K.C., *North Eastern India: The Problem and its Solution*. Calcutta, 1980.

Chauhan, R.S., *Society and State Building in Nepal*. New Delhi, 1989.

Chhandhoke, Neera, *The Conceits of Civil Society*. New Delhi, 2003.

Chopra, V.D., *Genesis of Indo-Pak Conflict on Kashmir*. New Delhi, 1990.

Clarke, Robin, *The Science of War and Peace*. London, 1971.

Cohn, Bernard, *An Anthropologist Among Historians and Other Essays*. Delhi, 1987.

Cohn, Bernard S., "The Command of Language and the Language of Command," in Ranajit Guha (ed.), *Subaltern Studies*, vol. 4. Delhi, 1987.

Collean, Roach, *Communication and Culture in War and Peace*. Newbury Park, California, 1993.

Connor, Walkar, *Ethno-nationalism: Quest for Understanding*. Princeton, N.J., 1994.

Dallmayr, Fred and G.N. Devi (eds), *Between Tradition and Modernity: India's Search for Identity. 20th Century Anthology*. New Delhi, 1998.

Danda, Dipali G., *Among the Dimasas of Assam: And Ethnographic Study*. New Delhi, 1978.

Darby, John and Roger MacGinty (eds), *The Management of Peace Processes*. Hampshire, 2000.

Das, Samir Kumar, *ULFA: A Political Analysis*. Delhi, 1994.

———, "Toward Developing an Agendum of Refugee Studies in Northeastern India," *Journal of North-East India Council of Social Science Research*, vol. 24, no. 2, 2000.

———, "Peace and the Limits of Democracy: Some Reflections on the Naga Peace Process," in C.J. Thomas and Gurudas Das (eds), *Dimensions of Development in Nagaland*. New Delhi, 2002.

———, "Civil Society and the Politics of Peace-Making in Northeastern India," in B. Datta Ray (ed.), *Agenda for North East India*. New Delhi, 2002.

———, *Ethnicity, Nation and Security: Essays in Northeastern India*. New Delhi, 2003.

———, "Terrorism and the Limits of Democracy: The Case of Contemporary Assam," in Omprakash Mishra and Sucheta Ghosh (eds), *Terrorism and Low Intensity Conflict in South Asian Region*. New Delhi, 2003.

Das, Samir Kumar and Paula Banerjee, *Civil Society Dialogue on Human Rights and Peace in the Northeast: A Report*. Kolkata, 2001.

Das, Suranjan, *Kashmir and Sindh: Nation-Building and Regional Politics in South Asia*. Kolkata, 2001.

Das, Veena, *Cultural Rights and Definition of Community* in Oliver Mendelsohn and Baxi Upendra (eds), *The Rights of Subordinted Peoples*. Delhi, 1994.

Dasgupta, Partha, *An Inquiry into Well-Being and Destitution*. Oxford, 1995.

Data, P.S. (ed.), *North-East and the Indian State: Paradoxes of a Periphery*. New Delhi, 1995.

Dawson, Pauline, *The Peace Keepers of Kashmir: The Un-Military Observer Group in India and Pakistan*. Bombay, 1995.

De Silva, K.M. *Managing Ethnic Tensions in Multiethnic Societies: Sri Lanka 1880–1985*. Lanham, New York, 1987.

———(ed.), *Ethnic Conflict in Buddhist Societies: Sri Lanka, Thailand and Burma*. London, 1988.

Desai, A.R. (ed.), *Expanding Governmental Lawlessness and Organized Struggles*. Bombay, 1991.

Dharamdasani, M.D., *Nepal in Transition*. Jaipur, 1997.

Donald, Daniel C.F., et al., *Beyond Traditional Peace Keeping*. Hampshire, 1996.

Elliott, Carolyn M. (ed.), *Civil Society and Democracy: A Reader*. New Delhi, 2003.

Engineer, Asghar Ali (ed.), *Secular Crown on Fire: The Kashmir Problem*. Delhi, 1991.

Ferencz, Benjamin B., *A Common Sense Guide to World Peace*. London, 1975.

Fiaz, Shahid and Ranabir Samaddar, *Peace Process in Sri Lanka*. Kathmandu, 2001.

Forsythe, David P. *Human Rights and Peace: International and National Dimensions*. London, 1992.

Francois, Houtart, *Religion and Ideology in Sri Lanka: Essays and Research*. Bangalore, 1974.

Frankel, Francine, Zoya Hasan, Rajeev Bhargava and Balveer Arora (eds), *India: Social and Political Dynamics of Democracy*. New Delhi, 2004.

Galtung, Johan, *The Struggle for Peace*. Ahmedabad, 1984.

Gamage, Siri and I. B. Watson, *Conflict and Community in Contemporary Sri Lanka: Pearl of the East or Island of Tears?* New Delhi, 1999.

Ganguly, J.B., *Peace and Development in Tripura: Problems and Prospects*. Guwahati, 1999.

Ganguly, Sumit, *Conflict Unending: Indo–Pak Tensions since 1947*. New York, 2001.

Garewal, Sher Muhammed (ed.), *Pakistan Way of Life and Culture*. Lahore, 1988.

Gauhar, G.N., *Hazratbal: The Central Stage of Kashmir Politics*. New Delhi, 1988.

Gellner, N. David, Joanna Pfaff-Czarnecka and John Whelpton, *Nationalism and Ethnicity in a Hindu Kingdom: The Politics of Culture in Contemporary Nepal*. Amsterdam, 1977.

Gilchrist, R.N., *Indian Nationality*. New Delhi, 1986.

Granville, J.A.S. and Bernard Wasserstein, *The Major International Treaties of the 20th Century*. London, 2001.

Guha, Amalendu, *Medieval and Early Colonial Assam: Society, Polity, Economy*. Calcutta, 1991.

Gulati, M.N., *Pakistan's Downfall in Kashmir: The Three Indo-Pak Wars*. New Delhi, 2001.

Gupta, Dipankar, *The Context of Ethnicity*. Delhi, 1996.

———, *Culture, Space and Nation State: From Sentiment to Structure*. New Delhi, 2000.

Gupta, Shekhar, *Assam: A Valley Divided*. Delhi, 1984.

Gusfield, Joseph R., *The Culture of Public Problems: Drinking, Driving and the Symbolic Order*. Chicago, 1981.

Hall, Stuart and Paul du Gay (eds), *Questions of Identity*. London, 1996.

Hasan, Mushirul (ed.), *Islam and the Nation: Muslim Identities in South Asia and Beyond*. New Delhi, 1998.

Hawkins, Darren and Melissa Humes, "Human Rights and Domestic Violence," *Political Science Quarterly*, vol. 117, no. 2, 2002.

Hazarika, *Bolin Human Rights in India: Socio-Political and Legal Dimensions*. Jorhat, 2003.

———(ed.), *Human Rights and Democracy*. Jorhat, 2004.

Hewitt, Vernon, "Ethnicity, Subnationalism and Federalism in South Asia," *Hull Papers in Indian Politics*. Middlesex, 1989.

Hobsbawm, Eric, *Age of Extremes*. New Delhi, 1995.

Horam, Mashangthei, "Waiting for the Peace that Never Comes," *Economic and Political Weekly*, August 3, 1974.

———, *Naga Polity*. Delhi, 1975.

Houss, Charles, *International Conflict Resolution*. London, 2001.

Hussain, Asad Asif Anwar, *Conflict in India: A Case Study of Nepal*. New Delhi, 1979.

Hussain, Monirul, "Tribal Movement for Autonomous State in Assam," *Economic and Political Weekly*, August 8, 1987.

———, *The Assam Movement: Class, Ideology and Identity*. Delhi, 1993.

———, "State, Identity Movements and Internal Displacement in the North-East India," *Economic and Political Weekly*, December 16, 2000.

Iftekharuzzaman (ed.), *South Asia's Security: Primacy of Internal Dimension*. Dhaka, 1993.

———, *Ethnicity and Constitutional Reform in South Asia*. Colombo/New Delhi, 1998.

Ignatieff, Michael, *Blood and Belonging: Journeys into the New Nationalism*. New York, 1993.

Israel, Fred L., *Major Peace Treaties of Modern History, 1648–1967*. New York, 1970.

Ivekovic, Rada, "On Whether to Acknowledge the Split/Sharing of Reason," *TransEuropennes*, vol. 23, 2003.

Jacobs, Jullian with Alan Macfarlane, Sarah Harrison, and Anita Herle, *The Nagas: The Hill People of Northeast India*. London, 1999.

Jacques, Kathryn, *Bangladesh, India and Pakistan—International Tensions and Regional Tensions in South Asia*. London, 2000.

Jahan, Rounaq, *Failure in National Integration*. New York, 1972.

Jalal, Ayesha, *Democracy and Authoritarianism in South Asia*. Cambridge, 1995.

Jalibi, Jammel, *Pakistan: The Identity of Culture*. Karachi, 1984.

Janice, Jiggins, *Caste and Families in the Politics of Sinhalese*. Cambridge, 1979.

Jayal, Niraja Gopal (ed.), *Democracy in India*. New Delhi, 2001.

Jeremy, Seabrook, *Freedom Unfinished: Fundamentalism and Popular Resistance in Bangladesh Today*. London, 2001.

Jha, Prem Shankar, *The Origins of a Dispute: Kashmir 1947*. New Delhi, 2003.

Jha, Shree Krishna, *Uneasy Partners, India and Nepal in the Post-Colonial Era*. Delhi, 1975.

Johari, J.C., "Creation of Naga Land: Triumph of Ebullient Infra-nationalism," *Indian Journal of Political Science*, vol. 36, no. 1, 1975.

Kabir, M.G. and Shaukat Hassan (ed.), *Issues and Challenges Facing Bangladesh*. Dhaka, 1989.

Kabir, Muhammed Ghulam, *Minority Politics in Bangladesh*. New Delhi, 1980.

Kadian, Rajesh, *India's Sri Lanka Fiasco: Peace Keepers at War*. New Delhi, 1990.

Kalla, A.K., *The Ethnology of India: Antecedents and Ethnic Affinities of People of India*. New Delhi, 1994.

Karan, P.P., *Bhutan: Environment, Culture and Development Strategy*. New Delhi, 1990.

Kaul, R.N., *The Wail of Kashmir: In Quest of Peace*. New Delhi, 1999.

Keck, Margaret E. and Kathryn Sikkink (eds), *Activists Beyond Borders: Advocacy Networks in International Politics*. Ithaca, 1998.

Keyes, Charles F. (ed.), *Ethnic Change*. Seattle, 1981.

Khan, Rasheeduddin (ed.), *Composite Culture of India and National Integration*. New Delhi, 1987.

Kohli, Atul (ed.), *The Success of India's Democracy*. Cambridge, 2001.

Kohli, Manorama, *From Dependence to Interdependence—Indo-Bhutan Relations*. New Delhi, 1993.

Kulkarni, V.B., *Conflict in Indian Society*. Bombay, 1981.

Kumar, B.B., *Tension and Conflict in North East India*. New Delhi, 1995.

Kumar, Maya Unnithan, *Identity, Gender and Poverty: New Perspectives on Caste and Tribe in Rajasthan*. Oxford, 1997.

Lakoff, Robin Tolmach, *Talking Power: The Politics of Language in Our Lives*. New York, 1990.

Lamb, Alastair, *Kashmir: A Disputed Legacy 1846–1990*. London, 1991.

Laquer, Walter, *The New Terrorism: Fanaticism and the Arms of Mass Destruction*. New York, 1991.

Lasuh, Wetshokhrolo (ed.), *The Naga Chronicle*. New Delhi, 2002.

Latiff, Abdul, *From Community to Nation: The Development of the Idea of Pakistan*. Ann Arbor Michigan, 1987.

Lavin, Michael D. (ed.), *Ethnicity and Aboriginality*. Toronto, 1993.

Lee, Tang Lay, "Refugees from Bhutan: Nationality, Statelessness and the Right to Return," *International Journal of Refugee Law*, vol. 10, nos.1 and 2, 1998.

Levene, Mark, "The Chittagong Hill Tracts: A Case Study in the Political Economy of 'Creeping' Genocide," *Third World Quarterly*, vol. 20, no. 2, 1999.

Lewis, John P., *India's Political Economy: Governance and Reform*. New Delhi, 1997.

Lifschultz, Lawrence, *Bangladesh: The Unfinished Revolution*. London, 1979.

Lijphart, Arend, "The Puzzle of Indian Democracy: A Consociational Interpretation," *American Political Science Review*, vol. 90, no. 2, 1996.

Ludden, David, *Making India Hindu: Religion, Community and the Politics of Democracy in India*. New Delhi, 1996.

Madhok, Bal Raj, *Jammu Kashmir and Ladakh: Problem and Solution*. New Delhi, 1987.

Mahajan, Gurpreet (ed.), *Democracy, Difference and Social Justice*. Delhi, 1988.

———, *Identities and Rights: Aspects of Liberal Democracy in India*. Delhi, 1998.

———, "Democratic Rights, Liberty and State Security: A Liberal Response," presented at the seminar on "Terrorism, Human Rights and Democracy: The Indian Experience," Department of Political Science, Rabindra Bharati University, Kolkata, 2003.

Mahmood, Safdar, *Political Roots and Development*. New Delhi, 1990.

Makil, Hafeez (ed.), *Dilemmas of National Security and Cooperation in India and Pakistan*. New York, 1993.

———, *Pakistan: Aspirations and Today's Realities*. Oxford, 2001.

Malik, Iftikhar, *State and Civil Society in Pakistan*. London, 1997.

Mamoon, Muntassir and Jayanta Kumar Roy, *Civil Society in Bangladesh: Resilience and Retreat*. Calcutta, 1996.

Mascaranhas, Anthony, *Bangladesh: A Legacy of Blood*. London, 1996.

McClintock, Anne, Aamir Mufti and Ella Shohat (eds), *Dangerous Liasons: Gender, Nation and Postcolonial Perspectives*. Minneapolis, 1996.

Mendus, Susan and David Edwards (eds), *On Toleration*. Oxford, 1987.

Millar, J.B., *Current International Treaties*. London, 1984.

Miri, Mrinal, *Identity and the Moral Life*. New Delhi, 2003.

Misra, H.N. *Bhutan: Problems and Policies*. New Delhi, 1988.

Misra, R.C., *Emergence of Bhutan*. Jaipur, 1989.

Misra, R.C. and Meenakshi Chaturvedi, *Bhutan in South Asia*. Jaipur, 1996.

Misra, Udayon, *Northeast India: Quest for Identity*. Guwahati, 1988.

———, "Movements for Autonomy in India's Northeast" in T.V. Sathyamurthy (ed.), *Region, Religion, Caste, Gender and Culture in Contemporary India*, vol. 3, New Delhi, 1996.

———, *The Periphery Strikes Back: Challenges to the Nation-State in Assam and Nagaland*. Shimla, 2000.

Mitra, Subrata Kumar, *Culture and Rationality: The Politics of Social Change in Post-Colonial India*. New Delhi, 1999.

Mitra, Subrata Kumar and R. Allision Lewis (eds), *Subnational Movements in South Asia*. Boulder, Col., 1996.

Mohanty, Dusmanta Kumar, *Indian Political Tradition: From Manu to Ambedkar*. New Delhi, 1997.

Mohanty, Manoranjan, Partha Nath Mukherjee with Olle Tornquist (eds), *People's Rights: Social Movements and the State in the Third World*. New Delhi, 1988.

Moogee, W. Christopher, *The Mediation Process: Practical Strategies for Resolving Conflict*. San Francisco, 1996.

Mohapatra, Bishnu, "Understanding the Discourse of Minority Rights in Contemporary India," presented at the workshop on "Minority Rights in India," International Centre for Ethnic Studies, Colombo and Centre for Studies in Developing Societies, New Delhi, 2001.

Mukarji, Nirmal and Balveer Arora (eds), *Federalism in India: Origins and Development*. New Delhi, 1992.

Mukherjee, Lt. Gen. J.R., "A Perspective on the North East" in Sekhar Basu Ray (ed.) *New Approach 2002: Our East and North East*, vol. 11, nos. 1 and 2, 2002.

Mukherji, A.B. and Aijajuddin Ahmed (ed.), *India, Culture, Society and Economy—Essays in Honour of Prof Asok Mitra*. New Delhi, 1985.

Mumtaz, Khawar, et al., *Pakistan: Tradition and Change*. Oxford, 1996.

Munck, Ronaldo and Purnaka L. de Silva (eds), *Postmodern Insurgencies: Political Violence, Identity Formation and Peacemaking in Contemporary Perspectives*. London, 1996.

Muni, S.D., *Pangs of Proximity: India and Sri Lanka's Ethnic Crises*. New Delhi, 1993.

Murty, Satchidananda K. (ed.), *The Divine Peacock: Understanding Contemporary India*. New Delhi, 1998.

Nag, Sajal, *Roots of Ethnic Conflict: Nationality Question in North-East India*. New Delhi, 1990.

———, *Contesting Marginality: Ethnicity, Insurgency and Subnationalism in North-East India*. New Delhi: 2002.

Nandy, Ashis, "Terrorism—Indian Style: The Birth of a Political Issue in a Populist Democracy" in Subrata Kumar Mitra and James Chiriyakandath (eds), *Electoral Politics in India: A Changing Landscape*. New Delhi, 1992.

———, *The Romance of the State and the Fate of Dissent in the Tropics*. New Delhi, 2003.

Naqvi, Jamal, *Inside Pakistan*. New Delhi, 1986.

Neog, Maheswar, "Atrocity in Assam," *New Republic*, March 21, 1983.

Nepali, G.S., *New Wars: An Ethno-Sociological Study of Himalayan Community*. Bombay, 1965.

Newdo, Donald Wilber, *Pakistan, Its People, Its Society, Its Culture*. New Haven, 1964.

Nuh, V.K., *Struggle for Identity in North-East India: A Theological Response*. Guwahati, 2001.

Nunthera, C., "Peace Accords as Instruments of Conflict Transformation: Arrangements that Work and Arrangements that Don't," presented at the workshop on "Dimensions, Dynamics and Transformation of Resource Conflicts between Indigenous Peoples and Settlers in Frontier Regions of South and South East Asia," Switzerland, 2002.

Oinam, Bhagat, "Dynamics of Ethnic Conflict in Manipur: Towards a Proposal for Solution," presented at the seminar on "Coming out of Violence: Resolving Ethnic Conflicts in North East India," Department of Political Science,

Gauhati University, Assam and Indian Council of Social Science Research, Northeastern Regional Centre, Shillong, in Guwahati, 2002.

Ostheimer, John M. (ed.), *The Politics of the Western Indian Ocean Islands*, New York, 1975.

Pai, Panandhikar V.A. (ed.), *Problems of Governance in South Asia*. New Delhi, 1999.

Pal, Izzud-Din, *Pakistan: Islam and Economics: Failure and Modernity*. Oxford, 1999.

Pant, Kusum, *The Kashmiri Pandit: Story of a Community in Exile in the Nineteenth Centuries*. New Delhi, 1987.

Parmanand, *Politics in Bhutan*. Delhi: 1993.

Patil, V.T. and N.K. Jha, *Peace and Cooperative Security in South Asia*. Delhi, 1999.

Paul, Madan C., *Dimensions of Tribal Movements in India: A Study of Udayachal in Assam Valley*. Delhi, 1989.

Peacock, Olive, *Minority Politics in Sri Lanka*. Jaipur, 1989.

Perera, Jehan, *Peace Accords in Nagaland and Chittagong Hill Tracts: An Audit Report*. Kathmandu, 1999.

Phadnis, Urmila and Ela, Dutta Luithni, *Maldives: Winds of Change in an Atoll State*. New Delhi, 1985.

Phukan, Surajit, "Assam a New Movement," *Sentinel*, June 26, 1988.

Phukon, Girin (ed.), *Political Dynamics in North East India: Essays in Honour of Professor Barrister Pakem*. New Delhi, 2000.

———, *Ethnicity and Polity in South Asia*. New Delhi, 2002.

Phukon, Girin and N.L. Dutta (eds), *Politics of Identity and Nation Building in Northeast India*. New Delhi, 1997.

Prabhakara, M.S., "Still Largely Symbolic," *The Hindu*, February 13, 1985.

———, "Imponderables in Nagaland," *The Hindu*, January 12, 1989.

———, "The Mailed Fist," *Frontline*, July 7–20, 1990.

———, "Bodos Hopes, Harsh Realities," *The Hindu*, October 4, 1990.

———, "Changing Face of Ulfa," *The Hindu*, January 17, 1993.

———, "What Did the Bodos Achieve?" *The Hindu*, March 11, 1993.

———, "The Progress of Assam Accord," *The Hindu*, October 19, 1993.

———, "The Northeast Turmoil," *The Hindu*, June 16.

Prasad, Pradhan, H., *India: Dilemma of Development*. New Delhi, 2000.

Puri, Balraj, *Simmering Volcano, Study of a Rural Society*. Calcutta, 1983.

Quddus, Muhammed A., *Pakistan, A Case Study of Rural Society*. Calcutta, 1981.

Rahul, Ram, *Royal Bhutan*. Delhi, 1983.

Ram, Mohan, *Sri Lanka: The Fractured Island*. New Delhi, 1989.

Ramakant and R.C. Misra (eds), *Bhutan: Society and Polity*. Jaipur, 1996.

Rapoport, David C. and Yonah Alexander (eds), *The Morality of Terrorism: Religious and Secular Justifications*. New York, 1982.

Rapport, David (ed.), *Inside Terrorist Organizations*. London, 1993.

Rawls, John, *Political Liberalism*. New York, 1993.

Ray, Baren, *India: Nature of Society and Present Crises*. New Delhi, 1983.

Ray, Jayanta, *India–Nepal Cooperation Broadening Measures*. Calcutta, 1997.

Ray, Parama, *Indian Traffic: Identities in Question in Colonial and Post-colonial India*. New Delhi, 1998.

Raychaudhuri, Tapan (ed.), *Perceptions Emotions Sensibilities: Essays on India's Colonial and Postcolonial Experiences*. New Delhi, 1999.

Richter, Justin and Christian Wagner (eds), *Regional Security, Ethnicity and Governance*. New Delhi, 1998.

Rizvi, Hasan-Askari, *Military, State and Society in Pakistan*. London, 2000.

Rose, Leo (ed.), "The Nepali Ethnic Community in the Northeast of the Subcontinent," *Ethnic Studies Report*, vol. 12, January 1, 1994.

Rose, Leo E., *Nepal: Strategy for Survival*. Bombay, 1971.

———, *The Politics of Bhutan*. Ithaca, 1993.

Ross, Mark Howard, *The Management of Conflict: Interpretations and Interests in Comparative Perspective*. New Haven, 1993.

Rotberg, Robert I. (ed.), *Creating Peace in Sri Lanka: Civil War and Reconciliation*. Washington D.C., 1999.

Roy Burman, B.K., *Indigenous and Tribal Peoples: Gathering Mist and New Horizon*. New Delhi, 1994.

Roy, Devasish, "The Discordant Accord: Challenges towards the Implementation of the Chittagong Hill Tracts Accord of 1997," *The Journal of Social Studies*, vol. 100, April–June, 2003.

Roy, Sanjay K., *Refugees and Human Rights: Social and Political Dynamics of Refugee Problem in Eastern and Northeastern India*. Jaipur, 2001.

Rupesinghe, Kumar and Khawar Mumtaz (eds), *Internal Conflicts in South Asia*. London, 1996.

Rustomji Nari, *Bhutan: The Dragon Kingdom in Crises*. Oxford, 1978.

Sahadevan, P. (ed.), *Conflict and Peacekeeping in South Asia*. New Delhi, 2001.

Saberwal, Satish, *India: The Roots of Crises*. Oxford, 1986.

Sabratam, Lokmanan, *Ethnic Attachments in Sri Lanka: Social Change and Cultural Continuity*. Basingstoke, 2000.

Salaluddin, Ahmed Akbar, *Pakistan Economy and Society: Traditional Structure and Economic Development in Tribal Society*. London, 1980.

Samad, Yunus, *A Nation in Turmoil: Nationalism and Ethnicity in Pakistan 1937–1958*. New Delhi, 1995.

Samaddar, Ranabir and Helmut Reifeld (eds), *Peace as Process: Reconciliation and Conflict Resolution in South Asia*. New Delhi, 2001.

Samaddar, Ranabir, *A Biography of Indian Nation 1947–1997*. New Delhi, 2001.

Sandel, Michael, *Liberalism and the Limits of Justice*. Cambridge, 1982.

Saraswati, Baidyanath, *Culture and Peace: Experience and Experiment*. New Delhi, 1999.

Sayeed, Khalid B., *Politics in Pakistan: The Nature and Direction of Change*. Delhi, 1980.

Schellenberg, James A., *Conflict Resolution: Theory, Research and Practice*. New York, 1996.

Schendel, Willem Van, "Stateless in South Asia: The Making of the India–Bangladesh Enclaves" *Journal of Asian Studies*, vol. 61, no. 1, 2002.

Seevaratnam, N. (ed.), *The Tamil National Question and the Indo–Sri Lanka Accord*. Delhi, 1989.

Sen, Geeti (ed.), *Indigenous Vision: People of India, Attitudes to the Environment*. New Delhi, 1992.

——, *India: A National Culture*. Delhi, 2003.

Sen, Jahar, *India and Nepal: Some Aspects of Cultural Contact*. Simla, 1992.

Sen, Rangalal, *Political Elites in Bangladesh*. Dhaka, 1986.

Senaviratne, H. L. (ed.), *Identity, Consciousness and the Past: Forging of Caste and Community in India and Sri Lanka*. Delhi, 1997.

Shah Mehtab Ali, *Foreign Policy of Pakistan: Ethnic Impacts on Diplomacy*. London, 1997.

Shah, Ghanshyam (ed.), *Social Movements and the State*. New Delhi, 2002.

Shapiro, Michael, *Language and Politics*. Oxford, 1984.

Sharma, Manorama, *Social and Economic Change in Assam: Middle Class Hegemony*. Delhi, 1990.

Sharma, S.L. and T.K. Oommen (eds), *Nation and National Identity in South Asia*. Hyderabad, 1999.

Siddiqi, Ayesha Agha, *Pakistan's Arms Procurement and Military Build-up 1979–1999: In Search of Policy*. Basingstoke, 2001.

Simkhada, R. Shambhu, *Study of Peace Zones with Special References to Nepal's Zone of Peace Proposal and Its Political, Economic and Security Implications*. Ann Arbor, Michigan, 1987.

Singh, B.P., *The Problem of Change: A Study of Northeast India*. Delhi, 1987.

Singh, Bhupinder, *Indo–Pak Conflict Over Kashmir*. Patiala, 1983.

Singh, Gurnam (ed.), *Ethno-Nationalism and the Emerging World (Dis)Order*. New Delhi, 2002.

Singh, Raj Kumar, *Less Tasty Indo–Nepal Political Relation (1947–1997)*. Patna, 1998.

Sinha, A.C., *Bhutan: Ethnic Identity and National Dilemma*. New Delhi, 1991.

Sinha, A.C., et al., *Hill Cities of Eastern Himalayas Ethnicity, Land Relations and Urbanizations*. New Delhi, 1993.

Sinha, Raghubir, *Religion and Culture of North Eastern India*. New Delhi, 1977.

Smart, Ninian and Shivash Thakur (eds), *Ethical and Political Dilemma of Modern India*. Basingstoke, 1993.

Spencer, Jonathan (ed.), *Sri Lanka: History and the Roots of Conflict*. London, 1990.

Srivastava, S.K. (ed.), *Modernization in Nepal*. Varanasi, 1986.

Stacy Leigh, Pigg, *Disenchanting Shames: Representations of Modernity and the Transformation of Healing in Nepal*. Ann Arbor, Michigan, 1990.

Stern, Jessica, "Pakistan's Jihad Culture," *Foreign Affairs*, November–December, 2000.

Stern, Robert W., *Changing India*. New Delhi, 1993.

Subramanian, Narendra, *Ethnicity and Populist Mobilization: Political Parties, Citizens and Democracy in South India*. New Delhi, 1999.

Sundaram Soma Daya, *Scarred Minds: The Psychological Impact of War on Sri Lankan Tamils*. New Delhi, 1998.

Suryanarayana, P.S., *The Peace Trap: An Indo–Sri Lankan Political Crises*. New Delhi, 1988.

Swaminathan, V.V. *Problems of Peace and Security in Asia*. New Delhi, 1986.

Talukder, Maniruzzaman, *Group Interest and Political Changes: Studies of Pakistan and Bangladesh*. New Delhi, 1992.

Tambiah, S.J., *Sri Lanka: Ethnic Fratricide and the Dismantling of Democracy*. Delhi, 1986.

Tarapot, Phanjoubam, *Insurgency Movement in Northeastern India*. New Delhi, 1993.

———, *Bleeding Manipur*. New Delhi, 2004.

Tarrow, Sidney, "Mentalities Political Cultures and Collective Action Frames: Constructing Meanings Through Actions" in Morris and Muller (eds), *Frontiers in Social Movement Theory*. New Haven, Conn., 1992.

Teng, Krishan, *Kashmir Article 370*. New Delhi, 1990.

Thakur, Basant Krishna, *Kashmir, The Tangle–Untangled*. Nagpur, 1995.

Tilly, Charles, *The Politics of Collective Violence*. Cambridge, 2003.

Timur, Borhauudin Mohammed Abbas Aziz, *The Ganges Water Dispute*. New Delhi, 1982.

Uchikawa, Sluji (ed.), *Pakistan's Crises: Political and Economic Analysis*. Japan, 2000.

United Committee, Manipur, *The Greater Autonomy of Manipur: A Demand of the People of Manipur*. Imphal, 2003.

Varma, Ravi, *India's Role in the Emergence of Contemporary Bhutan*. Delhi, 1988.

Varshney, Ashutosh, *Ethnic Conflict and Civil Life: Hindus and Muslims in India*. New Delhi, 2002.

Vayryaen, Raima (ed.), *New Directions in Conflict Theory: Conflict Resolution and Conflict Transformation*. London, 1991.

Ved, Sudhir D., *The Crises of Changing India*. Delhi, 1974.

Verghese, B. George, *India's Northeast Resurgent: Ethnicity Governance, Development*. Delhi, 1996.

Vijayalakshmi, N., *Politics, Society and Cosmology in India's North-East*. Delhi, 1998.

Wallace, Paul (ed.), *Regional and Nation in India*. New Delhi, 1985.

Wallersteen Peter, *Understanding Conflict Resolution: War, Peace, and the Global System*. London, 2002.

Walter, Barbara F., *Committing to Peace*. Princeton, 2002.

Walzer, Michael, "The New Tribalism: Notes on a Difficult Problem," in Omar Pahbour and Micheline R. Ishay (eds), *The Nationalism Reader*, Atlantic Highlands, 1995.

———, *On Toleration*. New Haven, 1997.

Weeks, Richard V., *Pakistan Birth and Growth*. Princeton, N.J., 1964.

Weidemann, Diethelm (ed.), *Nationalism Ethnicity and Political Development in South Asia*. New Delhi, 1991.

Weiner, Myron, *Sons of the Soil: Migration and Ethnic Conflict in India*. Princeton, N.J., 1978.

Weiner, Myron, *The Indian Paradox: Essays in Indian Politics*. New Delhi, 1989.

Weiner, Myron, "Bad Neighbors, Bad Neighborhoods: An Inquiry into the Causes of Refugee Flows," *International Security*, vol. 21, no. 1, 1996.

Weiner, Myron and Mary Fainsod Katzenstein, *India's Preferential Policies: Migrants, the Middle Classes and Ethnic Equality*. Chicago, 1981.

Weissberg, Robert, *Political Tolerance: Balancing Community and Diversity*. Thousand Oaks, 1998.

Wignaraja, Ponna and Akmal Hussain, (eds), *The Challenge in South Asia: Development Democracy and Regional Cooperation*. Karachi, 1989.

Williams, A.J., *A Critical Analysis of Community Education and Socio-Economic Change in Nepal*. Ann Arbor, Michigan, 1990.

Wilson, Richard (ed.), *Human Rights, Culture, and Context: Anthropological Perspectives*. London, 1997.

Winslade, John, Gerald Monk, *Narrative Mediation: A New Approach to Conflict Resolution*. Jossey Bass, San Francisco, 2000.

Wolf, Eric R., *Pathways of Power: Building an Anthropology of the Modern State*. Berkeley, 2001.

Wriggins, W. Howard and James F. Guyot (eds), *Population, Politics and the Future of Southern Asia*. New York, 1973.

Young, M. Crawford, *The Politics of Cultural Pluralism*. Madison, 1976.

Zaidi, A. Akbar (ed.), *Regional Imbalances and National Question in Pakistan*. Lahore, 1992.

Zakaria, Fareed, *The Future of Freedom: Illiberal Democracy at Home and Abroad*. New Delhi, 2003.

Ziring, Lawrence, *Pakistan in the 20th Century: A Political History*. Karachi, 1997.

About the Editor and Contributors

The Editor

Samir Kumar Das, a member of the Calcutta Research Group, teaches at the Department of Political Science, University of Calcutta. Prior to joining the University, he was on the faculty of the Department of Political Science, Presidency College, Kolkata. He specializes in and writes on issues of ethnicity, security and migration. His previous publications include *Ethnicity, Security and Nation: Essays on Northeastern India* (2004); *Regionalism in Power* (1998); and *ULFA—A Political Analysis* (1994).

The Contributors

Paula Banerjee is a member of the faculty in the Department of South and South East Asian Studies, University of Calcutta, India.

Subir Bhaumik is the Bureau Chief, East India, BBC.

Pradip Kumar Bose is a member of the faculty of the Centre for Studies in Social Sciences, Kolkata.

Sumantra Bose is a member of the faculty in Comparative Government, London School of Economics and Political Science, London.

Shibashis Chatterjee is a member of the faculty in the Department of International Relations, Jadavpur University, Kolkata, India.

Committee of Concerned Citizens was formed in order to facilitate dialogue between the Government of India and the

PWG (People's War Group) in Andhra Pradesh. The Committee is based in Hyderabad, India.

Parimal Ghosh is a member of the faculty in the Department of South and South East Asian Studies, University of Calcutta, India.

Dipak Gyawali and Ajaya Dixit are the co-editors of *Water Nepal* and well-known environmentalists of Nepal.

Mubashir Hasan was the co-founder of Pakistan People's Party and the first finance minister of the Zulfikar Ali Bhutto government of Pakistan. He is also one of the most well-known peace personalities of Pakistan.

Amena Mohsin is a member of the faculty in the Department of International Relations, Dhaka University, Bangladesh.

Jehan Perera, an economist from Harvard University, is currently the Media Director of National Peace Council of Sri Lanka.

Ranabir Samaddar is the Director of Calcutta Research Group, India.

Oren Yiftachel is a member of the faculty in the Department of Geography and Environmental Development, Ben Gurion University of the Neger, Beer Shera, Israel.

INDEX